THE FAMILY OF GOD

THE FAMILY OF GOD

A Symbolic Study of Christian
Life in America

by W. LLOYD WARNER

GREENWOOD PRESS, PUBLISHERS
WESTPORT, CONNECTICUT

Library of Congress Cataloging in Publication Data

Warner, William Lloyd, 1898-1970.
   The family of God.

   Reprint of the ed. published by Yale University
Press, New Haven, which was issued as A Yale paper-
bound, Y-45.
   "Consists of sections of [the author's] The
living and the dead ... revised and supplemented."
   Bibliography: p.
   Includes index.
   1. United States--Religion--1945-
2. United States--Social life and customs--
1945-   3. Symbolism.   I. Title.
[BR526.W3 1975]   209'.73   75-11494
ISBN 0-8371-8206-9

Originally published in 1961 by Yale University Press,
New Haven

Reprinted with the permission of Yale University Press

Reprinted in 1975 by Greenwood Press,
a division of Williamhouse-Regency Inc.

Library of Congress Catalog Card Number 75-11494

ISBN 0-8371-8206-9

Printed in the United States of America

To the memory of
Alfred Kroeber

Contents

Charts

Acknowledgments

The acknowledgments and dedications published in the five Yankee City volumes hold for the present one. It is hoped that the reader will relate them to the present recognitions of indebtedness.

I wish to express my gratitude to the authors and publishers for their permission to use quotations from their publications. I feel a particular debt to Harper and Brothers, for permission to use materials of my own published by them.

Part I

*The Family, the Emergent Collectivity,
and Sacred Symbolism*

Introduction

Social anthropologists have long recognized the close relation of the family in other societies to the meanings and significances of sacred symbols, to the divine beings of classical antiquity, to ancestor worship in China and Africa, and to the vast number of totemic systems whose believers and celebrants, scattered throughout the world, are groups of kindred organized in clans. Sir James Frazer's *Golden Bough*, Émile Durkheim's *Elementary Forms of the Religious Life*, Robertson Smith's studies of the ancient Semites, all readily come to mind as important examples of the many scholarly works that have contributed to our understanding of the sacred symbol systems which are found in and created by the family structure. The present volume investigates the meanings and functions of Christian symbolic life in America. It will be maintained that Christianity's basic meanings lie deeply within the moral and species structure of family life. Our evidence was gathered by field and library research in community and national studies on the living and the dead and on Christian beliefs, rituals, and "myths." Although most of the research was done in Yankee City, a small New England city, other communities were studied as well. Valuable research by other investigators on the distribution of Christian belief throughout the United States has been drawn on. The nature of sacred symbolic life in this country is such that, despite important variations, the basic meanings of our religious symbols are much the

3

same in all regions. When one studies Memorial Day
rites or the significance of the Mass in New England or
the Far West, much of what is learned holds for the
rest of the nation.

This volume analyzes both Catholic and Protestant
symbolic behavior, opening with a discussion of the
continuing dialogue between the secular and sacred systems of belief in the emergent great society. Chapter 2
broadens the inquiry about the relation of family structure and the collectivity to sacred symbol systems by
use of evidence from three other societies. These are
examined to bring out explicitly some of the essentials
of the problems we face and provide comparisons with
our own system.

The two chapters of Part I are mostly new. All other
chapters, reconstituted and edited, are from the author's
The Living and the Dead [114f], the fifth volume of
the Yankee City Series. The present book is entirely
concerned with religious and other sacred behavior;
the earlier one covered a broad spread of many other
symbolic subjects as well as theory, method, and the
use of evidence. The methods used in both volumes
follow those in *Black Civilization*. [114a]

For the convenience of the reader and in order to
avoid a multitude of footnotes, references to source
material are by bracketed numbers indicating items in
the Bibliography, where the customary publishing data
will be found. Where more than one reference to a
single work is involved, the page numbers are given in
brief footnotes to the text.

CHAPTER 1

The Continuing Sacred-Secular Dialogue in an Emergent Society

Rational and Non-rational Meanings in an Emergent Social System

Many of the present directions of the symbolic life in this country contain strange contradictions and paradoxes. Full examination of some of them sometimes leads beyond these conceptual contradictions to a deeper understanding of the nature of our culture's symbolic life. Some of them may be easily studied. In the American collectivity the use of rational, empirical, and technical symbols, with their non-moral meanings and values, is rapidly increasing, both absolutely and relatively, in terms of the society and of most individuals in it. [114*f*] Yet, despite the probable validity of this empirical hypothesis, the non-rational, moral beliefs and values of this society—those having to do with the ongoing, not to say eternal, life of the species—are growing in strength and enlarging the social areas of their recognized legitimacy and daily application.

Moreover, for purposes of successful adjustment to the world around them, the decisions of individuals and the symbols used by them must be increasingly rational and intellectually autonomous; increasingly too, the

non-rational meanings, beliefs, and values originating
in the moral and species matrix of the family become
more crucial and necessary, and are more often used
for the training, development, and maintenance of
well-adjusted personalities.

Finally it is proposed that, while the sacred symbolic
life of our emergent technological society is continuing
its centuries-old retreat from the attacks of secular
rationality and technological empiricism, this retreat is
no longer necessary. [5] The sacred symbols of religion
and the moral beliefs and values that support them,
particularly those of the human family, can help re-
order the meanings and values of science, thus aiding
and abetting the advancing use of the rational, em-
pirically derived symbols and facts of our technology;
and, in so doing, they can strengthen and give energy to
religious symbols and the collective unity. [24]

Whatever the truth of these paradoxical hypotheses,
we can in truth begin by saying that the interplay of
the opposing symbols, beliefs, and values of the non-
rational, moral, and sacred structures and the rationality
of the expanding technology, is a basic theme that we
Americans and others must continue to explore with
great care. Here lies the area where perhaps we will
learn the most about the development of these fundamental systems of meaning; and more importantly,
here we shall learn what kinds of new beliefs and values
are coming into being and what traditional ones are
holding and asserting their validities for the moral
control of the increasing rationality of our mental life.
We shall also state here that no one can fully understand symbolic behavior, or develop an adequate methodology for studying it, unless he relates what he is

doing to the moral and technological orders. This shall be a major task of this volume.

For the purpose of clarity it seems necessary to define briefly some key terms. Later these will be restated and amplified. [114f]

Symbols and their systems are composed of signs and their meanings. They refer to and stand for other objects, real or not. They evoke and express feelings and values. *Symbol systems* function in part to organize individual and group memories of the immediate and distant past and their expectancies of the future, and by so doing strengthen and unify the persistent life of each. Those symbols which evoke memories of past events for the individual or the group are greatly contracted and condensed, often modified beyond the power of the individual or group to recognize their full references. Such condensed systems arouse the emotions of individuals and the sentiments of the group. Generally speaking, symbol systems which direct the attention of the individual or group to the past and relate him to it tend to be social logics, to be nonrational and evocative rather than rational and referential.

Meaning is culture-bound and species-bound. The contexts of the society and the species in which particular signs are used must always be considered. Meaningful existence within the organic species and the cultural tradition is controlled and determined by each of these closed systems. The adaptations of each to the rest of nature are necessary and have most important influences, but the experience felt, the effects achieved, and the meanings of the world outside man and his culture, are always mediated and transformed by the limitations and needs of the human organism in its cultural context. Direct experience with nature is necessary and unavoidable, but the meaning of the experience is always transformed into what is significant to the animal and social life of the group. A changing American culture, spreading its expanding technology across and into the natural world of things, constantly increases its store of meanings for natural reality; yet the new experiences felt and recorded are transmitted through the changing yet traditional cores of meaning of that culture and are bound within the organic limitations of the species. Scientists should not forget that myth and so-called "scientific reality" alike attribute meaning to human life or nature only as man experiences each within the confines of his own species.

The term *species* emphasizes the group character of man's animal nature and behavior rather than the individual. It emphasizes the unconscious, non-rational and adaptive aspects of human thought, emotion, and behavior rather than the irrational. A principal distinction between non-rational and irrational behavior is that the former is adaptive and the latter is not. The first holds human beings together and is creative; the latter pulls them apart. [114*f*]

So much for the species context of meaning. Now let us examine the social context and the meanings of the moral and technical orders. As conceived here, the American society is a vast, interconnected set of relations comprised of constituent parts, the whole composing a social system. The constituent parts are the structural form of our life, consisting of interrelated social positions which order all the activities of those in the system, the technology which instrumentalizes the system and adapts the whole society to nature, and the symbols, beliefs, and values including the conscious and unconscious feelings, the rational and non-rational principles which motivate and determine the behavior of those in the American social system. All of the parts are emergent and changing, each within itself, each to the other, and each within the total system which is the larger American society.

The application of technical, scientific, and rational knowledge and the skillful use of tools and machines to provide for the material needs of the populace make up the technological subsystem which controls and transforms the natural environment. By morally ordering the relations among those who fill its different economic and social statuses, such as managers and workers, buyers and sellers, parents and children, and husbands and wives, it regulates the human species environment and thus provides the rights and privileges, the obligations and duties, for those who interact in the total social system.

All these adaptive subsystems are mutually dependent. The symbols of the moral order, those which convey the group's meaning for the rules governing human conduct—beliefs and values about right and wrong, good and bad, and what is to be rewarded or punished —are integral parts of the basic moral relation of the society with the animal life of the species.

The moral order, by its direct involvement with the interactions of individual members of the species, helps channel their feelings into meaningful and cohesive relations, thereby permitting the powerful life energies of the species to be culturally expressed. [1] In this matrix, particularly in the family system, the growing individual, while he learns the rules, experiences the negative and positive social sanctions of criticism, physical punishment, bodily rewards for acting or failing to act according to the precepts of the moral order. The moral order aids the technological in helping the individual to learn, use, and invent symbols which refer to and express outer physical reality. The environmental forces of animal life are felt by the moral order, and the knowledge of technology presses heavily upon it, forcing it to adjust itself to the natural environment. Social control of the species and the natural environment must be constantly synchronized, and continuing adjustment is required between them. [114*f*]

Non-rational symbols are a basic part of the animal and moral organization of man. They express and evoke the feelings and sensuous observations of animals in an interactive group. The signs and gestures used are not private but part of the basic sociality of man. They relate to his deepest emotions. Within them flow the vital energies and emotional significance of species behavior. When individuals grow up these symbols are not stripped of their egocentric meanings but undergo modification and become part of the symbolic equipment of mature men and women, remaining deep within their mental and moral selves. Such symbols are not unadaptive because they are non-rational; on the contrary, these evocative symbols, directly related to the species organization of man, allow this part of man's essential nature to be expressed and justified without the restrictions of cultural and moral life interfering. With their aid, man remains a *full* participant in the life of his species. Without their aid, he encounters painful difficulties.

It is not until attention is turned to the sacred symbol system that the purest form of symbol system is found, combining species and social symbols. This system of supernatural adjustment reduces and helps to control the anxieties and fears felt by members of the species because of insecurity in the natural and moral environments. Man's inability to control parts of the environments on which he depends for his individual and group survival is the source of his deepest anxiety and accordingly a prepotent influence on sacred rituals and beliefs. It only need be mentioned that his anxieties come from his experiences with the real threats of his natural environment and the equally real ones of his species existence as well as from the fearful fantasies of his moral and social life.

Let us now turn our attention to the other important concept mentioned earlier. What is meant by *emergent?* The most general meaning, that of the dictionary, speaks of the appearance of new properties in the course of development and the arising of entirely new elements during the several phases of an entity's career. This, of course, includes all kinds of objects, both human and non-human. The term as we use it is more limited and of greater scientific utility. In brief, it means that the processes of change are in themselves integral parts of the social system. The very nature of the American social system, if it persists in being what it is, must be in continual change. Each part has within it something coming into being and something ceasing to be. Moreover, the cultural past is continually being absorbed into the present and the present into the future, and each loses part of its identity by this process of absorption.

The whole emergent process, moving in the direction of continual experimentation, heterogeneity, specialization, increasing division of labor, as well as velocity, is partly restrained and contained by social forms and pressures which provide common experiences, values, and beliefs. The general tendency toward symbolic heterogeneity and diversity is counterbalanced by that toward symbolic homogeneity and uniformity. Tendencies that make men and women different and difficult to approach in terms of their separateness from the commonalities are counterbalanced by those symbolic processes which lead them to the common places of the cultural past and of the cultural experience of today. The fundamental *core* values of our society, those that lie deeply buried within the accumulated experiences of the human species here in our culture, are continuous processes that might finally undergo modifications by the emergence of new forms but actually maintain their basic order because they derive their energies from what, for lack of a better term, I shall call the "eternal" nature of the human species.

For people living in this fluid world, the symbols of individual autonomy, with individual choice-making and individually used beliefs and values, are absolute necessities. As here used, individual autonomy is both moral and intellectual; the individual applies social and intellectual symbols, as an individual, to himself and others. The fact that he is autonomous does not mean that he is completely different and separate from his group and from the core values of his group; rather, it means he has within himself the intellectual and moral ability to make decisions necessary for immediate action.

As our society becomes more extended and more diverse, individual decision-making necessarily becomes more frequent, complex, and demanding. When the individual moves from status to status, from place to place, and, as he must sometimes, from moment to moment, in the emergent great society, he must redefine who he is and what he does primarily on his own initiative. One must suspect that greater social complexity and rapid social change in the inner and outer worlds of everyone increase the need for individual symbols for decision-making, for intellectual and moral autonomy, and that they instigate our society's high evaluation of individuals with these capacities. Now to turn to another part of the argument, with new evidence for its support.

The functions and autonomy of the multitude of local communities throughout the United States are diminishing radically. Almost all primary interaction used to take place in towns and cities, where face-to-face relations characterized the group life of men and women. At the present time the emergence of the great, complex organizations that enter all parts of our lives —technological, moral, and sacred—is bringing into being a larger, national community where direct action, communication, and face-to-face relations now occur.

A great primary society now exists. The many local groups are still important and necessary parts of our social apparatus but now, instead of having only their own kind of autonomy, they are integral parts of the larger American, not to say world, social system. These changes have developed a great society which continues to emerge and become something more than what it now is. Covariantly changing with the structure of this

great society, symbol systems are developing which relate men more effectively across different cultures and
divisions of labor.

The present great diversity of American symbol systems is related to the high division of labor and extreme
complexity of the social structure. Two contrary tendencies operate in the symbolic behavior of contemporary America. Since early settlement there have been increasing diversity, heterogeneity, and exclusiveness, now
to the point of individuation. On the other hand, as
the American society grows more complex and the
symbol systems more diverse, a second tendency—an
opposing but necessary one—operates. There is an increasing generalization and standardization of public
symbols understood by all levels and all kinds of members of the society. Some of these public symbols, such
as the communication of certain mass media and of
certain kinds of sacred symbols [51], are highly stereo-
typed and, as their names suggest, have common acceptance by diverse groups within the masses of the
people. Whereas the segmenting symbolic process is related to the diverse structural units, to social differentiation, and to the increasing tendency of America to
form each new individual into a semi-autonomous unit
and private social system of his own, the second or
unifying tendency is directly related to the social need
to maintain a minimum cohesion and a larger solidarity. [81] Over all, integrative symbol systems which
everyone understands and which evoke common sentiments, values, and beliefs for all members of the society
are expressions of this second tendency. They provide
the symbols which are exchanged by everyone in the

group and are the materials most fitted for common use. [82]

Complex societies must have a common core of basic understandings known and used by everyone, or their complex symbolic superstructures will not stand. They need general symbol systems that everyone not only knows but feels. We must now take a close look at the nuclear family and the role it plays in our technological society.

The Moral Order of the Family and Sacred Symbol Systems

The family system externally is related to, integrated with, and functions for this larger moral and symbolic system. Internally, the family controls impulse life, distributes affection, orients the younger generation to this system, and provides a moral form for species life. The two, the internal and external controls, are in probable opposition. [114c] Obviously there is greater need in our complex society for a family system constituted to let us train our children for diverse occupations and activities, to interact socially and economically in the diverse and changing social systems. Training cannot be for fixed and permanent tenure of the individuals in one position; American families must train their children mentally and morally for decision-making, for movement and individual choice in a changing society of changing individuals. To allow men and women to move from occupation to occupation and between various statuses, demands the training and forming of persons capable, with minimal effort, of adjustment and continuous re-adjustment.

To move easily in the circulation of personnel, the members of families cannot be too closely attached to their kindred or they will be held to one location socially and economically. This is true for both the family of birth and the family of marriage for each individual. It is also true for the individual moving from his family of birth to his family of marriage. Consequently, for structural congruence the individual's families of birth and marriage must be loosely related—the relation of two semi-autonomous units. The training of children by parents in the family of birth must allow them to internalize the symbols and values of the group so that they will be motivated to choose for themselves.

This loose family order provides for greater maneuverability and flexibility. The younger generation is more easily adapted by the society to its new ways that are partly in change; this necessarily means that the symbols and the training for using these symbols must allow the individual to operate freely and easily with them and within the complexities and changes of contemporary technological society.

The increased diversity and integration of different groups and social levels as well as of symbols and their systems, have been accomplished and maintained by training the younger generation's developing members for individual decision-making and moral autonomy— by autonomous families partly freed from the restraints of the families of the father's father and the mother's father or, in social-anthropological terms, from the past as it is present in the persons of the second descending generation. Therefore the traditions of the past have fewer opportunities to make their demands and to control the development of generations of grandchildren by the grandparents.

Wider integration of the society and growing family autonomy also increase the expression of affection and control within the family; or perhaps the same amount of affection is distributed among a smaller number of kindred. Fewer direct relations with other kindred to allow affection-giving seems to be a constant experience for many in this society. The confinement of emotion within the small family increases the possibility that more hostility and love will be intensely felt and thus will have to be controlled and properly distributed. Consequently there is a greater problem of reducing hostility and placing it elsewhere. Since for many the larger kin group no longer functions in our society as it once did, the outside non-kin group tends to take over the affection and hostility that can be bestowed; therefore, the functions of friendship groups are important. The greater problem of handling unconscious impulse life is also related to our feelings of control and taboo around sexual expression within the family. The changing meaning of the mother image in infancy, childhood and adolescence, and maturity is a crucial one in America. It is necessary that the individual free himself easily from his family of orientation and the affections placed there; yet given our family system, this is much more difficult to do than it once was.

The changing place of the autonomous families and their members requires re-evaluation and re-symbolization of themselves, the society around them, and the kinship persons to whom they are related. In a rigid society only age-graded family definitions and evaluations are present; in an open and flexible society such as ours, with free access to status, this means changing social perspective and constant redefinition.

Despite all this, the core of family and species life remains largely fixed and impermeable; the basic emotional core and its experiences and the nucleus of each family role today are still similar to the past. Part of this, of course, is that the family system lies buried more deeply in species life than any other social institution. Consequently the central usages are the same; the meanings of the symbolic apparatus at the sacred and secular levels change but little as compared with changes in the rest of the society. Still it is possible to say that the family symbols and the family structure at the sacred symbolic level diverge into two ideal extremes, both satisfied by empirical data, and both merging in various religious imagery. At the one extreme, traditional Catholic and certain Protestant sacred beliefs are present where the family symbols are clearly defined and function to evoke, express, and strengthen the deep species and social meanings of human experience in the family. All family symbols are present in this kind of symbolic and structural arrangement. At the other extreme, the family sacred figures have lost many of their meanings and definitions; consequently they do not express and evoke the feelings and beliefs which reinforce the traditional values of the society. Sacred beliefs are vague and, for some, nonexistent. [114f]

The great value placed on species life by the traditional church was a fundamental point of attack in the Protestant revolt. The meaning of eternal life as it flows through the species and finds its most significant expression in the generative processes was, and is, a mystery of the most sublime importance in the symbolic life of the traditional church. Male and female fulfilling their symbolic functions in species behavior are necessary and central parts of the most sacred level of its belief system; not male or female as moral beings only, but male and female entire in all their procreative life-giving and life-fulfilling significance. [23]

A consequence of family autonomy in the symbolic behavior of our own culture is that the core of family life increasingly becomes the central social experience that all Americans share. They who live in diversity accordingly use logical and non-logical symbols referring to and expressing the values and emotions resulting from their deeper experiences during their lives. Although diverse in form, such symbols may arouse common feelings. One merely has to mention such popular ceremonial days as Mother's Day, Thanksgiving, Christmas, and the like, to make this clear.

Another consequence of family autonomy is that most commonly shared symbols tend to be founded more on the deeper emotional and moral life of the family and less on the broader and less emotional experiences of the larger society. Therefore, although it may be losing its utilitarian functions, the family is becoming increasingly significant as an emotional matrix for the non-logical and evocative symbolic life of the group. Meanwhile, and contrary to this, the rational and empirical symbols of the technology are related to the broader and less emotional experiences of the group. Primarily related to the natural environment and to the rational processes for controlling it, they have grown and spread as the national society has grown and spread; they have developed and increased their power and significance as the great society has taken the place of the multitude of local communities.

Therefore, at one and the same time, the secular, technological symbol systems, with their rational beliefs and values, have increased in importance both relatively and absolutely while the deeper and more emotional and evocative systems of meaning that are related to the family as a moral and a species order have also become more significant. As the local community systems of value have contracted and retreated, and as the older moral order has been absorbed into the larger national society, the non-logical structure of the mental life of most individuals has, as a consequence, been molded increasingly in the autonomous family. The result of this is the development of a greater use of autonomous symbols, both at the moral and evocative levels and at the secular and technological levels; and as such, when viewed in this context, the paradoxes earlier stated cease to have the same significance as when viewed in propositional form.

Let us now restate them.

That the use of the rational technical knowledge along with its symbols and values increases in amount and kind, and continues to spread over larger areas of our system is demonstrably true. That individuals are increasingly, intellectually and morally, autonomous and necessarily must confront and solve problems that often demand scientific rationalism is a correlate of the first proposition.

Both are true because our emergent society is moving in the direction of increasing heterogeneity, economically, socially, and symbolically; at the same time, the multiplicity of local community controls lessens as the great national society continues to strengthen and elaborate its over-all symbolic, moral, and technological systems. The moral, technological, and symbolic life of our local communities continues and will continue but, as the power and significance of the great national society expand and grow in importance, their social strength contracts for more individuals and for more of the mental and moral activities of the collectivity.

Meanwhile the family, that hardy, eternal institution of our moral and species existence, modifies itself as it takes on the task of helping form the new individuals of the new generations, those who must live successfully in the great society now coming into being. Within its immediate and ultimate and, I hope, its inexhaustible powers, our ancient moral order is nurtured and protected. [23] In it a multiplicity of moral and symbolic tasks takes refuge. Many of those which formerly were effective parts of the multitude of local communities, and accordingly experienced and learned by the individuals developing in them now are being absorbed by the families.

As we have seen, many of the local tasks at all levels of adjustment including the symbolic have been absorbed by the national society. The nuclear family, now itself increasingly autonomous, trains the young and, more and more, controls the deeper non-logical moral and symbolic life of the mature. While allowing each, the young and the old, flexibly to yield to and use the rationality of science and technology, the family at the same time forms these individuals as sons and daughters, fathers and mothers, and husbands and wives, within its ancient mold into moral and mental beings who, in the emergent process, maintain the central signifi-

cances of man. As such, the family and the human beings which it helps create determine the fundamental
symbolic life, secular and sacred, of our onward moving
existence.

The non-logical moral order, whose principles of
truth and methods of reality testing are not dependent
on the empirical data of rational science, has validities
and significances testable only in the feelings and beliefs
and behavior that are integral and necessary parts of
the unchanging nature of the human species. These
truths and their symbols, overtly and covertly stated,
are not necessarily local for they are not dependent on
locality; they are not only American, for they are elsewhere; they are not just for today or tomorrow, they
are wherever man is, wherever he has been and will be,
for they are eternal. [17]

At the sacred level these fundamental symbols and
values created and formed in the family continue in
the images of God the Father, the Mother, Their Son,
and, through Him, all of us. At the secular level,
despite continuing attack, is the basic secular (and
mystical) symbol of the Brotherhood of Man, a powerful image founded on the basic truths of man's family
nature. [102a, 102b]

When men of the age of steel and atomic fission see
Oedipus Rex they easily respond to its beauty and to
the thoughts and feelings of a dramatist who lived many
years before Christ's birth. What makes it possible to
arouse their sympathy, their fear, and pity, and gives
human meanings to Oedipus, the man "who walked-in-
pain," are the shared experiences and feelings that all
men, ancient Greeks and those now alive, must have
by virtue of living in families. All people, however

primitive or civilized, deep within them hold these fears in common. Each of us can walk in pain with Oedipus, since we share common feelings and a common conscience with him. Through this human symbol, born out of myth and fashioned by the literary arts, we are allowed to express that which we cannot say. Oedipus' fate of killing his father, marrying his mother, and the awful tragedy he experienced as a moral being when he learned what he had done arouse the deepest emotions in men of every culture. Everyone can understand and share in the tragedy of such a man:

> His staff groping before him, he shall crawl
> O'er unknown earth, and voices around him call:
> "Behold the brother-father of his own
> Children, the seed, the sower and the sown,
> Shame to his mother's blood, and to his sire
> Son, murderer, incest-worker."

The meanings of the moral and sacred orders in all cultures more often than not lie deeply bound beneath rational existence in the solid core of species life. It is no accident that most religious beliefs are fundamentally based on the simplest realities and on the relations of family deities. These figures, coming out of the unity of the family, express as no other human symbols can the desire of all men to be one, yet separate, for as the sons of God in His family they can all be, or could be, brothers.

CHAPTER 2

Family Symbolism and the Sacred Collectivity: A Comparison

The sacred symbolism in America insofar as it is expressed in Christianity necessarily will have its unique qualities and characteristics. It serves and expresses the significances of an enormous collectivity in an industrial society that strongly emphasizes scientific beliefs and values. These symbols and those of other faiths, such as the Jewish, are integral parts of an emergent process in many ways unique. One would suppose that the influences of the huge diverse collectivity and the movements of emergent change would in themselves greatly modify Christian beliefs and practices. Yet there are reasons to believe that the ecumenical movements among both Protestants and Catholics gain in strength and significance, that the accomplished and planned amalgamations of Protestant churches, and the resurgence of Christian life generally, are indications of American Christianity moving toward integration rather than separation and possibly moving. toward closer similarity if not unification with the faiths of other cultures.

Whether these hypotheses and indications be true or not, before investigating the symbolic evidence for purposes of more objective analysis and evaluation of our own life, we need to inspect more closely the relations of the social structure and family organization to sacred symbolism and the effects of social change on sacred belief. To do this we will use the comparative method and, in this chapter, with field evidence from social anthropology, we shall examine these problems as they exist in other religions and societies. The totemic religion and simple society of the Australian aborigines, with little or no change, provide a sharply contrasting case for our own; the Siberian Chuckchee allow us a view of sacred symbolism reacting to rapid change in another society, much simpler than ours. We shall also view the social structure of the complexly organized African Bantu with an elaborate hierarchy and economic life more nearly like our own than the other two.

From these we can prepare to look at our own society, its sacred symbols, and the significance of family life for Christian symbolism. Let us begin with the Australian totemites.

Family, Clan, and Sacred Totem

The Murngin, a hunting and gathering people of North Australia, are very simply organized, having no political or economic system and no superior or inferior social classes. [114a] They are organized by three fundamental types of social structure, all founded biologically —those of age, sex, and family kindred. Their age and sex differences are expressed in age-grades where for certain purposes men are formally separated from women and organized by, and initiated into, a few age groupings. The kindred are divided into families and clans and these are re-grouped into two larger territorial clans (moieties). The age-sex divisions and the families and clans with an elaborate kinship structure dominate and control all the life of the Murngin. Those functions ordinarily performed by economic systems and political institutions in other tribes and nations are exercised by the family, clan, and age-grade.

When an individual is born he is a member of a family, a clan, one of the two major moieties, and is given his or her place in the age divisions and in the social group of his or her sex; thus, to speak in Murngin terms, before he is born he is all that he will ever be as a member of his group. The act of birth permanently places a woman in all respects; a man must move by initiation through the three ritual age levels.

All are born equal and die equal. The only social distinctions are that women are spiritually inferior to men, and children are subordinate to adults. The older age status for men is ritually and socially superior to all other statuses.

The religion of the Murngin, like that of the Arunta of Central Australia whose "elementary forms" of religion Émile Durkheim interpreted, is totemic; as clan members they are in ritual relations with spiritual species of plants and animals. Each clan has a sacred well or pool in which live its several higher and lower totems, the dead ancestors, and unborn souls. An individual, male or female, is born to and "inherits" his clan and his totems from his father. Before birth a man's soul, it is believed, must come out of his clan well and enter his mother; only after this can he and his soul be born. At approximately his sixth year he is ritually circumcized and enters a higher age level;

at sixteen to twenty years he is initiated into a higher
social and sacred level; at forty years he is shown the
high and very secret totems of the old men of his clan
and enters the highest age level. At death he returns
to the souls of the dead, to his clan's mythological
ancestors and totems, there to live forever in the sacred
clan well. A woman's soul follows the same circular
route, with the significant age initiations absent.

The religious rites of the Murngin are very elaborate
celebrations held during the dry season when food is
plentiful and male celebrants can congregate in large
numbers. It is a ritual season of great excitement following a dull season when food is scarce. The principal
ceremonies are related to a sacred myth. Each of the
hundreds of dramatic dances and sacred songs which
compose a ceremony, climaxed by the appearance of
the totemic emblems, is a dramatic representation giving expression to the sacred story of the myth.

Each myth and its totemic ceremonies describe symbolically how each clan was organized, its history, its
relations to all other clans and to each of the two major
clans or moieties. The myth tells, and its ritual songs
and dances make manifest, how the clan ancestors captured the totem and by force took it from their women;
thus men became dominant, more spiritual, in control
of ritual power, and the conductors of the all-powerful
totemic rites. The women lost ritual power, were less
spiritual and more profane; now they are only the
secular gatherers of food to provide for the celebrants of
the totemic rites. Most totemic ceremonies are used to
initiate the males into higher age grades. Circumcision,
in honor of Bapa Indi, the Great Father Python of the
python clan, lifts a small boy into the young men's

class; in the initiation rite of the eighteen-year-olds the huge trumpet emblem of Bapa Indi is first seen. The many totems are spiritually higher and lower, the more powerful being "deeper down in the totemic well."

The mental life and symbol systems of the Murngin are not highly differentiated as they are in our complex society and in other complex social structures. Their two principal symbol systems are language and religion. Dancing, singing, painting, drawing, and art generally are parts of the ritual life of the tribe and have their meaning and being within the religious context.

Most of the mental life of a Murngin lies implicit in his myth and ritual. Most of his learning is simple: a simple secular technology and an easily learned moral order relate him to nature and man; his cosmology and cosmogony are founded on his totemic religion. The cohesive, highly integrated moral system is reflected in the undifferentiated religious symbol system. The stone-age technology has a rudimentary but highly practical body of knowledge which effectively relates the male hunters and the female gatherers to the world around them. Plants and animals as technological *facts* are the family's food supply; as *symbols* they are transitory embodiments of ultimate sacred reality, the totemic species. Thus the passing present members of the human species and those of other species around them live in organic fact, yet have their eternal being, spiritually, in the sacred symbols of the supernatural.

Evidence is ample that Murngin sacred symbols largely are intellectual and moral representations of the family, clan, and moiety kindred, and of the age-sex divisions. The data show the totemic emblems to be collective representations of the father's family, his clan and moiety, intellectually formed by the collective hypostatization of the sex principle and masculine dominance. All totemic beings have kinship and family terms and, as members of the clan, are spiritual kindred. The "totem-god," the Great Father Python for example, is a sacred symbol of the clan generally. During ceremonial times Bapa Indi, the Great Father, becomes manifest in a huge wooden trumpet covered with the consecrated blood of his masculine celebrants. Then, in particular, he is the potent symbol of the older, more spiritually potent men's part of the clan.

Thus among the Murngin the facts clearly bear out the hypothesis that the family and its collective structures are collectively represented in their sacred symbol systems. They also demonstrate a close connection between the low technological development and the use of rational and non-rational symbols of totemism to solve most problems of this sacred society. Here secular thought is not important: it describes and acts in the technology; it does not explain. This is for sacred, non-rational thought to accomplish. Throughout this system of symbol and structure the family is the ultimate point of reference, the creator, the end and beginning for the ultimate meanings of human existence.

The Sacred Ancestors

Let us now turn to a very different kind of social system, a complex one with a high division of labor. Many of the people of Africa who speak Bantu live in such complex societies; some of the old indigenous cultures had well-developed governmental and judicial systems, advanced agricultural technologies and economic systems that supported large populations within the

political controls of one Bantu nation. [94] The basic
social fabric uniting local populations into cohesive
units was and is the kinship system, which may be
patrilineai or matrilineal. In the patrilineal groups the
father is the absolute head of the household. He is
master of several wives and their children, who live in
huts organized into a "kraal" with a fenced yard.

A cluster of kraals with their several gardens, common
lands, and grazing grounds compose a village, adminis-
tered by a local chief or head man who has a considerable amount of economic control and authority. Several villages may be regrouped into a larger subdistrict,
and several subdistricts into a district, the latter a still
larger political unit with a larger territory and a larger
body of citizenry. The district chief exercises political
authority and has considerable political power over his
province. Finally, there may be a still more extensive
organization, the kingdom, comprising several prov-
inces, ruled by a paramount chief or king. The court of
the paramount chief is often filled with many functionaries whose offices are staff divisions of the complex one
occupied by the king. The king or paramount chief
has great political, juridical, and economic power.

This social system, once typical of pre-industrial western Europe, appears to be and is complex, yet the principles of organization are simple and must be understood to comprehend fully the religious system. The
father, we said, is the head of his several families and
his kraal. The relations of those beneath him are all
familial. Ideally the most important relation for the
maintenance of this unit is that of the eldest son to his
father. The relation of the local headman is conceived
as being that of a father to his people; his and his

people's conduct is governed accordingly. The same paternal definition is extended upward to the office of the rulers at the higher levels of this hierarchy which control larger bodies of subjects.

The king is often in name the father of his people. His and his subjects' rights and duties are ordered in this basic pattern. Richards says, "The sub-chief and the chief . . . assume the functions of the patriarchal head of a family, transformed and on a larger scale. They are addressed by the 'father' term and become the object of a quasi-filial sentiment. Like the father, also, the chief is in control of food resources." [1]

The attitudes of respect and obeisance from the subjects and the degrees of subordination and political power increase as the offices of the hierarchy ascend, but they do not change in kind. The child who has learned how to behave with proper respect for his father and has the ability to compete in the family yard with his male siblings from his father's several families has learned the basic rules of conduct for his adult relations with his head man, chief, and king. He need but add a few flourishes to his manners and elaborate his etiquette to be a polished courtier at the high court of the king.

We are obviously before a social structure very different from the Murngin's. In addition to a larger territory inhabited by large populations there is a hierarchy which places people in superior and inferior relations. The Murngin are democratic and simply organized; the Bantu, aristocratic and complexly organized. The family and the father in each system are of absolute importance for it. The father's clan and moiety in Australia are expansions of the family—they only

1. Richards [94], p. 144.

redesign its membership; in Africa the nuclear family
and the father's status are extended into an elaborate
hierarchy.

The Bantu worship their ancestors much as do many
other people, including the Chinese. The ancestors are
the most sacred symbols they possess. Unlike the Murngin, everyone cannot take the lead in the religious exercises. The father has this important function for his own
family. He is the only one who is permitted access to
the family ancestors. The ritual which he conducts is
a sacrifice, usually an offering of flour or beer—the
bread and wine of the country—to his family's ancestral
spirits. On very important occasions a cow may be sacrificed. Many authorities say that the intellectual and
emotional core of ancestor worship throughout the
Bantu is the cult of the father and the immediate family gods. The intimate family relations which the father
previously had with the living are continued after their
deaths; the worship of their family spirits, recently
dead, gives meaning, power, and direction to the religious beliefs and processes of an entire Bantu nation.

Just as the father and head man and the chief and
king have analogous functions, the latter greatly extended and more important, at their levels in the economic and political hierarchy, so do they in their religious life. [94] The ancestral spirits are stratified and
allocated to each level. Richards declares,

> the same hierarchical organization can be observed
> in the case of those ancestral spirits who are be-
> lieved to be responsible for the general welfare and
> prosperity of the people. Just as the father's right
> of access to the family ancestors is one of the sources

of his authority in the kinship group, so the chief's privilege of approaching the tribal deities is one of the essential functions of his leadership, and fixes his whole position in the economic scheme. The immediate family ancestors perform quasi-paternal functions, since they bless their own descendants with prosperity—increase of cattle, fruit trees, and crops—and protect them from sickness. Like the father, these personal ancestors are members of one definite family . . . and are responsible only for their own descendants.[2]

Richards goes on to say that for some tribes communal ancestors are those of the paramount chief and that he, in the capacity of a priest of his ancestral line, sacrifices to the national gods. He is, says Junod, "a son of the gods not only their protégé." [3]

Examination of the liturgical forms of the Bantu sacrifice yields further insight into the nature of their symbolic processes and contributes to our understanding of the general problem of sacred symbol systems. The sacrificial rite is a ceremonial meal in which the ancestral spirits and the living kindred participate and commonly share consecrated food. The flesh of the slaughtered cow is divided among members of the community of the living and dead kindred according to the rules governing those of an ordinary meal. The sacrificial ritual meal among these people is a collective representation which expresses the social structure of the family life and that of the larger collectivity. Richards says, quoting Willoughby,

2. *Ibid.*, p. 154.
3. *Ibid.*, p. 155.

The Gods have therefore to fulfill not only the
general obligations of the human father to succour
and provide for his family, but they are, as he is,
parties to the marriage contract of the earthly children . . . the sacrifice in itself is a public meal. It
is, in fact, a replica of the family meal—in a sense, a
meal shared by god and worshippers alike. The
evoked spirit and his ghostly kinsmen feed upon
the victim, and the sacrificer and his living relatives share the feast with their unseen guests.[4]

The translation of the meanings of an ordinary meal
of kindred to those of a sacred rite shared by them and
their gods was first identified and named by Robertson
Smith [105] and Ernest Crawley. [27] We must spend
only a brief moment here with their theories, and later
we shall return to them. Smith, viewing the ritual meal
as an expression of group life, said that it bound the
living among themselves and in the minds of the worshippers united them with their gods.

Among the Bantu the sharing of food on earth binds
people together, and active eating binds unseen members of the family group with the earthly. The same
rights, obligations, and duties which govern those who
share the common meal among the living bind those
among the dead who share a ritual meal with them. To
quote Richards again, "The spirits appealed to in daily
life are the ancestors of the family group. The ritual
meal binds the living and the dead to fulfill their part
in this complex scheme of family obligations." [5] The

4. *Ibid.,* p. 186.
5. *Ibid.,* p. 187.

father sacrifices to, and eats with, his family ancestors and obligates them to provide for him and those for whom he is responsible. The king sacrifices to, and eats with, the tribal gods and thereby ritually expresses their obligations to look out for him and his people. Those among the living who have or have not the right to partake are precisely those who can or cannot partake of the ordinary family meal; and those among the sacred ancestors who can partake, be it king's meal or commoners', are those who when alive were in the kinship circle.

The gods are not equal among themselves, but unequal—like those who worship them—in a hierarchy. The family god bows before the might of the tribal deity. Each god increases the area of his influence and the number of people over whom he holds control in exactly the degree of his increase of position within the social hierarchy.

Chart 1 pictures the relations among the social institutions and sacred symbols of the Bantu. Down at the right of the lowest lateral line is the term father and the small rectangle to represent his status; to the right of him is a larger rectangle for his family and house area. Ascending from him are the head man, the district chief, and the king, each with his group and territory.

To the left of the father on the lowest lateral line, and a little above him, are his immediate ancestors, and they, in the chart, are connected with the dead of the family locally organized.

Thus the unity of the dead and the living at the family level is organized.

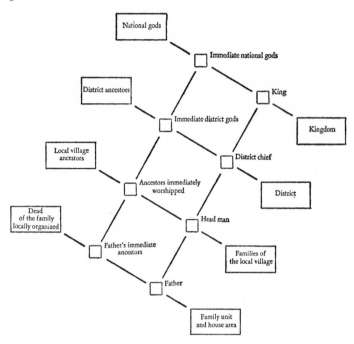

Chart 1. The Bantu Family: Social Structure and Sacred Symbol System

At the next level, the lateral extension runs from the left and the several families of a village, through the head man on to the right and local village ancestors. Above are the lines for the district and its ancestors and the king and the national gods; thus the national gods of the state are rightfully placed at the pinnacle of the chart and are reached from the lowest point where the father and his family are located. But the conceptual and emotional image of the great gods of the state at the pinnacle and those who worship them are founded on, and significant only because of, the nuclear family, a father and his family.

The Family Blood Mark and the Sacred Fire

The last people we shall discuss before turning to our own society are the Chuckchee. [6] These people, living in the far north of Siberia, on the Pacific Ocean, now earn their living by keeping large herds of reindeer. Formerly they were a fishing group, as some of their nearby kinsmen still are. The Chuckchee are very simply organized. They live in small or large village bands which move at least seasonally to give their flocks new pasturage. The basic unit of their social system is the family and the larger kin group called the *varat*. These people have no purely political, economic, or associational institutions. They are dependent upon their kinship system, the family, and varat for the maintenance of their social life. [6]

The varat is patrilineal. Males and females are born into the father's varat group and the boy remains there, but when the girl marries, she joins her husband's, thereby emphasizing the strong patrilineal principle of reckoning relationships. To obtain the girl, her prospective husband works in the camp of the father for the right to take her away with him.

In addition to the family and varat, the Chuckchee have an institution referred to as marriage companionship. Two or more Chuckchee men enter a binding agreement by which they have access to each other's wives. This agreement is a serious one since the men accept all the responsibilities of blood revenge and all the fundamental duties of a varat member.

The religious system is a simple one. There is a belief in spirits and, although everyone has access to them, the shaman is in closest and most effective contact.

There are two basic sacred symbolic rites, investiture of the sacred blood mark and the maintenance of the purity of the sacred fire. When a child is born, it is given the father's blood mark in a religious ceremony. This rite, it is believed, removes him from the dangerous position he occupies at birth; since he has just arrived from the powerful world of the spirits, he is still felt to be a member of the spirit group until by the formal initiation of the blood mark he enters his father's group.

At marriage a daughter moves from her father's camp to that of her husband's father and becomes a member when given the blood mark of her husband's people: the son's wife is given her husband's blood mark.

When Chuckchee men organize a marriage companionship and (in effect) create a new varat for themselves, they ceremonially exchange blood marks, thus symbolically stating the new relationship. However, the blood mark exchange is felt to be more than a mere exchange of symbols, as will be clear when the sacred fire symbol is discussed. *The active effect of the symbol exchange is to make the symbolic rite the thing it stands for; the men feel they are one and so bound by the sacred rite's mysterious action.*

Each group of kindred possesses a sacred fire. No other fire can be mingled with it, no alien fuel used with it, no outsider's food cooked upon it. No one not belonging to the family group can remove a brand from it. The mother's people are barred from the fire; only relatives of the male line may mingle their fires and exchange faggots. The Chuckchee's religious emblems, fetishes, and charms are symbolically connected with and derive their power from the sacred fire. The fire symbolizes and expresses the sentiments aroused in the varat group. The Chuckchee are deeply attached to this sacred symbol (we should say symbol system, since there are a series of complex sacred practices centered around the fire).

Symbol and referent often become one in their practices. At times, because of economic advantages, several poor men pool their herds, but they keep their fires separate. Occasionally through misadventure the faggots from their fires may mix. When they do, a purification ceremony is held, and the formerly separated groups become one varat. The combining of the symbols automatically forces the combination of the groups they symbolize. The maintenance of the power of the symbol is more important to the people involved than the maintenance of their social structure.

The sacred fire and the blood mark are two sacred symbol systems which express and are formed by the same social reality—the group of kindred. What the totemic emblem of the clan is in Australia, the sacrifice in Africa, the tablet and temple in China, the blood mark and fire are to the Chuckchee. The symbols differ in form but are the same in function.

We have said that the reindeer economy is a comparatively recent development among these people. Their change from a maritime to a land existence has resulted in certain modifications of their social structure and, in conformance with these changes, the symbolic practices have also changed. The reindeer herds at first were small, and little change took place in the social organization. An old man and his sons took care of the flock and lived together with their wives and children. The work of this patrilineal, patrilocal group was

strengthened occasionally by the prospective sons-in-law
working out their obligations before taking away the
daughters of the family. But the herds grew. Some old
men became reindeer wealthy, and their herds were too
large to be cared for by their sons. Instead of inventing
a purely economic institution to solve this problem, the
Chuckchee modified the varat system.

The rich owner hired young men from the outside
as his assistants. They received their wages in animals.
However, these aliens, new to the camp and new in the
social system, were regulated by family usage. They, too,
became adopted sons-in-law and the husbands of the
man's daughters, but the daughters were not taken to
the camps of their husbands; they remained instead at
the father's home. Thus, to accommodate the new economy to the society, the whole system of residence was
reversed.

The symbolic rites also shifted. When the marriage
took place, instead of the daughter receiving her husband's blood mark, the husband received her father's.
He was made a member of the father-in-law's family
and varat and was liable for blood revenge. Furthermore, he used the sacred fire, and its emblems (fetishes)
became his. This method of adjusting the social structure to the new technology also resulted in an adjustment of the symbolic structure; it shows clearly how
sign and symbol express, and are expressions of, their
social structure.

So much for the sacred symbols and family life of the
three societies. Before leaving them, let us briefly compare them for our purposes.

The sacrifice to the ancestral gods of the Bantu and
their collective sacred meal are liturgical rites closely

resembling Jewish and Christian worship. (The Murngin, too, have a sacred meal, but it is not of great ceremonial importance to them.) The Australian totems and their "worship" in the image of the father and other kindred by the clan and moiety closely parallel the ancestor worship of the Bantu. The shifting social structure of the Chuckchee is interrelated with the shifting public worship and the significance of their blood mark and sacred fire. All symbol systems, in different ways, are related to the family structure.

We have examined very generally the relations of the family to the changing social structure in the broad spread of the American society. We have viewed the family and the social structure of three other societies and briefly viewed the relation of the symbol system to the family and the larger social structure. It is now time to turn to our own society and study the meanings and significances of Christian symbolism, Protestant and Catholic, as related to family imagery when it is interpreted in the context of the American social structure. Detailed evidence from the close study of an American community will be used.

Several important questions will guide our inquiry:

What is the nature of Christian symbolism in America?

What, if any, are the relations of rites and beliefs to the unity and diversity of the emergent social structure of the American collectivity?

What are the significances of the emergent processes of the American collectivity—increasing social differentiation combined with the old and new processes of homogeneity—for the presence or absence of faith among the churches and denominations?

Given increasing rationality and secularity, what is happening to the faith of America and the traditional non-rational sacred symbol systems?

Above all, what is the meaning and significance of the contemporary American family for understanding Christian symbolism in America?

Part II

God's New Kingdom

Introduction

The broad perspectives of the American family in the great emergent national society and of the human family in other societies as a potent matrix of sacred symbols, presented in Part I, prepare us for use of empirical evidence about Christian practice and belief. Most of the field work on the changing beliefs and values of Protestantism concerning man, God, and itself here presented was done in Yankee City. The first chapter in Part II interprets some of the meaning of the Protestant revolt; it also briefly reviews research evidence on the unity and diversity of belief among Christians in this country. To establish nationally the universe studied locally in American communities, the results of a careful study are used. The sacred beliefs of ordinary laymen, ancient doctrine, and modern faith, including those about the Trinity, the Father and His Son, Heaven, Hell, and the hereafter, are identified and counted. Catholics and members of all Protestant denominations supplied the facts on the conditions of contemporary belief in America.[1] Unity of belief and membership are in fact far greater than the apparent diversity.

The second chapter in Part II analyzes the symbols of a Tercentenary Procession which celebrated the history of New England as viewed through the eyes of the socially dominant Protestants. The procession was not

1. This excellent study done by other social scientists is not yet published.

staged for religious reasons, but among other ideas un-
covered by its symbols was the changing significance
that Protestant beliefs and values possess for present
believers. New meanings were added, and old ones
ignored or covertly attacked. The early fathers of New
England's theocracy lose their sanctity and some their
identity and, as anonymous figures, are symbolically
targets of today's hostility.

The evidence for Part II is from interview and observation. All the clergy were interviewed many times,
sermons were collected, congregations observed, and
their members interviewed. Church histories (there
were several good ones) and other religious documents
were collected. In a society that does not have writing,
such as that of the Australian aborigines, the field
worker's ultimate authorities on religion are the old
men of the tribe. They cite the ways and words of their
ancestors to validate and sanction their own sacred beliefs and actions. In a literate community those who
know and care have their own religious beliefs and
practices which can be heard and observed, but citations
for ultimate authority and the more profound truths,
particularly for the clergy, are also in sacred and semi-
sacred books and the written works of theologians and
holy men. [110] The several Catholic and Protestant
versions of the Bible are of course the best examples,
but the Roman Missal, the writings of authoritative
Protestant and Catholic theologians, liturgical and other
"guides" for the church seasons and Sunday sermons
are important data for the field study of American religion. Evidence from all the above categories was collected and used in this analysis.

CHAPTER 3

The Protestant Revolt and Protestant Symbolism

Christian Unity and Diversity

On a spring day of 1635 they came down the river and landed. Pushing through the salt grass onto high ground they fashioned rude shelters for their families and then built a meeting-house for God and their own collectivity. These Puritan founders of Yankee City were devout, hardheaded men. They knew what they wanted. Yet with all their reliance on common sense, logic, and their own ability to "figure things out" they, too, were driven by non-rational forces which surged through them and others like them in Europe and America—forces beyond their control or understanding. An autonomous conscience separated each of them from the English collectivity, and what a later prophet of their faith called self-reliance took them away from their homes across the Atlantic to an unknown wilderness. They were now "free" to order the unordered world around them in the image of themselves. This they proceeded to do. [83a]

Together and separately, in conflict and peace, these pious men founded a Protestant city and with other settlements established Protestant New England. [75] Here the values, sacred beliefs, and moral ideas of the Protestant revolt against the rule of established authority and the sacred symbols sanctioned by this authority grew and matured.

The early settlers of Yankee City were farmers, but not long after their arrival they began the enterprises that in time made them largely a seafaring people. According to local records the first wharf was built in 1655. By 1700 interest in commercial enterprises had grown to such an extent that the land along the river, hitherto held in common, was divided into river lots. "For two hundred years," says Samuel Eliot Morison, "the Bible was the spiritual, the sea the material sustenance of Massachusetts . . . For two centuries and more, the tidal waters [of the river] . . . midwifed hundreds of noble vessels; and Yankee City was the mart for a goodly portion of interior New England . . . [As early as] 1660 ship-building had become a leading industry in Yankee City . . ." By the time the Constitution was signed, "the lower river from Haverhill to Yankee City was undoubtedly the greatest ship-building center of New England, at this period as in colonial days." [1]

Following a brief depression after the Revolution, the people of Yankee City quickly regained the prosperity they had enjoyed before the war. They continued to harvest great oak logs from up the river and turn them into ships, the cordage industries flourished, fishing prospered, the distillation of rum and the rum trade yielded splendid profits. Capitalistic enterprises such as building bridges across the river and canals around the falls, and trade in lumber, farm, and manufactured produce with the populations of the interior, contrib-

1. Morison [78], pp. 101–2.

uted their portions to the renewed prosperity. A class of powerful merchant princes had firmly established their dynasties.

From 1790 to 1812 the mouth of the river harbored the greatest shipbuilding center in New England and the United States. At the same time the sea industry was led by some of the most astute men in the country. Yankee City supplied many—some say most—of the great names among merchant princes of the time. We have noted that the population almost doubled from the Revolutionary War through the period up to the census of 1810. From 1790 to 1806 the duties collected on imports tripled, while the sea-carrying trade in general grew enormously.

A high civilization had been established and a powerful economy founded which poured great wealth into the city and the rest of maritime New England. A great war had been won and a vigorous new nation established. A powerful party, the Federalists, dominated by the wealthy merchants of New England and the southern planters, through the instrument of the Constitution was running the country. Here Yankee City reached her greatest moment.

Some of the great names associated with the mercantile empires centered in Yankee City were the Lowells, the Jacksons, and the Tracys, as well as the more lately arrived Bartlets and Browns. In Yankee City as elsewhere in the harbor towns of Massachusetts, says Morison, "there was a distinct class of merchant princes who lived in magnificent style, surrounded by suggestions of oriental opulence." After the Revolution and up to the War of 1812, "they clung to the ways and fashions of colonial days or of 1790 at the latest, unwilling to admit even by the cut of a waistcoat that Robespierre could change the world." (This was the period from which an overwhelmingly disproportionate number of the floats in the Procession were taken.)

With their wealth the great merchants first built elegant mansions, such as the Dalton and Tracy houses, in the center of town and established country estates a few miles distant. Just before the turn of the century they started building along Hill Street, using the craftsmen whose competence had bested Europe in the building of ships. They surrounded their homes with gardens, filled them with furnishings and the other facts and symbols of European civilization. "Federalist architecture has here left perhaps her finest permanent trace. Hill Street," Morison remarks, "winding along a ridge commanding the river, rivals Chestnut Street of Salem, despite hideous interpolations of the late nineteenth century. The gambrel-roofed type lasted into the seventeen-nineties, when the Yankee City merchants began to build square, three-storied, hip-roofed houses of brick, surrounded with ample grounds, gardens, and 'housins.' . . ." [2]

Within these houses, dressed in the "small clothes" and "tie wigs" of court life of the eighteenth century, the great families accumulated the wealth, prestige, and power that ruled Yankee City and soon, with families from similar cities such as Salem and Boston, dominated the life of New England.

The embargo and catastrophic War of 1812 ended this period. [26] Yankee City did not recover from the destruction of her shipping and commerce, not only by

2. *Ibid.,* p. 153.

the war itself but by the government policies of the
southern and western agrarians, first under the leadership of Jefferson and Madison and later under new men
from the western states. Other cities in Massachusetts
—though not all—did retrieve the places they once held.
Boston rapidly rose to be the great metropolis of New
England. Evidence of the decline of Yankee City and
the end of the period of power and glory was fully sum-
marized at the time (1825–26) by Caleb Cushing, able
son of a prominent local family. After speaking of the
embargo and the war he declares: "During that calam-
itous period, our seamen were thrown out of employ-
ment; our traders lost their customers; the farmers, who
had looked to us for foreign commodities, and of whom
we had purchased lumber, and provisions, left our mar-
ket,—and our merchants were compelled to sit down
idly and see their ships rotting in the docks."

It is small wonder that in 1812, with ruin about them
—a disaster of federal policy—many contemplated what
the rest of the United States has called treason and
plotted among themselves to join Canada and once more
become a part of the political union of British peoples;
or considered secession, a movement that culminated in
the notorious Hartford Convention. During the transition from the sea to the land they saw their respectable
and profitable way of life being destroyed by the agrar-
ian South and the West, and by the forces of democracy
that came from revolutionary France as well as from
the new frontier states which espoused the cause of
France against that of Britain. Once the transition had
been made, all New England learned what Francis
Lowell and others had quickly understood, and they too

became integral parts of a continental United States and were able to continue in the great traditions established by their fathers.

Their descendants and those successfully incorporated into this superior status dominated Yankee City; they conceived, presented, and controlled the great Procession (as we shall see in the next chapter) which expressed for all their contemporaries the history of the town. Their sources of income and economic power have changed, but the roots of their social prestige lie deep within the living traditions which took form and became a way and style of life in the decades before the Revolution and until the War of 1812. After a brief return in the days of the clipper ships (1850–60), the sea culture disappeared forever. Reluctantly Yankee City returned to the land and in time built factories for textiles, transformed her comb and silverware arts from hand to machine manufacturing, and, with the aid of "the new shoe people" from outside, built the great shoe industry that now supports her people.[3] A large proportion of the people are now ethnic, including Catholic Irish, Jews, French-Canadians, Greeks, Poles, and others.[4]

Contemporary Protestant churches of the community, some of them lineal heirs of the "first parish," others more recent and intrusive, reflect most of the diverse tendencies of American Protestantism. Despite the Reformation, some liturgical Protestant sects, such

3. For a history of manufacturing, particularly of the shoe industry, see Warner and Low [114e].

4. See Warner and Srole [114d]. Only a few of "the new people" have been rewarded by achieving a secure status at the top social level of the society.

as the Episcopalian and Lutheran, cling tenaciously to the ritual style and much of the basic doctrine of the traditional church. [34] Some have moved in diverse theological directions away from the ancient core; others have gone to the limits of secularity, leaving little to distinguish them from many secular organizations. [108b] Indeed, lodges and secret societies, such as the Yankee City Masons, are more religious in doctrine and ritual than certain modern churches. However, the churches to which we will give our present attention, including the Congregational, Presbyterian, Baptist, Methodist, and at times the Unitarian, all well established in Yankee City, possess soundly founded theologies and public ceremonies, including the Lord's Supper and baptism. The ritual usages of the Unitarians in Yankee City largely depend on the minister and the dominant parishioners. In some cases Communion is a regular part of the service, expressive of the ancient doctrine of the sacrifice held by those who participate; in others the sermons are intellectual kin to the lectures of a modern psychologist or social scientist. [82]

The task of making unequivocal statements that will hold beyond Yankee City for the Catholic Church and all Protestant denominations in America at first seems insuperable. The mere number and diversity of the Protestant groups seem far too complex and contradictory. Yet brief inspection of easily available materials on membership in church organizations shows "that ninety per cent of the church members in America are found in twenty denominations and over eighty per cent within thirteen denominations." [82] The same authoritative book, *A Primer for Protestants,* by James Hastings Nichols, declares that "more than four out of five American Protestants belong to one of the six great families of Protestant Churches: Baptist and Disciples, Methodist, Lutheran, Anglican and Episcopalian, Presbyterian and Reformed, Congregationalist and Christian. These same six families include nine tenths of the Protestants of the rest of the world."

Since Roman Catholics belong to "the one Church" and the variety of Protestants are members of but "six great families" and these and others are rapidly moving toward unity of federated action, if not amalgamation, structural variation seems low and decreasingly so. But a question still remains; we must ask if there is great variation or strong unanimity among American Christians about their faith in traditional sacred beliefs. Do Catholics and Protestants actually believe in the Trinity and the Divinity of Christ, and in other major articles of the Christian faith?

Most of them do. Nine out of every ten Protestants and nine out of every ten Catholics faithfully believe in the Trinity.[5] Ninety-two Catholics, eighty-seven Protestants, and seventy Jews out of every hundred of each faith in the United States declare that they have a sure conviction that God exists. Eight of every ten Protestants and Catholics, but only four of every ten Jews, conceive of Him as a Loving Father.

There is surprising agreement but still considerable variation, national research indicates, among members of the several Protestant denominations. Some Protestant churches outscore the Catholics in the percentage of their members who hold to certain items of basic Christian doctrine. For example, the Baptist percentages outranked or tied Roman Catholic in their belief

5. John L. Thomas, S.J., of St. Louis University, and others, mss. on American religious beliefs.

in the immortality of the soul, the existence of an actual Heaven and a Hell, in the Bible as revealed truth, and the real importance of religion in their lives.

For most articles of faith, the Baptists score highest and the Congregationalists lowest among Protestant church members. The Presbyterians, whose historical sources of belief have been often nearer those of the Congregationalists, are less close to them and often more like the Baptists for the proportions of their members who have faith in a particular doctrine. For sureness of faith in the divinity of Christ, the Baptists score ninety out of every hundred members, and the Congregationalists but sixty-two, the Presbyterians eighty-one; for belief in the Trinity the Baptist percentages are ninety-five, the Presbyterian eighty-nine, and the Congregationalist eighty-three; and for belief in the Bible as revealed truth, ninety-three Baptists, eighty-nine Presbyterians, and seventy-six Congregationalists out of every hundred are in the affirmative.

Despite the considerable diversity in belief and ritual among Protestants, it is possible to ask and hopefully seek answers to the following questions: What is the nature of Protestant symbolism? How does it differ from Catholic signs and their meanings? Why are many Protestant beliefs and practices different from, yet very similar to, those of the liturgical faiths?

They Gathered at the River, Separately

When the first new church was built and Yankee City founded, the parishioners placed their own authorities within the new house of God. They not only brought the absolute authority of the Holy Word with them but paid two pastors, a junior as well as a senior, to help

them interpret it. They controlled, and in turn were
controlled by, their local clergy. From the beginning the
two ministers and their flock fought against the "elders"
in Boston who ruled the colony's Calvinistic theocracy,
refusing "obedience and subjection" to them as "the
duty of brethren."

Soon a few families moved several miles inland, still
on land granted to the original settlers. Their new settlement "demanded the right to establish a parish" and
be independent. A half-century of contention passed
before they were allowed to do so. Meanwhile, coastal
trade and the building of small ships developed a third
settlement, which became Newtown or the Port. It
emerged as the urban center of Yankee City. In Newtown "the seeds of a mercantile and shipbuilding aristocracy were beginning to sprout." They, too, demanded
a separate parish. The first parish tried and failed to
prevent it; not until 1722 was reluctant approval given
for a separate church. [39a]

Thus, revolt against authority and the need for local
and individual autonomy continued to stir those who
had begun the struggle in England. [83b] Within them
their internal conflict and the ethics of revolt were
brought to America. From the very beginning the local
settlements fought against central authority, established
by those who once led the revolt which resulted in the
founding of the colony. Yet, when confronted with the
same separatistic spirit in their midst, the parishioners
of the parent settlement of Yankee City fought tenaciously against the demands of offshoot settlements for
freedom of worship and self-control.

From its beginning "the decaying and languishing

state of religion was of deep concern" to the pious of Newtown. An association was formed "to redress in themselves and families any irregularities, and next to admonish their neighbors of the same." According to one of the accounts, to strengthen the state of religion in Yankee City the members of the association called on the young communicants of the church

> and endeavored to counsel and advise them to continue "in the sincere practice of those duties that are incumbent upon them by their public confession of Christ." A committee was appointed to "converse with ye wife of" one of the parishioners, "concerning the disturbances she gives him, when he is going to perform family prayers." One of the committees visited "ye taverns by ye waterside" and reminded the landlords of "ye order required to be kept in their houses" and ordered the constable to walk "ye streets after the evening exercise is over on the Lord's day, that the Sabbath may not be profaned."

A local church history reports that "the religious hysteria of the time was more violent in Yankee City" than elsewhere in that part of Massachusetts. The Rev. Caleb Cushing, lineal ancestor of a great family in Yankee City and the nation, commented at the time, "Many New Lights and new doctrines and corrupt errors threatened to overrun the country. Indeed, the many trances, visions, and dreams and wild extacies and enthusiastic freaks and phrensies, which have abounded in some places, have cast a great damp on the work and much cooled the fiery zealots, and we hope God will in mercy prevent the growth of those errors which seem to be creeping in space . . . and spare his people, and not give his heritage to reproach, Etc."

The great English evangelist, the Rev. George Whitefield, at about this time visited Yankee City. He was often obliged as the apostle of the "great awakening" to preach in barns because the conservative churches were closed to him. Because of his evangelism, sixty-odd families left the first and third parishes and, in what is locally called the Presbyterian Schism, founded the fourth church. In 1746 they built the Old South Church, one of the most beautiful structures in New England. (The bones of Whitefield lie in a vault beneath the pulpit.) A chronicler of the times, a member of the first church whose family remained loyal, calls Whitefield an "astonishing fanatic (who) in his sermon entitled 'The Seed of the Woman and the Seed of the Serpent' classed the people of (this) Parish with evil spirits, and is kind enough to inform us that a council of the Trinity was called to decide upon the creation of the lovely creature Eve. . . . He was accustomed to stigmatize (women) as weaker vessels, as the means whereby sin entered into the world . . ."

Still later divisions took place, and in the nineteenth century other churches including the Catholic and Greek Orthodox invaded this Puritan sanctuary.[6] The Irish and French Canadians each established a Roman Catholic church, the Jews a synagogue, and the Greeks an Orthodox church. Slightly under half the people of Yankee City are now Catholic, but the predominant

6. See Warner and Lunt [114c], pp. 356–66, for a discussion of the churches of Yankee City.

spirit of the town is Protestant and the dominant people in the community are largely Protestant.

The principal Catholic church, although drawing from all class levels, is largely composed of members with ethnic backgrounds. By actual count it is low in membership from the two upper and two middle classes, but has a high proportion from the two lower levels. The three Congregational churches have a significantly high membership from the lower and upper-middle classes. St. Paul's Episcopal church has a high proportion from the two upper levels and a low representation from the two lower levels. The Unitarian church also has a sparse membership from the two lower classes, but more than would be expected by chance from the lower-upper and upper-middle classes.

Oral Protestantism and Visual Catholicism

The church buildings located throughout Yankee City, consecrated and ritually set apart, contain the sacred places where those who believe come together to communicate with, and offer public respect to, their god. Extending high above the other buildings, the white spires of many of them gleam in the sun's rays against the dark borders of the river. The simple, unadorned lines and obvious utility of many of these meeting-houses give them an aloof, pure appearance— an aesthetic grace by which their builders strove to satisfy the spiritual needs of their congregations. All are beautiful, but some are architectural treasures, cherished and proudly cared for by the faithful. Within their walls the sacred world of the community lives and takes on collective form. The powerful Father, the gen-

tle Son, and sometimes his lovely Mother are here to
be found by those who seek.

Not far from Hill Street stands a sacred building that
is different in architecture and beauty from the other
churches in Yankee City. Its style is not traditional in
New England; the congregation is comparatively new
in Yankee City. Yet the massive church building gives
an appearance of being older than the simple traditional New England churches. It is the principal Roman
Catholic church of the city.

Entering it one sees a huge painting of Christ over
the altar, a very physical Christ, nailed and bound to a
heavy, almost threatening wooden cross. The human
flesh of his face and body show the cruel marks of man's
sadism. Crucified and dying, he dominates the whole
shadowy interior of the building. Below and to one
side of the altar is a smaller representation of the Christ,
his body taken from the cross and cared for by his sor-
rowing Mother, the Virgin Mary. The building is
named the Church of the Immaculate Conception. Thus
even in name it is set apart from the others. [23, 66]

The Protestant pulpits are bare and largely free of
decoration. Sometimes flowers grace them during services on Sunday. Despite the artistic excellence of the
interiors of these churches, there is a bare quality about
their walls. Their enclosed, precisely defined pews express a cool restraint and aloofness. In these consecrated
edifices, Catholic and Protestant, separated from the
profane world of secular life, men go to find and communicate with their god. Whom do they find there?
What is the sacred world they enter? Who are the sacred
beings they worship? And, for the social scientist, what
is the meaning of what they do, think, and feel?

Let us enter this world with the reverence and respect it demands and is due. But let us examine it with detachment to make sure we give the facts of religious life the same scientific respect paid those from the other realms of man's collective life. Perhaps in so doing we will learn more fully why the symbolic world of the church holds truths which modern science must learn if it is to understand and help man to know himself.

The worship of the Catholic Church emphasizes visually connected symbols whose basic appeal is non-logical. [66] The worshiper participates in the drama of man and his fate acted out before him while watching the symbolic actions of significant sacred characters. He hears the sacred words as part of this visual action system. The words themselves are important, but their communicative functions are tremendously strengthened by the context of visible symbols. The collective rite incorporates all the worshipers. For those who officiate at the daily Mass, the principal Catholic rite, all the senses of the body are directly involved. Vicariously, and sometimes directly, the worshipers also participate with all their bodily senses. They, too, see, taste, smell, feel, as well as hear, when they experience the sacred relation with God. They, too, vicariously and sometimes directly, and with the whole body, act out what is symbolically defined for them to think and feel. The *whole* human body, as well as all the senses, may be involved in public (group) worship with other members of the community and the species. Thus the act of communication with God by the communicant can be a total one; all of him can be involved.

Protestant worship has shifted the use of sensuous visible symbols to a minimum and oral-auditory ones to a maximum. For the clergy and the congregation the sermon, prayer, and hymn are the central parts of Protestant ritual. Muscular movements are minimized, the unobservable movements of the tongue being those principally used, reinforced by bodily gestures which tend to be signs equivalent to those of sign language. More often the gestures are those of the individual minister rather than prescribed and officially sanctioned symbols.

But the Protestant final symbol of authority is the *written* word. [88] The oral word is reduced to written form. The marks of a written word are often symbolic substitutes for oral words which are symbolic substitutes for the sacred drama, itself a symbolic form. The activity of the eye and its field of vision are held to the limitations of the words on a page. Form, shape, color, texture, movement, rhythm, and all the varieties of visual imagery which stimulate the whole man are transformed into the arbitrary arrangement of a mechanical alphabet. Gratification from symbols expressive of immediate visual perception is greatly reduced. The sensuous, visible world around him has disappeared. The eye must first accept the emotional and mental discipline of written words. What words stand for may arouse deep emotions, but the principal intrinsic virtue of written alphabetical word-signs is that they in themselves have nothing to excite the emotions or the imagination. The written or orally communicated word may be a non-rational symbol, but it tends to stand for rational concepts more often than the dramatic, visible action symbols displayed to communicate to others. [15]

Sermons, prayers, and hymns—as we said, the principal forms of Protestant public worship—are founded on the written word of the Bible. Each emphasizes oral, non-visual, communication. [120] In them the sensuous satisfactions of life are rigidly limited. To arouse the communicant's emotions these several ritual forms are dependent on the evocative qualities of words (and their meanings) and on the (animal) tone qualities of those who speak and the emotional significance given them by those who listen. The lyrics and music of the Protestant hymn provide the greatest opportunity for the evocation and expression of feeling. The non-rational feeling systems of the whole man can be involved by "a good rousing hymn." The sermon and prayers of some ministers may violently stir the passions of a congregation.

In the values of Protestantism, the reliance on "the word" is not only an expression of increased "rationality" but, more importantly, an exacting way of reducing the use of the several senses, for controlling the bodily needs and containing the appetites once satisfied directly or vicariously by dramatic symbols. When the visual signs are largely banished and the learned word substituted, the whole man—the man of the species—is held in stricter control. When the rational mental life is emphasized, in some churches, the non-rational world of the species is largely eliminated.

Visual schemes of thought that are intuitive and come most frequently from within the organism,[7] often characteristic of the symbolic order of sacred rituals, are not easily reducible to referential language. In daily interaction they are used most often by children. They readily communicate feelings about bodily experiences

7. Piaget [89a], pp. 43-9.

with the inner and outer world with other beings like
themselves, so that those who feelingly respond to these
communications can fully understand and respond to
their impact. But those who try to make referential
sense out of such words usually fail to learn what the
child means—children understand children but adults
supposedly better prepared for understanding, to whom
the same communications may be sent, often fail.

The symbols of non-rational communication help to
order the varieties of experience felt by organisms, and
though such symbols may report on outer reality, their
central task is to communicate the sensuous feelings of
the whole body and the accumulated experiences of
the species. They do not atomize the world into discrete
units or reform and transpose it into the rigid, abstract
mental structure of rational life. For example, the meaning of a man's love for his mother permeates all levels of
his being. The sacred world and its symbols incorporate
all of man; they have to do with entireties. The mysteries of life, including man's love of God, always involve the entire meaning of man. These include man
the animal, as well as the moral and spiritual being.
Such symbols, including art and religion, express men's
relations to each other and their place in the great
physical world and the greater supernatural universe
surrounding it. These mysteries do not and cannot
yield to rational inquiry. They need, and respond to,
non-rational understanding in which the whole man
communicates and can be communicated to. The non-
rational symbols which express these mysteries can be
only partly understood by rational inquiry. The realities
they express when translated into logical and scientific
discourse lose much of their significance. The very

process which attempts to make them logically meaningful may destroy what they really express. The expressive "language" of art and religion is most often successful in ordering these meanings into communicable forms.

Protestant churches, particularly the "respectable" middle-class ones, are often perplexed by problems raised by their stern limitation of worship to oral rites and symbols. Some churches—the more emotional ones, such as the Holy Rollers, the Shouting Baptists, and those of the Pentecostal faith—have evolved systems to provide for species expression. The congregation, led by their pastors, abandon rationality and the logical meanings of words, substituting violent gestures, bodily movement, and shouting, which permit the faithful to express what they feel and allow them to believe they have evoked the Holy Spirit. These "excesses" disturb the respectable and since, more often than not, such churches have a lower-class membership, they often arouse the scorn of middle-class Christians. It seems probable that the poverty of symbolic expression characteristic of the ordered worship of Protestant churches which minister to the lower classes makes it impossible for the cravings, longings, wishes, desires, and frustrations of the faithful to be expressed in sanctioned forms. The older symbols, characteristic of the traditional liturgies, which evoke and express the species and impulse life of man are lost to them. Some of the ecstatic emotional outbursts where the emotions of the whole congregation burst forth, where strange tongues are spoken and men and women writhe on the floor in spiritual ecstasy, are most likely to be the compensatory substitutes of the less inhibited and more emotional lower classes for the satisfactions they once felt in church rituals.

The solidly respectable upper-middle-class churches which emphasize decorum and the use of the rational word sometimes find that many of their own parishioners are little involved in the sacred symbols used. Many fail to find the spiritual resources either in themselves or in the forms of worship to feel confident that there is real communication with the sacred world. The cold, alien rationality of science more easily invades their sanctuaries. The seminaries, the ministers trained by them, and the laity who feel their influence are often vulnerable to the persuasive power of scientific materialism, for the mental world of their sacred life is strongly founded on a faith in rationality and logical communication. Such a condition often disallows the grace to believe; it eliminates the sacred and spiritual symbols from the mental life of many of those who once believed.

The Symbols of Masculinity, Femininity,
and Procreation in Protestantism

The Calvinists who founded New England and their descendants are regarded by most scholars as worshipers of a masculine God; the Puritan faith usually is characterized as "masculine." Lecky declared Puritanism to be "the most masculine form that Christianity has yet assumed." In his *History of European Morals* he says that ". . . in the great religious convulsions of the sixteenth century the feminine type followed Catholicism, while Protestantism inclined more to the masculine type. Catholicism alone retained the Virgin worship, which at once reflected and sustained the first."

He added, "It is the part of a woman to lean, it is the part of a man to stand." [8]

During the Tercentenary celebration of Yankee City, a sermon to commemorate the spiritual significance of the event was preached by a leading Protestant clergyman. Among his other remarks he declared, "The Christianity . . . brought to Massachusetts . . . adapted its adherents for every kind of human endeavor that was adventure, self-reliant, rugged and idealistic . . . The masculinity, the strength and ruggedness in the Puritanism which formed us are the absolutely essential ingredients of any religion which is worth while . . . Puritanism brings people not to their knees but to their feet."

Although such statements about the masculinity of Puritanism are largely true, they fail to grasp the real significance of the Protestant revolt. Manifestly it did eliminate "worship" of the Virgin Mary. The Mother was removed from the temple and her many feasts and vigils destroyed. At the manifest level it is true that the male and his virtues were extolled and such values reified into the attributes of divinity. Yet these, important as they were, are dependent on, and expressions of, a more important revolt against existing values and their symbols.

The Protestant revolt against the reified symbols of the traditional social structure, particularly that part of the liturgy which expressed and bestowed moral approval on the species, greatly modified the ritual and belief system of Christianity about sexual life. It was not represented or freely expressed by Protestant sacred symbols. Liturgical life was reduced to a few crisis

8. Lecky [63], p. 368.

events believed to have occurred in the life of the male Christ. The longings, feelings, and deep physio-psychological attachments that had been a part of mediaeval and late Roman Christianity and the great religions that preceded them became suspect and were violently attacked and abolished. The moral revolt against female symbols of the species increased through time until the mother and the woman largely disappeared from worship and only the male Jesus and the other male figures of the Trinity remained. [23]

The fundamental movement was against the great value placed on species life by the traditional church. The meaning of eternal life as it flows through the species and finds its most significant expressive act in human procreation was and is a mystery of the most sublime importance in the symbolic life of the traditional church. Females and males fulfilling their symbolic functions in procreative acts were necessary and central parts of the most sacred level of its belief system; not males or females as moral beings only, but males and females entire in all their procreative life-giving and life-fulfilling significance.

Although woman was banished from the Protestant pantheon, the revolt against her was not so much an attack on her for what she is in herself as a person but as the procreative partner and the one who symbolizes and arouses the erotic impulses of men. The revolt was not against her as the mother but as the central symbol of species life. The celibate priests can cry, "Hail Mary, full of grace, the Lord is with thee," and know at that solemn moment he is speaking of the procreation of God in a human female womb and that he is a male "other Christ" participating in a symbolic act expressive of the impregnation of a woman. But the Protestant minister, in status male and sexually active, cannot be so mentally free as to perform such a ritual lest his manifest sexuality affront the moral values of his congregation. To the priest, Mary with "the charm of virginity" *is* the queen of purity, "the eternal idea of true chivalry." To the Protestant minister, sexually free from the vows of the celibate, it is congruent that she be the remote and distant woman necessarily accepted, for she is recognized in the Holy Word.

The elaborate and growing cult of the Virgin, which will be discussed later, symbolically and non-logically expresses the central and focal point of species life: the procreative, fecund woman sexually conceiving, bearing, and caring for her child. Her sacred symbols reinforce species existence and make it manifest and meaningful in sacred form. More importantly, they greatly strengthen the masculine symbols of species existence. Her cult makes it easier for most men and women to "understand" and feel at the unconscious levels the significance of the Divine mysteries. Her presence as the Divine woman more fully involves men as males in the sacred world; the male aspects of God functioning as procreator and procreated are more clearly stated, thus providing a more unified emotional experience for the morally trained organism. The symbols of the whole family, male and female, father and mother, are represented and become channels of expressive significance for the worshipers. [23, 66]

With the female largely eliminated, there is less scope in Protestantism for male sexuality to express itself in religious symbols. The Lord God Jehovah is there and present but he tends to be a distant Father. The Holy

Ghost has lost his significance as the symbolic spiritual being of masculine creativity. The Christ remains a male but an "asexual" one. These symbols of species life, focused on the procreative function uniting males and females and maintaining the physical connection of the generations of men and women, have greatly weakened. For the very reason that Catholicism is strongly influenced by the female values and symbols, the male role is strengthened, not weakened, in the drama and myth of Christian life.

During the early periods of Christianity, following the Jewish theological system, women were not of positive importance at the sacred level. They were reduced to a subordinate sacred position. The spread of Christianity through the Mediterranean, where it felt the warm, sensuous influence of Grecian, Italian, and other cultures, gradually increased the position of women until the role of the Virgin became of great importance and finally one of the central positions in the Christian pantheon. [23] During the Middle Ages the secular ideals of chivalry and courtly love came to full flower in the aristocratic values and beliefs expressed by the symbol of the unattainable, perfect woman. More importantly, for our present purposes, it was then, too, that the long development of the sacred symbol of the Virgin, an ascetic and sensuous sacred ideal of womanhood, received great recognition by the faithful. While the secular troubadours were singing the knight's chivalrous and perpetual love of the unattainable woman, using symbols of erotic love, the clergy and the laity were offering prayers to the sacred woman whose cult as the Virgin and Queen of Heaven flowered in the rites of the Church. [53]

Tristan's "love of love" dominated the passion of the knight for his unattainable lady. Sublimated desire, transformed to the highest secular level of moral purity, transfigured passion into images of moral perfection. Huizinga in *The Waning of the Middle Ages* says, "The knight and his lady, that is to say, the hero who serves for love, this is the primary and invariable motif from which erotic fantasy will always start. It is sensuality transformed into the craving for self-sacrifice, into the desire of the male to show his courage, to incur danger, to be strong, to suffer and to bleed before his lady-love. . . . The man will not be content merely to suffer, he will want to save from danger, or from suffering, the object of his desire." [9]

Some writers believe the use of the symbol of the sacred woman was deliberately fostered by Church authorities; it seems more likely to have been an integral and "natural" expression of the non-logical, emotional needs of the Church and its celibate priesthood.

From the middle of the twelfth century onwards [says De Rougemont] there was a succession of attempts to promote a cult of the Virgin. It was sought to substitute "Our Lady" for the "Lady of Thoughts" of the heretics. At Lyons in 1140 the canons instituted a Feast of the Immaculate Conception of Our Lady. . . . It was all very well for Saint Bernard of Clairvaux to protest in a famous letter against "this new feast unknown to the custom of the Church, disapproved of by reason, and without sanction from tradition . . . a feast which introduces novelty—the sister of superstition and

9. Huizinga [52], p. 67.

the daughter of fickleness"; and it was all very well
for Saint Thomas, a century later, to declare in the
clearest terms that "if Mary had been conceived
without sin, she would not have required redemption by Jesus Christ"—the cult of the Virgin filled
what the Church felt, in face of the danger threatening it, to be a vital necessity.[10]

The chivalrous courtly knight and the unattainable,
perfect woman on whom his unfulfilled desire was expended, the celibate priest and the pure and undefiled
Virgin in whom the clergy found a perfect symbol for
its own chivalrous love, are the secular and sacred symbols and statuses which express the moral ideals of
Christians.

The secular structure of society has changed, the
chivalrous way of life with its knights and ladies has
long departed, aristocracy has lost its unchallenged
noble position. But the great hierarchical structure of
the Catholic Church has remained and its celibate
clergy still venerate with combined filial and chivalrous
feelings the sacred and unattainable symbol of the
Virgin. She, lovely and beautiful, as the Queen of
Heaven and the Mother whom no man has sexually possessed, is still the perfect symbol for the celibate expression of sublimation and unfulfilled desire perpetu-
ally unsatisfied. "Romantic love," Bertrand Russell declares, "as it appears in the Middle Ages, was not
directed at first towards women with whom the lover
could have either legitimate or illegitimate sexual relations; it was directed towards women of the highest
respectability, who were separated from their romantic

10. De Rougement [98], p. 111.

lovers by insuperable barriers of morality and convention." [99b]

The ideals of courtly love survive, transformed and weakened, in the arts and in the frustrated wishes of most contemporary women. The knight in the tournament competing in physical combat for the approval of his unattainable lady was gone long before Yankee City was founded, but he still survives there in the secular world of the motion picture, television, and other mass media. There in costume dramas he still appears, combining the thrills of love and death to satisfy the wishes of those who yearn for perfect love and the need of men to feel the vicarious pain of the sacrifice of self. Here the cowboy, too, on his great horse nobly rides forth to battle, to kill and be killed, to rescue pure womanhood from villainy. Honor and self-sacrifice dominate his thoughts and control his actions. The violence of the tournament is transformed into gun battles in the never-never land of the Old West, where the hero and his mounted horsemen, contemporary Tristans and Knights of the Round Table—still champions of purity and morality—fight and conquer the champions of evil and villainy. The Lone Ranger today, Sir Galahad yesterday; once Lancelot and Tristan, now Gary Cooper and Gregory Peck in "High Noon" and the "Gun Fighter."

The revolt against the sacred life of the traditional church and the non-logical, emotional order of the species has been carried beyond Protestantism to its ultimate extreme in the Marxian philosophy, now the state religion of several nations. The Marxian symbol system reduces all their sacred symbols to the dull logic of a technique and the discipline of a technology.

The symbols of the family and those of the species expressing themselves in the forms of sexual, filial, and parental relations were ruthlessly attacked in Marxian literature. The ethics, morality, and doctrines of family life were subordinated to those of getting and sharing food. Those hostile critics who say Marxism reduces man to an animal or perhaps to the alimentary canal are wrong. In this materialistic doctrine emphasis is not on the nature of the animal but on the development of new technical *controls* over the environment through the social evolution of *new forms of technology,* thus changing the symbols and values of the group without counter-controls of the species and the society operating to control the technology. The technology in this new theology is primary and dominant. The ethics and basic social values of the group are officially reduced to the dependent position of being weak effects of this elemental First Cause: the Holy Ghost of Marxian mysticism.

The Freudian movement is in part a secular revolt against the extremes of "protestantism" as it is felt by modern men whether they be Jewish, Protestant, or Catholic. Although founded on the individual rather than on the group and the species, Freudian concepts lead modern men to recognize the worth of species life. Freudian thinking is still technological, perhaps necessarily in a scientific age. The rationale of the psychological interview reduces feeling to the mechanism of the libido and the feelings and affective life of the unconscious to the mechanical control of personality constructs. Personality becomes a "topological" mechanism; nevertheless, sexuality is recognized, accepted, approved, and allowed expression.

Some of the Protestant churches in Yankee City have staged a counter-revolt. There has been a resurgence of the sacred symbolic life. A liturgical renaissance has flowed through the worship of such diverse groups as the Episcopalians and Unitarians as well as Methodists, Congregationalists, Presbyterians, and Baptists. The *use* of non-verbal symbols to refer to the world beyond the symbols of reference—to the world made meaningful by the deep feelings men have as members of the species and as participants in the ordered daily events of their society—now seems to be increasing. [102*a*]

There are many indications that we have reached the limits of the Protestant revolt and that a counterrevolution supporting and using evocative symbols is developing. The present may be the extreme limit to which the technological symbols of Marxism and similar systems will take us. It may be the high-water mark of what was once called the Protestant revolt. No social system, no matter how great its needs for rational conduct, can carry a rationality founded on technological empiricism to the point where the needs and demands of the physical and social life of the species are no longer recognized and sanctioned in the symbols and values expressing the spiritual life of the group. [102*b*]

Mother's Day: the Return of the Woman
and Her Family to the Protestant Pantheon

Perhaps one of the most significant changes in the contemporary Protestant church has been the recent introduction of several special family days into their sacred calendar—all of them coming out of the influence of the laity on the church. The church calendars in Yankee City now give an official place to the mother.

There is an official Family or Mother's Day on the second Sunday of May—coincidentally the month especially dedicated to the Virgin Mother in the traditional liturgical calendar. Mother's Day began as a secular holiday to allow sons and daughters to express their feelings for their mothers ceremonially. Its observance spread very rapidly throughout the United States. It became one of the most popular of all holidays. Ministers incorporated it into their Sunday services and preached sermons devoted to the mother. Many of these sermons express most of the sentiments and values evoked by the Mother of God in Catholic rituals. Some ministers interrelate the symbols of the human and divine mothers.

The Congregational liturgy suggested for Mother's Day and used in Yankee City includes a poem in free verse, "For All Mothers—A Litany," which not only comprehends "what is divine" in a mother's love and establishes the image of all women in the form of each man's mother, but also remembers the mother of Christ and views all women in her image.

MOTHER'S DAY

Scripture Reading: Ruth 1

For All Mothers—A Litany

From slowness of heart to comprehend what is divine
   in the depth and constancy of a mother's love,
     Good Lord, deliver us.
From the unreality of superficial sentiment, from commercial exploitation, and from all lip service to motherhood while we neglect the weightier matters of justice and mercy and love,

Good Lord, deliver us.
By our remembrance of the mother of our Lord standing by the cross of her well-beloved Son,
Good Lord, deliver us.
That it may please thee to open our ears that we may hear the Saviour's word from the cross, "Behold thy mother,"
We beseech thee to hear us, good Lord.
That it may please thee to give us grace from this hour, with the swift obedience of beloved disciples, to take unto our own every woman widowed, bereft, hard-pressed in life,
We beseech thee to hear us, good Lord.
That it may please thee to touch our hearts that we may behold our mother in every woman—

The Virgin Mary as the Mother of God with her own day and month assigned to her in the liturgical churches has been welcomed back, again the sorrowful mother who stands "by the cross of her well-beloved son." Indeed it would be strange and difficult to understand in a country with a secular cult rapidly becoming sacred if in time she were not recognized and her cult re-established. Furthermore, it seems probable that the original Mother may have some of the new values attached to her image in the rituals of the liturgical churches. Instances are at hand in some communities (not Yankee City) of statues of the Madonna being displayed by Evangelical churches on Mother's Day. Mother's Day is still a festival to celebrate the moral worth of the human mother, but now she is an idealized figure securely placed in the ordered worship of most Protestant churches and a significant part of liturgical revivals. It seems possible that this mother symbol may draw closer to, and again be identified with, the Virgin Mother of God. Whatever may happen to the symbol of the mother, the family through her inclusion is once more ceremonially honored in Protestant public worship. [77]

Along with the recognition of the mother by a day set apart there has been a movement, although less popular, to give the father recognition. Some churches have instituted a children's day. Thus the whole family, mother, father and children, is being structured once more into the symbol system of Protestantism. A few years ago the Puritans in Yankee City did not so much as recognize Christmas or Easter; today their descendants are giving ritual recognition to collective symbols expressive of the whole family structure—the strongest being the mother's. Species life and the family structure are indeed reasserting themselves; in new images, the mother and her family have returned to an honored place in the Protestant ceremonial calendar. [51]

Despite losing many of its functions in contemporary life, the family still organizes much of the emotional and species life of the individual. As such, it is a basic creator and referent for systems of common and uncommon evocative symbols whether they be sacred or secular. As world religious or political ideologies spread over the earth, becoming more universal and less tribal, they must increasingly depend for their evocative meanings and emotional validity on symbols which have universal sentiments back of them. The family is the only social institution which provides men of all cultures with such powerful and compelling experiences. It seems probable that as family life becomes more private and less public and increasingly the source of affection and emotional development of the individual, and as other institutions take over more of the practical functions of the family, its symbolism will increasingly dominate the sacred life of this and other groups.

The Protestant Revolt: Sex, Status, and Symbols of Power

Since the Protestant revolt at the moral and secular level was against authority, and since the authority system was masculine with descent of prestige, power, and position from father to son, it might be supposed that its attack would have been against the power and moral ascendancy of the father. Furthermore, since the movement was successful, it might be assumed that the status of the father would have been reduced and limited. It was not; the Puritan father, as well as his successors in New England, was an all-powerful tyrant. The pastor, the father of his flock, was also notoriously authoritarian and autocratic. The theocratic rule which dominated the early years of Yankee City and long after informally exercised powerful control demonstrates that the father and male rulers cast in his image were very powerful men. Meanwhile they were reinforced and sanctioned by the authority of the sacred male symbols; the virtual elimination of the cult of the Virgin had left a father god all-important. Why was the father not attacked? Why were male statuses, created in his image, strengthened and given power by this "reform" movement? What was the moral part of the revolt against? [11]

11. My problem here is a structural and symbolic one. It is not my purpose to examine the problem of corruption within the Church.

It was not against male authority as such, but the *form* of this authority; the target of the attack was the system of fixed status for men. In feudal society the family functioned to fix permanently the place of the individual. He was born to, and stayed in, one closed position. The fluid Renaissance Protestant and industrial societies, all terms for the several aspects of one basic change, emphasized the movement of free individuals and openness of status. The Puritans who came to Yankee City to improve their *economic* and *religious* status also came to improve their *social* position. All were integral parts of a systematic change from an old to a new system. Birth into a family of a given status no longer fixed the entire career of the individual or all of his activities within one status. He was freer to do what he might to be the master of his fate. He could move.

The woman's position remained largely fixed. She did not act on her own but according to her family status. True, given the new freedom of men to marry outside their status she, too, could marry above or below her status. In American culture women have always freely changed family status at marriage but until recently, long after the tide of Protestant revolt had reached its limits, they have been subordinate and under male dominance in the family roles which fix their status in the whole community. Masculine dominance limited a woman's right to make individual decisions running contrary to the rigidly defined roles of mother, wife, daughter, and sister. It should be noted that, with one exception, each of these roles in varying ways denies her sexuality. Daughter and sister are asexual and taboo. In daily life the moral attitudes toward the mother exclude sex; she, too, is taboo. Only the role of the wife is openly defined as sexual. Sexuality, impulse life, and the relaxed indulgence of the physical life of the organism were subordinated by Protestants to the harsher demands of daily tasks, sensuous pleasure to the virtues of work. Thus the emphasis on work as an end in itself, the disapproval of pleasure and idleness, the fear of impulsivity and joy in the senses and their condemnation as sins, are parts of a larger concern: the limitation and control of species life, denying it full expression at the moral and sacred levels.

In Yankee City, during the early years, there were additional reasons for the rigid control of women. Its social system was founded on the family; in fact, it was more fully dependent on the family to maintain order than was the older system. The loose social organization of Protestantism, largely free of the hierarchy of social, political, and church ranking, was more in need of the family to insure stability and security than the previous one where the controls of the larger systems of ranking unified and held people together. Each local society in early New England was greatly dependent on the autonomous family for order. The male's free movement, his increasing freedom to choose for himself, to move from role to role, from place to place, to change his functions and status, all helped to loosen this fluid system. Tightening the controls and limiting the position of women and the relations of men and women served as a counterforce, hence the rigid rules controlling a woman and her behavior in her several family roles, particularly her relations with men. The firm regulation of the status of the woman and the relations of men to it provided a foundation for the masculine moral and symbolic worlds. Free her and chaos might result; subordinate her and the fluid economic and social worlds largely inhabited by males could increasingly develop and absorb the physical and psychic energies of men. But within the family, usually the socially approved haven for the intimacies and indulgences of species life, the stern father rules his sons and daughters in relations of obligation and duty; the dominant husband and the submissive wife perform their procreative duties to be fruitful and multiply. We must remind ourselves that the difference between the culture of Calvin and the Latin culture of Catholic Rome are of degree only, for the latter, too, has its own asceticism. Yet, no matter how far the similarities of these two subcultures are credited, the great difference between them as to how they morally order and symbolically express the non-rational world of the species must be recognized as an important and significant characteristic.

We have spoken earlier of the ascetic rules controlling the celibate priest and his release in the sublime symbols of the Virgin Mother and her heavenly family. We need to examine such sexual controls in relation to the priest's place in the structure of the Church and his delegated authority to control sacred symbols of absolute power. We must then compare the status of the priest with that of the Protestant clergy to understand something more of the meanings of the Protestant symbol systems.

The status of the celibate clergy, a rigidly controlled sexual position, slowly developed in the Church structure as an expression and integral part of the ascetic, negative Christian ideals controlling the relations of the sacred and profane. The rules governing the position "married the clergy away" from their biological families into the body of the Church where the entire person is encompassed in one status. To understand the present condition of the clergy, a glance at the past is necessary. Originally celibacy, as most people know, was not required and the clergy married, yet throughout early Christianity there were strong feelings about the impurity of sex; [70] consequently the clergy, as the professionally purest of men, were felt to be most subject to ascetic ideals. As the structure of the Church grew more powerful, ascetic ideals forced celibacy on the entire clergy. At first celibacy "was an act of virtue," later it was "an act of duty," and by the fourth century marriage of the clergy was considered criminal. Yet "marriages" of the clergy continued to be openly celebrated. Lecky comments, "An Italian bishop of the tenth century epigrammatically described the morals of his time, when he declared, that if he were to enforce the canons against unchaste people administering ecclesiastical rites, no one would be left in the Church except the boys; and if he were to observe the canons against bastards, these also must be excluded. The evil acquired such magnitude that a great feudal clergy bequeathing the ecclesiastical benefices from father to son, appeared more than once likely to arise." [12] It was not until late in the Middle Ages that the power of the pope and the feelings of the faithful were sufficient to force celibacy on the clergy. Today this ecclesiastical status is now entirely extricated from the family system and community control.

12. Lecky [63], p. 330.

The hierarchical organization of statuses to which the parish priest belongs, as a member of the lowest ecclesiastical rank, is a rigorously organized system of authority in which power supposedly resides at the top and flows from the absolute power of God himself. By virtue of ordination, spiritual power enters the status and person of the priest as part of the Church structure, lifting him above the laity who occupy no official position in the hierarchy. The symbolic tasks he performs, the symbols of his habiliments, and his way of life outwardly manifest the structural realities of the Catholic social system and the relations of the clergy and the laity.

The Catholic doctrine of infallibility by which the pope for certain purposes speaks as the voice of God and as an ultimate and final authority is part of the structure of spiritual absolutes making up the symbolic life of the Church. This infallibility of the pope and the doctrine of the "real presence" allow pope and priest within rigidly defined limits to talk with the spiritual authority of God himself. Symbolically each doctrine reinforces the others. Ultimate truth always and forever resides in the worldwide local use of the symbols of the Mass. In this ceremony the Church, the clergy, the hierarchy of local bishops, the pope, and countless congregations express their unity in a miraculous, magical symbol that makes them one.

The priest who performs the ceremony of the Mass does so through the absolute sacred power vested in him by his bishop and through the sacrament of ordination, the latter a principal rite of passage of the Catholic Church which sets the man who is a priest apart so that he is "another Christ." The apartness not only transforms him spiritually but socially and biologically. When he takes vows of celibacy to remove himself from the moral and biological claims of procreation, he acknowledges the authority and discipline of the sacred hierarchy of consecrated officials which ultimately connects him in ritual union with the pope and through him with the absolute power of God. Historically, through some two thousand years and many generations of ordination, it is believed he is "one with Peter" and related to Christ himself.

When it is firmly believed by the faithful of Yankee City and elsewhere that the spiritual power of the symbols the priest controls is so great that he can bring God himself to the altar and incorporate him into the physical bodies of men, a number of consequences follow. The principal ones are that the priest himself, within the limits of his status in the hierarchy, exercises absolute spiritual power and authority; but the hierarchy, composed of ascending levels, each under the discipline of an immediately superior status, often removes decision-making from the local community of Yankee City and places it far from America in an alien culture. Through the priest the faithful are spiritually oriented to a local and a world society. The priest, as a being set apart, is removed from the immediate control of the family and community structure, this by training and by the symbolic separation. He is by personal training and the status he occupies in a better position than the minister to perform his difficult tasks. That he is a human being and sometimes fails must be recognized, yet more often he succeeds.

The Protestant clergy, on the other hand, are bound locally to the family life of the community. Through their wives and children their lives are inextricably interwoven with the biological and social cycles of pro-creation. Protestant clergy are locally controlled. Protes-tant hierarchies, if any, tend to be nationally rather than internationally centered. Power tends to be local. The congregation can "hire and fire" the clergy. The clergy are less set apart than priests. The symbols they manipulate have no absolute power *within* them; their sacerdotal authorities, if any, do not speak with symbols of intrinsic authority. Minis-ters must depend on their moral autonomy if they are to exercise control. The structure which weaves local-ities together being loose and often weak, a personally powerful local pastor, as the histories of the churches in Yankee City demonstrate, may become dominant and wield great power to the point of schism. But the sacred symbols he controls are intrinsically weak. God is not in them in the same way as he is believed to be in the Catholic Mass. The minister can never exercise the power the priest can express daily.

Because of the belief of the faithful in the power and influence of the symbols of the several sacraments, the Catholic hierarchy accumulates and controls great power. Because of man's dependence on its symbols, the church itself is a reservoir not only of great spiritual strength but of temporal power. Since most of the sacraments have to do with the spiritual sanction of human crises and their rites of transition, including birth, marriage, and death, or with maintaining grace-ful relations with sacred power, and since the sacra-ments controlled and performed by the clergy bring God himself into the immediate situation, the depend-ent and subordinate position of the vast mass of the laity is very great. This condition can exist only so long as the laity are faithful and believe. When faith goes, power departs, too. Because they refuse to recognize the power of faith and belief, the economic determinists and those who interpret power as only economically founded fail to understand many of the phenomena of contemporary and historical America and Europe. It might well be argued that it is the power of faith in an economic system which maintains it, or that the lack of a powerful faith in an economic system results in its abandonment. Obviously, not all change can be accounted for by this interpretation, nor is this intended. Yet scientific exploration and interpretation of the persistence or modification of many economic and social systems must also be founded on moral, spiritual, and symbolic, as well as economic, evidence.

Concomitant variation has continued from the time of the Reformation and the Protestant revolt; the sacred symbol system has shifted, the status order has changed from fixed to open, the technology from early hand to later machine; the division of labor from simple to complex; all concurrently, so that they are synchronized into a socio-technical-religious order in which the changing parts are moderately, if sometimes discordantly, congruent with each other. To say that one necessarily *caused* another is scientific nonsense. That technological shift and economic change *caused* the social and symbolic shifts or that a religious ethic shifted the economy, I believe, is false.

That radical changes in the technology will affect the social and symbolic orders obviously follows, for a moderate degree of congruence, equilibrium, and cohesion between them is necessary. However, that a new symbol system and powerful social order can change the technology of a culture has been demonstrated by no one better than by those who, following Marx, believe exactly the opposite: the Communists in Russia.

The Protestant reaction against the close attachment to the family of birth and social orientation and its fixed status in the group, combined with the feeling of repugnance for too open symbolic expression and satisfaction of the emotions, expelled the woman from the holy pantheon. The man who leaves his fixed status in fact or attitude is likely to be the man who emotionally "leaves" home. [48b] The deepest emotional, if not social and legal, tie to the family of birth is the mother. If the individual is to be freed from his family of birth and if fixity of status is to be reduced and freedom of movement increased, the intense attachment to the mother must be reduced. Her meaning to her children must be changed. They must be able to free themselves from her and get away. It is probable that the revolt against the closed and fixed position (of the men) of feudal society and the elimination of the Virgin from Protestant worship were both parts of the larger changes which resulted in a more flexible western European culture. All are integral parts of the shift in the treatment of the species in the moral and symbolic life of Yankee City.

CHAPTER 4

The Protestant Community Legitimates Its Past

The Citizens of Yankee City Collectively State What They Believe Themselves to Be

During the early period of our research, Yankee City celebrated the three-hundredth anniversary of its existence. Forty thousand people came from all over the country to be a part of the historic event. Natives gone to the West and to the great metropolitan cities returned home and others born elsewhere came there for this historic moment, many seeking ancestors and hoping to identify with a known and desirable past. The people of Yankee City had spent the major part of a year carefully preparing for this tercentenary celebration. Everyone was involved: the aristocracy of Hill Street, the clam-diggers of the river flats; Protestants, Catholics, and Jews; recent immigrants and the lineal descendants of the Puritan founders. Fine old houses and other places of prestige and pride throughout the city were selected and marked with permanent signs which told of their importance and significance.

Five days were devoted to historical processions and parades, to games, religious ceremonies, and sermons and speeches by the great and near great. At the grand climax a huge audience assembled to watch the towns-

men march together "as one people" in a grand historical procession. This secular rite, through the presentation of concrete historical incidents, stated symbolically
what the collectivity believed and wanted itself to be.
Those who watched saw past events portrayed with
symbolic choice and emphasis in the dramatic scenes
of the tableaux which passed before them. At that moment in their long history the people of Yankee City
as a collectivity asked and answered these questions:
Who are we? How do we feel about ourselves? Why are
we what we are? Through the symbols publicly displayed at this time when near and distant kin collected,
the city told its story.

Forty-two dramatic scenes representing over three
hundred years of history (1630–1930), beginning with
an idyllic view of the continental wilderness—"the
forest primeval, before man came"—and concluding
with a war scene from contemporary times, passed before the official reviewing stand and the vast audience.
Among the scenes were Governor Winthrop bringing
the Charter of the colony, the landing of the founding
fathers of Yankee City on the banks of the river, a local
witch trial, as well as episodes from the French, Indian,
Revolutionary, and other wars of American history.
All had immediate significance for Yankee City, and
most of the scenes were important in the history of the
nation. Among the personages portrayed were Lafayette,
George Washington, Benjamin Franklin, and William
Lloyd Garrison.

Extraordinary care had been taken to make each
scene historically correct. Local, state, and national histories were consulted by an expert committee to be sure
that each occasion, each character, the actions depicted,

the clothes worn, and the stage settings were authentic. The Boston Museum of Fine Arts supervised the production of most of the floats, constructing authentic models of the historical characters and incidents.

The total sign context of the parade from the beginning "Before Man Came" until now, the very movement of the trucks that carried the floats, each vividly portraying things past, all showed time going by. "Events" from the distant but diminishing past moved toward the present in preordained "inevitability," supposedly bound to the imposed irreversibility of chronology. They came into the eyes and present worlds of the audience, then once more disappeared into the past like the historic events they represented. What was put in and left out, selected and rejected, became symbols which revealed something of the inner world of those involved and the present beliefs and values of the collectivity.

The great Procession passed before the dignitaries of an official reviewing stand who were the city's official representatives. Then, in effect, the collectivity officially accepted the significance of the signs that it had fashioned and now offered publicly to its ceremonial leaders: the sign-maker accepted his own signs in self-communion. On such a memorable occasion what meanings flowed from the past to be again part of the present? At the particular moment in time and place when the group see the symbols they have made and chosen, what are they saying to themselves? And to whom, other than themselves, are they speaking? This question is necessary, since what they say about themselves will be partly determined by the audience to whom they communicate it. The city's Tercentenary Committee made all this quite evident. On several occasions the chairman and others declared that the Procession would help to establish "understanding among citizens of diverse racial origins and points of view" and "teach our children the importance of our city's past." It was clear they were also talking to themselves, for they said, "We will learn of our own greatness and the important part we have played in this country's history."

Despite the successful use of expert knowledge, the authentic reconstruction of each event, and the overriding emphasis on evidence and fact, the significance of each event selected (and rejected) was not a matter of reference and rational sign behavior but of collective emotion and evocative symbolism. The story's plot, its characters, actions, minor and major episodes and their development, as well as the opinions and attitudes of the audience and the producers, were significant symbolic evidence which could be collected and analyzed. Each dramatic episode and the entire procession were examples of pure symbol. They were fabricated signs whose present meanings referred overtly and explicitly to past events in the life of the community and the nation. But beyond this, they were evocations and present products of the past emotional life of the group *as presently felt*. As symbols they were collective representations which conformed to Durkheim's classical definition of collective rites. Collective representations, he has said, are signs which express how "the group conceives itself in its relations with objects which affect it." Within their meanings is collective power individually felt, the condensation of the "innumerable individual" mentalities of past generations whose social interactions produced and maintained them. All societies uphold and reaffirm "at regular intervals the collective sentiments and collective ideas" which help to maintain their unity. They achieve this unity at times by means "of reunions, assemblies and meetings where individuals being closely united to one another reaffirm in common their common sentiments." [35a]

More important than the rational and scientific, not to say Puritan, moral resolve to "create understanding" and teach by "learning of their own greatness," the people of the community unknowingly revealed their non-rational, unconscious feelings and beliefs about themselves. In talking to themselves, in presenting their own signs to themselves, with their own meanings given to these signs as they were offered and accepted, revalued and reconceptualized, they were dealing with George Mead's "significant symbol." They were saying not only what history is objectively, but what they now *wished* it all were and what they wished it were not. They ignored this or that difficult period of time or unpleasant occurrence or embarrassing group of men and women; they left out awkward political passions; they selected small items out of large time contexts, seizing them to express today's values. Thus, at times they denied or contradicted the larger flow of history and the intentions of yesterday's understanding, often repudiating beliefs and values that were once sanctioned or honored.

In wish and fear, in guilt and hidden emotion, they were using the unconscious symbols of Freud or perhaps Jung. But since the individual concepts of Freud do not fit the group phenomenon present, and Jung's *"racial* unconscious" although collectively founded carries false implications, we must examine these signs of meaning as the expression of the unconscious emotional group-life of the species, given cultural form in the experience of each individual.

The condensation of collective experience expressed in the forty-two tableaux was much greater than the condensation of an individual's dream, for the latter at best reflects only one lifetime, whereas the images of this procession dealt with a span of time which covered the total meaning of the lives of tens of thousands of individuals who had lived, died, and passed on their collective and individual significance to those now living. The forty-two dramatic scenes were intended to represent historical truth and recreate the past for three hundred years of experience—for the actions of thousands of men and women who had once lived, their accumulated total being many times the city's present census. This represents an incalculable number of events, of comings and goings, deaths and births, failures and triumphs, beginnings, endings, and continuities, which make up the lives of individuals who compose the living history of the group. Any one of these events, any one of the forgotten thousands, had a significant story whose meanings, properly unraveled and told, could inform today's people of their beginnings and their past. Yet most of them, both events and individuals, have disappeared without identifying trace. They have not been "forgotten," for most of them were never remembered. Yet they were woven into the fabric of group life.

During the three hundred years of its history thousands of families, each biologically and socially founded, emerged, matured, and dissolved in death. They were the solid foundation on which the generations of Yankee

City built and maintained community life. Which were remembered, and their presence and significance celebrated, when Yankee City "took stock"? The solid superstructure of institutional life, the church, the school, and the government—town, state, and national—each during these three hundred years had its own continuing life, changed its meanings and forms or held firmly to its way. What of them and their past? What is their significance to the present collectivity? What influence did the economic life of Yankee City exert, with its old and new forms, with inventions and new technologies supplanting older ones and new economic institutions taking the place of, or reordering, those that had gone before? What were the meanings of the economy in the great collective rite?

Finally, not only had these countless events flowed continually through three hundred years—not only had individuals lived their collective lives in the institutional and economic matrix—but the events, the individual lives, and the social relations of the community had been evaluated at the time of their existence and later re-evaluated. Individuals had felt these social beliefs and values as joy and sorrow, pain and pleasure, triumph and despair. As a collectivity at various times they had felt them as the upward swing of well-being and high hope or as despair and suffering, accordingly as life moved quietly or convulsively along. Such emotions had also been expressed in the collective symbols and life of the time. Are they, like those who felt them, dead? And if still active—as I believe they are—how are these collective memories stored and expressed in the signs and meanings of today? What has happened to these "delayed" communications from the past as they

are transmitted and transformed through the generations, and learned and re-expressed today? How do contemporary members of Yankee City publicly recognize
and evaluate them in a collective ritual designed for
such a purpose? What does the community's "available
past" signify to the interested or apathetic present?

In brief, what is remembered of things past? Which
of past beginnings, endings, and continuities are marked
with significance? Which have mental and emotional
signs placed upon them saying in effect: "Look at these
objects. Understand and feel again through them what
was once true and what, when you recognize and value
its significance, will be true again."

Despite the careful historical research of specialists in
the fine arts and the social sciences and the knowledge
of local antiquarians to insure that the events depicted
and the objects marked were historically correct and
individual characters properly portrayed, the whole at
certain levels of understanding was like a dream, perhaps a collective fantasy. Tableau after tableau moved
dreamlike across the minds of the beholders. External
and fixed, they moved out of the past across the reviewing eyes of present beholders in exactly fixed time relations, yet their deeper meanings disregarded time. They
told a moving, non-rational story of how things should
have been, while giving moral approval to what a God-
fearing community should approve; or covertly nudged
the audience to enjoy, perhaps unconsciously and vicariously, some of the same forbidden pleasures their ancestors experienced more directly and consciously.

For the investigator these symbols of things past provide a long shaft sunk deep into the dark interior of the
mental life of Yankee City, and in this symbolic "stock-

taking" the non-rational levels were tapped and brought into view. The unconscious world of the species living out its existence within moral and intellectual forms is present and active. In what ways did it find cultural expression? What parts of its meaning gained access to these rigidly controlled symbols? These answers found, what new knowledge can they give us about the moral forms which constitute the structure of social life in Yankee City and America? To begin to answer these questions, we must guide our search with an explicitly understood procedure.

The Tercentenary had three phases: its early planning, organization, and assignment of authority; the activation and ritualization of the community as a whole in preparation; and the celebration itself. Each is important for understanding the significance of the entirety. Based on larger theory and method, each demands its own techniques of inquiry. In the opening phase the major committees were selected which organized, planned, and directed the entire proceeding. A brief examination of their membership is necessary to learn what kinds of persons and social attitudes and values were involved in the community's conceptualization of what Yankee City is or should be to its people. It will answer such questions as: What ethnic and class levels were represented? How did their beliefs and values influence the dramatic ceremonies? What kinds of significant or insignificant tasks were assigned to representatives of the various social groups? How did the lower-class levels and the various ethnic and religious groups share the responsibilities of the production with the higher classes and the descendants of Puritan ancestors? Who controlled the celebration and had the power to choose the symbols? What effect did these persons or groups have on the kinds of symbol selected and how were they defined and presented to the public?

The second phase consisted in activating and organizing all the people of Yankee City to make them integral and active participants in the preparations and the celebration itself. This was done partly by organizing further committees and enlisting the aid of the city government, schools, churches, men's and women's organizations, and also civic, business, and industrial organizations throughout the city to sponsor the floats. Sponsorship involved some degree of congruence or relation between the social meaning of the sponsoring group and the meanings of the symbols they selected.

After the preparatory phases the celebration opened on a Sunday with sermons by the clergy, a showing of ship models and pictures by the local historical society, and visits to a Navy cruiser anchored in the harbor. This was followed on Monday by the Washington parade, when the first part of the two-day Procession took place; on Tuesday by garden displays, sports, and other activities; and on Wednesday by the second part of the great Procession, when the other forty-two tableaux were shown. The festival ended the following Sunday with a service on Old Town Hill.

A member of the central controlling committee was assigned to write a series of connected historical sketches, more than forty in all, each a little chapter which dramatized the local importance of a national hero or event and, in so doing, traced chronologically the history of the community. During the months before the Procession these sketches were published at regular intervals in the local paper, which had a large circulation among all groups and classes.[1] They were further used in the public and parochial schools for history and civics courses and as texts for little plays the grade-school children wrote and produced for their own entertainment. The public response to the published articles was highly favorable; their topics became subjects of ordinary conversation among old and young. Letters to the press by the older inhabitants about the various episodes, discussions at home and at social gatherings, public congratulations of the committee and the author of the series, demonstrated the broad appeal of the articles and the response to them. We learned by interview that a large number of local people had clipped and mailed them to distant friends and kindred.

Most of the local audience on the day of the Procession carried some of this knowledge with them in viewing the floats. Much of what they "saw" had been learned or brought back into memory by reading and talking about the series of stories. For the Tercentenary the most important function of the little vignettes was that each was designed to provide the background for a float in the Procession. It functioned as the text and authentic source from which a small physical model was first prepared by museum specialists and a tableau of living actors in a dramatic scene, sponsored and prepared under supervision by a local organization, was later presented to the audience. The whole series of scenes, properly known and understood, thus became living chapters of the Yankee City Book of History made manifest in the Procession.

This arrangement of story and dramatic ceremony is

1. Fifty-two per cent of all newspaper subscribers in Yankee City, including substantial numbers from all class levels, took this paper.

of methodological importance to our study, for fundamentally it is a close analogue to the historical myths
and rites of primitive society. It proved possible to study
the collective rites of Yankee City by some of the same
procedures used successfully on primitive peoples.[2] The
origin myths of primitive groups and their legendary
accounts of how and why contemporary man came to
be, each portrayed symbolically in great totemic rites
that tell those who produce or see them the meanings
of life and the significance of the collectivity, were almost exactly paralleled by the historical stories of
Yankee City and the related dramatic ceremonies of the
Procession. The parallel is in fact even closer than this
suggests. Myths in primitive Australia and elsewhere
are socially sanctioned by tradition and belief, and their
ceremonies informally "supervised" and sponsored by
the old men who control the necessary knowledge and
social and sacred power. This was also true in Yankee
City. All floats chosen by religious, ethnic, and civic
sponsoring groups had to be selected from the "official"
history of the community set forth by the central committee. Each had to follow the "authentic design" established by the story and the sculptured model. All this
for purposes of "historic accuracy," to maintain a "dig-
nified and trustworthy" presentation of the city's past.
Such stipulations made it possible for a consistent story
to be told; the official "myth" and its control made certain that various ethnic, religious, and other status
groups could not insert discrepant versions of historic
truth.

The oral (non-literate) traditions of a simple society
are more easily maintained and transmitted by its re-

2. Warner [114a], pp. 244-411.

sponsible members than those of a complex culture, partly because the undifferentiated social system is slow to change and produces a symbol system which expresses meanings that all can feel and appreciate. There are few variant values or ways of knowing and believing. For the investigator the relation of the primitive social structure, of family, clan, of age and sex, to the collective representations which express present realities as well as past significance raises many basic questions about the relation of symbol and sign to social structure; but such theoretical problems are simple compared to those which must be answered for a complex modern society.

Although legends and myths of simple cultures are often historical in the sense that they purport to deal with past time and tell the official history of the group, they are all oral products of non-literate peoples who do not have the control of written documentation from the past to help them recall their history. The significance of this "delayed communication" of written history will be treated in a later section. Here we will deal only with some of its methodological and technical aspects in our treatment of the evidence and its effect on our interpretations. The crucial effect of the background of a written culture on method in this case is that it allows comparisons to be made between the historical facts of historians and the historical symbols of the Procession and its stories.

We can now ask and begin to answer: What are the meanings and functions of this great emphasis on historical accuracy and realism? What does it do for the diverse members of the present collectivity? For everyone, Catholics, Protestants, and Jews? And what do

these secular symbols express and evoke for the dominant Protestant group which fashioned and displayed
them?

The Secular Rites of Legitimation

The meanings and functions of (symbolic) drama, as
everyone knows, range from the most sacred rituals of
an established religion to those which are purely secular
in character. The drama of the Mass at the altar of a
Christ crucified, sacred processions on public streets, the
tragedy and comedy of the theater, the celebrational
themes of thousands of festivals and fiestas, among
them stern morality stories or those evoking licentious
abandon, as well as the skits and trivialities of vaude-
ville, radio, and television, are among the many varieties.
In each a story is dramatically portrayed, where the
actions of a hero and other characters embody the values
and beliefs communicated.

In the Yankee City celebration, to make the symbols
chosen for the Procession perform the function of evoking the past—to make them believable and manifest to
a diverse audience—was a most difficult task. How were
the signs to be fashioned and presented so that they
would mean something real and legitimate? It is our
thesis that most of the period of preparation immediately preceding the Procession was itself an unintentional, informal, secular ritual of consecration. Supposedly entirely devoted to the examination and selection
of historical facts referring to the past of Yankee City,
and their transformation into authentic concrete form,
the preparatory activities served primarily to perform
this function in such a way that the audience could

make the mental acts of affirmation necessary to accept the symbols as true. Faith in their scientific truth had to be established.

One may note in passing that because science has been wrongly viewed as founded only on skepticism it is too rarely recognized that those who practice or believe in it must found their skeptical search for truth on an ultimate faith in its modes of mental activity. Science, too, has its own values and unprovable beliefs. Like religion, it must have its acts of unreasoned assumption about, and acceptance of, the unknown; in brief, it must have its own myths.

There was a variety of ways theoretically available to those who produced the Procession to establish its symbols as real and legitimate. [115] Taking in the broad possibilities of cultures in general, the symbols used might have been consecrated by religious leaders invested with the power to mysteriously transmute them from ordinary into supernatural ones through rituals of sacred legitimation. Or at the secular level the belief system of the community might have been such that the organizers of the Tercentenary could have been invested with political power from an ultimate Leader, endowing them with this ability to establish faith; or with a political or economic doctrine, conformance to which would establish a sense of reality in the symbols. The symbols of the Procession might conceivably have involved belief in the conversion of ordinary men into extraordinary ones—for example, returned soldiers whose extraordinary courage, valor, and good luck in the face of death as champions of the people, or as defenders of the faith against the infidel, had changed them into heroes or martyrs whose meanings could be infused with the collectivity's values about its own survival.

To an extent this was true of the Procession; but its symbols and objects did not intrinsically carry *their own* proofs of validity. To evoke such meanings it was necessary to use and manipulate modern values and beliefs —to utilize "scientific" means. In a social world founded on Protestantism, the usages of sacred investment fail and the usual mystical ritual methods cannot accomplish such ends. The belief in the efficacy of the power of words and acts of ritual such as those of the Mass, which transform modern objects not only into transcendent signs of godhead but into God Himself, cannot be used. There can be no sacred icons, images of sacred investment, to speak the truths that need to be expressed. Nor is there a divinely or politically appointed authority capable of performing such acts of ritual consecration. No one would believe what he did. The souls of the ancestors cannot be called up ritually from the past to live in the present as they are in the totemic rites of simpler peoples. Something else needs to be done. The people of Yankee City, mostly Protestants and all skeptics in that they live in a modern science-based civilization, must settle for less—if not the souls of ancestors, then at least images that evoke for the living the spirit that animated the generations that embodied the power and glory of yesterday.

The techniques and authority of scientific reconstruction provided signs—incidents, costumes, settings, etc. —which supposedly referred to real things and happenings of the historical past. This faith established and the proper preparatory activities performed according to

prescribed standards, the symbols—the accepted com-
binations of sign and meaning—could be and were legitimated. To the audience (since the signs could be believed) their meanings were true, and this being so, all
or many of the evaluations and interpretations of events
portrayed could also be accepted and believed. To understand this, let us begin our analysis of the prelimi-
nary (second) period to present the evidence.

The first official announcement by the Tercentenary
Committee to arouse public interest and launch the
collective activity which culminated in the great celebration eight months later, appeared in a front page
story in the local paper. "The people of Yankee City
are to have an opportunity," it said, "to hear Professor
Albert Bushnell Hart of Harvard College, who will come
here to speak of the significance of the Tercentenary
Celebration and what other cities and towns are doing
to observe the great event. All persons residing in Yankee City are invited to attend and get the advantage of
Professor Hart's learning, as he is an historian of national reputation." It said further that he had written
"a special article on the subject" in which he declared
that the occasion "will be the greatest opportunity in
300 years for the people of Massachusetts *to take account of stock, to sum up what they have been doing
and to set it forth* [italics mine]."

This first document in the official files kept by the
chairman of the committee and used as evidence in our
study also told the people of the city that a "proper
observation" of the Tercentenary would not only be
"worth while in showing the development of 300 years,
but it will also have a valuable effect in *establishing
understanding among our own citizens of diverse racial*

*origins and points of view and demonstrate their rela-
tionship and importance to community progress* [italics
mine]."

To all races of traders, whether merchant princes of
seagoing fifteenth-century Venice, eighteenth-century
Yankee City, or their modern successors, taking stock
and setting forth their wares to the customers has always
been an exciting exercise. Balancing the books to show
a profit and demonstrating the success of an enterprise
to others as well as to those engaged in it, in fact and
symbol, lie at the heart of their economies and moral-
ities. Selling historic objects and symbolic events to
tourist pilgrims seeking "culture" or to nostalgic natives
returned to reinvest themselves and some of their money
in the world which first made them is even more worth-
while and exciting to these men. "Establishing understanding" in this kind of customer is doubly worth-
while, for it brings additional profits while teaching
buyers of "diverse racial origins and points of view" the
importance of the stock and their need to have it when
it is set forth.

Two weeks after this announcement the elder states-
man and keeper of the tribal knowledge came forth
from Harvard and made his appearance in Yankee City.
The great authority on American history reviewed the
great events and "paid a noble and well deserved tribute to the Massachusetts character and mentality which
sent so many famous men to the presidency, to the Senate and House of Representatives and to all parts of the
country." He left his paper with the committee. For
Yankee City and other Bay State communities it became
a guide and source book for their programs. From its

ultimate authority of science and learning first flowed the ability to believe.

Interestingly enough, considering the official desire to demonstrate the "relationship and importance" to the community's past of its ethnic citizens (almost half of the Yankee City population, most being Catholic), he did not speak at City Hall or a similar non-sectarian place but at Unitarian Hall, the meeting place of a very small, yet powerful, New England Protestant sect. With few exceptions those who attended were Unitarians, Episcopalians, Presbyterians, or Congregationalists. The executive committee of the Tercentenary was entirely so composed. The members of the subcommittee that selected the subjects for symbolic display and decided on the models for the floats and their suitability were entirely from the old-family aristocracy. Later, after these important decisions had been made, various groups chose the episodes they wished to sponsor. Included among sponsoring groups were "the citizens of French descent," "the Polish people," and "the Jewish community." Then came such sponsors as lodges, secret societies, and churches which represented citizens of "diverse racial origin," many from social ranks far below those who made the conceptual decisions. Only then was the committee greatly expanded to be sure "everyone is included," as everyone ultimately was, to guarantee the popular success of the collective rites.

After Professor Hart's departure the local historical authorities took over. Authenticity and exact reproduction of the events of history were the ideals dominating their efforts and purpose. The symbols had to be as objective and reliable as expert historical authorities and institutions could make them. The committee to select the events and choose the markers of historical sites included local historical authorities but consulted other authorities as well as local and national histories. These and other sources, such as the local historical societies, helped to ensure authenticity. Genealogical experts were employed; to increase the feeling of historic reality, descendants of original participants in the great events were interviewed and encouraged to re-enact the roles of their ancestors.

The Tercentenary stories appearing serially were written by a local citizen, as we have seen. The writer's family name was greatly respected by everyone; the family lineage went back to Yankee City's period of renown and was connected with important events portrayed in the Procession. The artist who directed the construction of most of the models was himself an authority on the history of the town and of New England and a member of the Boston Museum of Fine Arts. Moreover, he was a son of one of the aristocratic families of the city. Thus the directors strove for historical validity and reliability. In the rational aspect they were scientists, in spirit seeking to establish secular rather than sacred realities; non-rationally they were ritual functionaries consecrating and legitimating a secular rite.

When the Washington parade occurred, initiating the Procession, it was in "exact" accordance with the preserved full account of this event. "Washington" came from Ipswich attended by people playing the roles of those who originally accompanied him. He was met on the steps of the great mansion where he had originally been received. The same speeches—fortunately preserved—were given and replied to in the words originally spoken.

Each float in the main procession was heralded by a placard with its date and description prosaically and rationally set down. Immediately following came the historic tableau, played by living men and women each costumed according to the period. At one level of understanding they were, except for their movement, display cases in a modern scientific museum—well-labeled, authentic representations of ethnological reality. Behind them was authority expressed in expert design and workmanship.

Clearly this almost obsessive effort for scientific realism was an exemplification of the mentality of the people and a need to satisfy some vitally important demand for certainty. They did not look for sacred authority, as did their ancestors, to prove whatever they were trying to demonstrate, but for secular authority. Although they spoke as heirs of their forebears, and Yankee and Puritan values were everywhere being expressed—in their manner of "taking stock," "summing up and setting forth," as well as in professions of scientific purpose—the emotionally symbolic factors operating were of greater significance.

From the learned essay of Professor Hart and the study and efforts of those who followed him flowed the prestige of higher learning and the power to capture popular contemporary faith in modern science. From the authority of the latter's signs and facts came the ability to believe that the committee and their experts on local history could re-create the past and make it manifest in the signs displayed in the Procession and on the highly valued objects of the community. The physical presence of the "high priest" himself among them, giving a "noble and well deserved tribute to the Massachusetts character and mentality" while telling them what they must do to praise themselves by telling nothing but the truth, increased their desire and their will to believe. The facts of history, symbolically recreated through scholarly knowledge and the skills of the arts, were the ultimate and absolute sources of belief. Those who knew them were sufficiently authoritative to make their symbols of history legitimate and believable. To themselves and to others the search for, and emphasis upon, scientific fact and its reproduction in authentic representations were, as we have said, in effect a modern scientific ritual of consecration.

For this ritual to be efficacious in legitimating the endeavor and thus establishing faith in it, the action system involved had to conform to standards of objectivity, reliability, validity, and such other tests and judgments as will create in the minds of those concerned the feeling that they are in the presence of facts. The authority of "facts" could not be disregarded; their meanings had to be sought and understood. Once understood, they must carry ultimate weight. Thus the empirical symbols, in this case those of history, which refer to, and stand for, objective facts command very great respect in our society. The methods used to find and establish facts, and the outward signs necessary to create and reliably communicate their meanings, accumulate their own social power. Those who can manipulate these skills and whose delphic voices speak for facts and their meanings, once believed by their audience, possess a secular form of absolute power. At this moment in Yankee City, because the audience believed in scientific fact and skill and the authority of those who use them, they could identify with the images of what purported to be their individual and collective past and reaffirm their feelings and beliefs about what they were by faith in selected facts of history. Thus the whole period of preparation was a secular ritual of scientific consecration. Like priests at the altar, the members of the committee took ordinary things and, by the authority vested in them, transformed them into symbols of ultimate significance. The differences between priestly and "scientific" power are notable here because they throw further light on the problem of how the symbols of the Tercentenary were legitimated and made believable. The Christian priest, for example, performs a sacred ritual under the mystical power of God, and as His agent transforms ordinary things into elements of ritual significance which become, among other things, the symbols of an historic sacred event. He represents, and is authorized by, a church to perform this act. Ultimately he represents a community of men who believe in Christ. The ritual of the priest by intent and official pronouncement functions to make this transformation possible.

Secular rituals of consecration, although habitually functioning in our society, are not publicly recognized or authorized as such. If those engaged in the preparatory activities in Yankee City had believed that their intent was primarily to establish belief in their symbols —or, putting it speculatively, had their audience believed this was their primary purpose—it could not have succeeded. They needed to believe in the intrinsic power of historic fact and their ability to represent it. Their audience also needed to believe that the symbols of the

Procession were invested with this ultimate factual authority. Then the ritual drama of the Procession could be accepted, because the creation of its symbols was *not* recognized as a form of secular consecration.

To see clearly that the symbolic function of this period of preparation was not so much historical reconstruction as ritual consecration to establish belief in the values of the symbols chosen one need only think what might have happened had Professor Hart—from Harvard and Cambridge, in Massachusetts—not been invited to establish the ideology and voice the values and beliefs of the Tercentenary. Suppose Professor Charles Beard of Columbia and New York City, author of the *Economic Interpretation of the Constitution,* had been requested to write the founding document for the Procession. Let us suppose he had made his own kind of speech, with his characteristic values and beliefs, to launch the celebration. It seems unlikely that the historical facts as he would see them could have become effective symbols in the Procession. The preparatory ritual of consecration would not have achieved its end, for the community could not have identified with it; or, having admitted his facts as true, could hardly have incorporated them into its system of beliefs and values as symbols of its faith. Moreover, what he and Hart as *persons* stood for, as well as their places of origin, would give the latter the mark of approval and acceptance and the former probable doubt and disapproval.

Further, a committee composed, let us say, of third-generation Irish Catholics, all of Yankee City, all rightly respected professional historians, and all devoted to their home town, could not have hoped to establish the faith necessary to make the symbols of the Procession carry authority. In brief, while scientific processes were part of, and necessary to, the preparation, and historic facts were indeed collected and arranged in symbolic form, they were the lesser part of the enterprise and perhaps necessary only because they successfully disguised its real nature.

We have given our attention only to the Procession signs; we must also examine the problem of the ritualization of the objects of the community. Later we shall give a full description of the objects marked throughout the city, their chronological distribution, and their factual and symbolic significance. Here we must hold to the problem of their ritual consecration and the differences involved between their legitimation and that of the signs of the Procession.

The same careful procedure was used to determine the dates and history of the various things marked; the dates when houses were built, the time of their occupancy by distinguished families, and their association with important happenings were all traced. The houses and other historic objects were surviving facts of a living past; the people, their activities, and the historic events were gone and could only be represented by descriptive signs in the Procession, but the dwellings and public places where persons or families had lived and great events had taken place were a part of contemporary Yankee City. The problem was to turn them into objects of special regard and ritual significance.

The historical markers placed before the houses were signs, as were those that accompanied the floats. But, supported by the authority of the Tercentenary, they changed objects of present utility into those of ritual significance. In terms of the broader theory they moved from objects and facts into "intermediate signs" standing for something else and expressing values other than what they were unto themselves. The markers were needed to make them historically legitimate. Those who now viewed them knew that they came from, and were authoritatively blessed by, their intimate association with the ancestors. But to accomplish this transformation so that the meanings attributed would turn them from present objects into signs of past significance, their historical contexts needed to be known and verified to permit confident acceptance. They could then evoke the proper feelings about the glories of the past. These authoritative signs allowed everyone to share in the investiture of significance put upon them by the Tercentenary ritual.

The Period of Creation: Sexuality and the Images of Males and Females

Those in the reviewing stand, the Mayor and other dignitaries, saw the first float preceded by a sign announcing "The Forest Primeval." They saw a "maiden" standing "on the land of Massachusetts once covered with forests, where rivers, ponds, and damp marshes made open places." Under the titles, "Massachusetts' Great Birthday" and "The Wilderness," the two introductory historical sketches had said, "This year Massachusetts will celebrate its 300th Birthday." During the period "Before Man Came" the wilderness was untouched: "there was no government. There were no roads, no towns or cities, no churches, no schools or colleges."

The Forest Primeval of course came directly from Longfellow and the romantic conception of the wilderness. It is the world God called good before he created man. The place—the land, harbor, and river—are clearly marked as female. Nature is conceived as feminine. It is both pure and wild in its untouched state. By implication the masculine society later dominates and controls it. The men who farm the fields, who sail the boats, the technology that masters the wilderness and builds the roads, the towns, and the cities—they and their technical, moral, and sacred order are felt as masculine. This impression in the first scene is further substantiated by a later tableau called "1647. Aquilla Chase, Pilot and Fisherman. The first white man to cross the bar at the mouth of the river." The scene is preceded by those showing dominant male symbols, Columbus and Captain John Smith, related to subordinate feminine ones, the Indian "maidens" associated with the fruitful land. All these scenes show powerful males controlling and ordering the natural environment. The virgin wilderness, the land, New England, wild and dangerous yet pure, fruitful, and bountiful, yields to the strong masculine society and shares in the creation of contemporary Yankee City.

Although the minister of the First Church of Yankee City (Unitarian, and prominent in the Tercentenary) surely did not consciously have such an interpretation in mind when he preached the first sermon on the subject of the Tercentenary, his words give support to this interpretation. He told those principally involved in the celebration, as preparation for understanding their task, that "the masculinity, the strength and ruggedness in the Puritanism which formed us are the absolutely essential ingredients of any religion which is worth while." "Our fathers did what they did," he said, "be-

cause, banked up in them by their strength of spirit was
a strong, explosive vigor."

This theme of the "Great Birthday," when elements
of femininity, nature, and fruitfulness cluster closely
together in interaction with the explosive masculine
vigor of the dominant Puritan civilization, was related
to another which needs to be examined. Many of the
scenes in the Procession represented the beginnings of
things, when a given activity or institution had its inception. Only two, however, depicted the settling of
new earth, the first being "1635. Yankee City Is Settled,"
followed many scenes later by "1786. Westward Ho!
The Search for New Lands." These were the only two
where women shared the primary roles with men.
Where we find a creation period, of land being settled
by man, telling of the formation of things as they are
now, female and feminine symbols are emphasized.
When the city and the West begin, women are the principal symbols. Women's organizations selected and sponsored these scenes, thus giving them public meaning for
others to understand what Yankee City is and what they
themselves are.

There was only one scene and one moment in the
Procession when women were not in the custody of men.
In the beginning, "Before Man Came," the female
"Spirit of the Wilderness" was free—extricated from the
social consequences of her species condition. But she
was also outside the human world and the reproductive
cycle. In its time mythology the forest primeval was a
symbol of quiet, tranquility, eternal timelessness, when
nothing happened and all was still. Femininity, inac-
tivity, virginity, and timelessness are clusters of meaning expressed by the "Spirit of the River and the Wil-

derness," while after "her" contact with the dominant male civilization of the West she becomes the "mother" out of whom a great nation sprang. When man is not, time does not exist, for the symbols of time on which it depends are not there and the measurement of it and its human significance are lacking. For understanding the non-rational thought expressed by the forest primeval it is significant that as the "mother" *out* of whom all men come, "she" herself, eternally fruitful, remains the creative womb where there is no time. From her, by male contact, are born the generations of time-bound man whose linear events, arranged visibly in the moving line of the Procession, give spatial representation to the line of time moving from the past ever onward into the present.

The Yankee City of the Procession is masculine-dominated, its culture is masculine, and its significance and notable achievements are masculine.

Sexuality as a powerful driving force operating importantly in the lives of men and women and events of the time is nowhere depicted or consciously expressed in any of the forty-two scenes of the Procession or the Washington visit, nor is it present in the text of the supporting historical stories. Passion is not in them. In none of them is the passionate love of a man for a woman the dominant theme. Although female abstractions are used to express the meanings of the natural world, in none is woman symbolized by means of classical or romantic imagery as an embodiment of transcendent feminine ideals to which men subordinate themselves and their activities. Romantic love as a primary or secondary theme was not expressed in any of the scenes. Youthful beauty and sexual glamour as attri-

butes of Yankee City girls were not there; there was no
Juliet with her Romeo, no Isolde and Tristan dominating a scene. Present were costume displays and aristocratic elegance, with mature but unimportant ladies
who served as period pieces and as supernumeraries for
men of high position. Their presence often places the
appropriate status accent on a context for an important
male. The place of women is subordinate and, while
respected and often represented, is not important in the
dramatic developments of history.

Before further comment the research methods used
to verify these and other generalizations must be presented. In the signs of the Procession the facts of history
become symbolic products of present meanings. In our
research techniques we treated the forty-odd scenes as
"stories" told by those who presented them. Loosely
structured and unmanageable history had been in these
stories compactly re-formed into the symbolic scenes.
Heroes with their secondary characters were found acting out a plot, usually with dramatic outcome. The
meaning of each dramatic scene supported by the historical story and comments from some of those who
viewed the Procession made it possible to develop an
analytical procedure for establishing symbolic units that
could be identified and their meanings ascertained.

The procedure was as follows: The story line of the
plot was identified, the central character or hero determined, and secondary and supernumerary characters
identified and their symbolic functions so far as possible
ascertained. The negative and positive feelings attributed to the characters, particularly the hero, as the principal center of interest and identification were established through the treatment of the figures in the Pro-

cession and the historical stories told about them. In addition, the various symbolic elements of all the scenes could be counted to determine major themes and the overall grand design of the Procession. [48a]

There were forty-six leading roles or "heroes" among the dramatis personae; forty-one were male and five female. In four scenes a woman played the principal part; in thirty-eight, males were the principals; and in one scene there were two leads, divided between the sexes.

Among the five principal feminine roles two were wives and mothers of early pioneers and settlers; one was a victim of tragedy, member of a family in an Indian raid; one a "persecuted" old woman (and wife) charged and convicted of witchcraft; and one an abstract figure played by a young unmarried woman representing "the Spirit of the River," who was also the "Spirit of the Wilderness." In leading roles all the female figures representing human beings were subordinate to superordinate males; the female symbol of nature was alone on stage.

There were fifty-five secondary characters (not including the supernumerary "walk-on" parts), of which women played thirty-two. Twenty-two of these were Americans; seven were foreign or dark-skinned, including Cuban and Spanish señoritas, Indian girls—maidens and squaws—and three mythical symbolic figures: a Chinese moon goddess, the Winds of the Earth, and Columbia. Twelve of the twenty-two Americans were wives and mothers of prominent men, the remainder being customers in shops run by males, female congregations dominated by famous preachers, passengers on a famous clipper ship built by a great Yankee City inventor, and female high school students presided over by a famous male educator. Only one had an occupational role: a Red Cross nurse in World War I.

In sharp contrast, the male roles were most diverse and powerful, with marked prestige. All the principal male characters were superordinate and dominant. Along with the secondary ones, they covered the whole complex division of labor portrayed, though usually from the higher reaches of the society. Among them were presidents, admirals, generals and other high military officers, senators, signers of the Constitution, merchant princes and philanthropists, professors, famous lawyers, manufacturers; as well as sailors, soldiers, mechanics, and others on the less highly placed rungs of the occupational ladder. Great names were frequent.

From masculinity, presented as powerful and full of prestige, flowed the significant events that molded the life of the society; in it were contained the superior and authoritative virtues. Femininity was conceived as subordinate, and if superior socially, then because of a father or husband whose status established the position. In general, woman's position was dependent and given little interest or attention. In this collective rite there was little excitement in seeing or being a woman of Yankee City. The audience was meant to attribute its feelings of value to male, not female, images.

However, sex and sex attraction in women were not entirely absent. The sexually appealing woman, to whom direct sexual interest might be given by the audience, was placed in entirely secondary roles. All women whose sexual life was committed to a particular male and conventional custody were defined as American; however, around the edge of some contexts appeared several attractive women in secondary roles whose positions were sexually ambiguous—all exotic foreigners and racially different, outside Yankee City and American culture: for example, the Indian "maidens" and "squaws," attractive Cuban girls and Spanish señoritas. Although not in the same category, the Chinese moon goddess, in exotic and appealing surroundings, was an attractive female. The males with these ambiguously placed women were sailors, soldiers, and traveling salesmen, all occupations to which clichés are attached about unconventional sexual relations. Sex as a compelling force giving women power and esteem was not for these Yankee women. It was the sexually attractive Latins and the women of other races who were found with American males. The expression of impulse life is highly constricted and rational. The images of the Yankee women floated by in the Procession like the set pieces of a dream collected and recollected with the rational detachment of a scientific instrument. In this dramatic ritual the life of the species and the passionate and exciting events of three hundred years seemed to flow placidly through the cold chambers of the rational mind, not those of the passionate or overburdened human heart.

Such easy acceptance of this feminine role is surprising, for the committee in charge, which created the artistic conceptions for each tableau and passed on the fitness of each, was composed mostly of upper-class women. All could trace their ancestry back to colonial times. Several were, or had been, professionally trained and employed.

A closer inspection of the several contexts they created reveals something more than rational acceptance of the subordinate role of the mother and wife. Interpretation and content analysis are now necessary, for we do not have the necessary "psychological" materials or records of how decisions were made to relate the symbols presented to the actual historic processes which determined their presence. Two of the three most dramatic and emotional scenes had to do with a violent male attack on defenseless women and children and the persecution of Puritan women. These need more detailed analysis.

The twelfth float, "1679. The Trial of Goody Morse," was sponsored by the Yankee City Woman's Club. Those who played the roles were at the superior levels of Yankee City. All were of old Yankee stock. The float was designed by an older woman, the unmarried daughter of an old family. Perhaps the meaning of the subordinate role of women and possibly the guilt of contemporary man for their subordination is brought out by the sponsorship of the Woman's Club. The women perhaps publicly displayed their hostility for their unfair treatment and yet appear to forgive the men for what they do. The men who played the roles of "persecutors" acted out the guilt and possibly, it might be guessed, some of the satisfactions of being in such a dominant and superior position.

The sign which preceded the float gave the date and title with the explanation: "She was accused, tried, and condemned to death on the charge of witchcraft but subsequently released by the trial judge, thanks to her husband's persistent efforts. This was Yankee City's one witch trial." And, incidentally, the only scene with married devotion as one of its themes.

The heroine is clearly Goody Morse, the hero her husband; the "villain" is equally clearly the male magistrate and the theocratic law of the times. Although a female is mistreated by men and unjustly punished by the male law of the clergy and magistrates, the outcome is favorable. The magistrate turns from being a bad to a good man, her husband stands loyally beside her, making it possible to condemn masculine dominance while at the same time defending it. Three scenes later in the Procession the theme is repeated. The tableau follows a placard entitled "1697. Judge Samuel Sewall Repents," with the subscript, "After the witch panic subsided Judge Sewall, who presided over the witch trials realized the absurdity of the charges and did penance for his part in the persecutions by a confession in the Old South Church, Boston."

The story, one of the newspaper histories, declared:

> Samuel Sewall was the son of one of the first settlers of Yankee City. . . . He went to Harvard College and was graduated highest in his class of eleven. . . . became Chief Justice of the Bay Colony.
>
> Soon after he was made a judge some persons were accused of witchcraft. At that time almost everybody believed there were witches who did evil things. When it became his duty, with other judges, to try these persons in Salem he condemned to death those whom he thought guilty.
>
> A few years later he realized that there were no witches. So he wrote a letter saying he had made a mistake and was sorry. While it was being read to all the people in the meeting house he stood up so

all could see him and bowed his head. He never ceased to be sorry that he had condemned innocent people to death.

The outcome of the "plot" of this drama implies that the women who were the objects of the attack of the masculine clergy and magistrates were the victims of the evil ones who condemned them to death. The public confession and penance of the judge bring about a favorable outcome: rationality triumphs and the slaying of the innocent is condemned. Meanwhile male authority is both attacked and defended. The ambivalence felt for the male ancestors, the founders and fathers of the tribe, is also expressed; they were good despite their evil, misguided act. There is pride in the judge as an ancestor. In him rationality and masculinity triumph, the past is absolved of its crimes, and the present dominance of males forgiven. Still there is protest; the judge, symbol of masculine law and authority, is publicly humiliated in the confession of his guilt, recognizing the validity of the moral charges against him. In this masculine society the victims, by their involuntary sacrifices, are the moral agents who symbolize his guilt and its public recognition.

The Fathers Become Villains and the Past Is Made Present and Perfect

The period of the Early Fathers and the seventeenth century as a whole were given eight scenes in the Procession. Although outwardly all were presented positively and had such outcomes as befit the public stocktaking of the community, several attacked the traditional authorities. But they also defended them, for this was a family affair, to praise, not condemn; to display white linen, clean and freshly laundered for company. Yet the complaints of the subordinated and persecuted women, Goody Morse, the persecution of the Quakers, the felt guilt for the massacre of the Indians and the taking of their lands were all covertly present and occasionally openly expressed by these contemporary sons of the Early Fathers, inheritors of those who found and captured the promised land. Like their prototypes in Palestine they, too, found the deeds and words of their first ancestors not entirely tolerable. [108b] Still, if they were to maintain their own legitimacy it was mandatory for them to trace their ancestry to the very beginnings. Consequently, for the maintenance of their position it was necessary to invent new myths and new expressive rituals to hold the power of the ancestors, maintain it within the confines of the modern Christian ethic, and express all of the changes that occurred in the mental life of the group during three hundred years. The powerful influences of Channing, Emerson, the Unitarian movement, the New England renaissance in the arts and literature, as well as what was in fact the beginning of the Puritan Counter Reformation, combining with the influence of the scientific and rational enlightenment, made the invention of new myths necessary. [75]

Throughout our discussion of the symbols of the Procession we have dealt largely with heroes and the supporting secondary characters. Since all the scenes are dramatic episodes, and drama inherently has its heroes opposed by its villains, the question arises whether villains were present or in some way implied in the various floats from the several periods. In the minds of

those who composed, presented, and produced the
pageant, the villains were no longer the hated Redcoats
or the greatly feared British regulars who, by historical
account, sometimes threw the city's inhabitants into a
state of hysteria. There was no scene depicting the
"Boston Massacre," so popular in earlier community
celebrations. There were only two floats devoted to the
Revolutionary War. Colonel Little and his Yankee City
Men now set quietly off to Lexington, but there was
no visible or implied symbol indicating a hated antago-
nist.

Nor did the Red Indian, despite the bloody history
in which Yankee City spent her men and money, play
such a role. Yet this was a considerable phase of the
city's experience. The early accounts tell us that "at
the disastrous battle of Bloody Brook, September eighteenth, 1675 at South Deerfield during King Philip's
War 'the flower of the population of Essex' [the county
in which Yankee City is located] were massacred. There
were thirty men from the single town of Yankee City."
They were part of the company that marched to Deerfield. By January 1676 "sixty eight men" had joined
the local company. "The ratable polls at this time were
only one hundred and fifty nine." During the earlier
Pequot War in 1637, immediately after the city's founding with but twenty-two families, eight men were raised
in Yankee City.

No villainy is found in the once despised and greatly
feared French whose Catholic "idolatry" was considered
"an abomination" by the Puritan iconoclasts, constantly
under threat of bloody attack during the French and
Indian wars. In fact, only one float was devoted to this
long period of rivalry and warfare which finally re-

sulted in the destruction of the French empire and the triumph of English culture. In the placard, the text for the tableau, and the float itself we see the attack on the great fortress of Louisburg that once menaced the peace and safety of Yankee City and New England. The text, while telling of the heroism of the men from Yankee City who were part of the expedition, makes quiet fun of the early beliefs about Catholic idolatry. In the scene devoted to the Spanish-American War, where Yankee City forces are depicted in a camp in Cuba, the Spanish do not appear as villains; nor do the southern rebels or the Germans in the other war scenes. All these onetime enemies are no longer villains; but the men of Yankee City who fought them are heroes. Villains, as properly defined, were present and part of the history of the city. Although Benedict Arnold and Aaron Burr, traditional American villains and traitors, were once actually present in Yankee City, Arnold himself in a very prominent and powerful role, neither appears in the pageant (see pages 144 to 153 for why Arnold did not). Each of course would have made an excellent villain for the Procession.

Since this great public ceremony was a "stock-taking," and since merchants of history are likely to put the things of positive worth in their windows and ledgers for public inspection and quietly forget awkward items of the past, it might be argued that the hunt for a villain is futile and that the transformation of former villains into ordinary men who are not objects of hatred or contempt presents no problem. Closer inspection of the principal and secondary characters and their actions and the implied outcomes of their stories leads one to the same conclusion. No villain is explicitly presented, and there appear to be none off stage. Although this conclusion is justified as regards the spirit which animated those who composed the drama, further inspection shows that there are villains and that deep hostilities are expressed and projected on them. On some of these figures not only hatred but love is focused, but always in such a form that a second inspection is necessary to learn the full significance of the signs for such a tableau. Sometimes known names of prominent men —some historians would say great men—are quietly dropped and a scene becomes anonymous and depersonalized, their figures thus losing their individual meaning and becoming the targets of new meaning attributed to them by contemporary feeling in the community.

We will begin our analysis of these signs of villains and the present hostility to certain symbols of early history with one of the more explicit accounts. Early in the Procession appeared the fourth scene having to do directly with the history of Yankee City, entitled "1663. John Emery . . . a tolerant Puritan who defied the authorities by entertaining Quakers in his house at a time when they were outlawed." The tableau depicted Emery and his wife, ancestors of prominent families, and two itinerant Quakers standing before two stern magistrates who were the secular enforcers of the theocratic law of early New England. The sympathy of the audience for the Quakers is clearly bid for. Their local identification with John Emery would also cause a positive response for Emery and the Quakers and arouse opposition to the magistrates. The names of the magistrates are not given. They have become the representatives of an anonymous status and of the early Christian fathers who founded New England.

When it was announced that the Loyal Order of Moose would present the float of the "Tolerant Puritan," a quotation about him was given from one of the local histories.

> In 1663 John Emery was presented to the court at Ipswich for entertaining travellers and Quakers. From evidence sworn to by several witnesses, it appeared that two men, Quakers, were entertained very kindly to bed and table and John Emery shook them by the hand and bid them welcome. Also that witnesses heard John Emery and his wife say that they had entertained Quakers and that they would not put them from their house and used arguments for the lawfulness of it.

The story of the float is based on this historical text. It indicates who the implied "villains" are, but does not publicly name them. It says,

> Just for this act of kindness some stupid persons of the town had him taken before the court where he was actually fined, because at that time Quakers were not allowed to stay in the colony. Nevertheless, John Emery refused to say he was sorry, although he was obliged to pay the fine. He and others like him kept refusing to obey such cruel orders and after a time most people came to think as he did, and the Quakers were left in peace.

The language remains vague but, as we shall see shortly, there can be no question that those who designed the float knew exactly and specifically the names of some of the local persons who had been involved and to whom the symbols refer.

Before we can say specifically who these men were and by their identification get at some of the basic changes that have occurred in the collective meanings and representations in the mental life of Yankee City, we need to examine the symbols of the first tableau having to do with this land and its new people. It was preceded by the title "1635. Yankee City Is Settled." "Twenty-two men and their wives and children came up the Parker River in the spring of 1635 and encamped on its banks. They were the founders of the community." The float was sponsored by the Sons and Daughters of the First Settlers of Yankee City. The float of the "Tolerant Puritan" sponsored by the Loyal Order of Moose, which emphasized of course the belief that all religions must be respected and recognized, was a perfect symbolic fit for the membership of that group. The organization was composed primarily of ethnic peoples, of very diverse denominations and even religions, many of whom had only recently arrived in Yankee City. The Sons and Daughters of the First Settlers, on the other hand, were composed of the oldest Yankee and Protestant families. Yet both groups sponsored symbols expressing not only respect for the past but, as we shall show, hostility to the authorities and important men of the time.

The overwhelming majority of the scenes of the Procession dramatized actual persons whose names were given on the placards and further amplified by other names and descriptions of them in the text. This was particularly true for the earlier ones. With the exception of those having to do with early shoemakers, all, beginning with Columbus in 1492 up through the seventeenth and eighteenth centuries to the Revolutionary War, used a named hero, sometimes with several named subsidiary characters; yet this most important scene, the actual landing of the founders of Yankee City, remains anonymous and its people unidentified.

Once again it might be conjectured that their names were lost or not validated by historians. Such is not the case. The names of the leaders and many of the followers are well known. The small river they first landed on, the Parker, bears the name of the clergyman who led the band. The present real name of Yankee City was given it by this leader, calling it after his home town in England. One of the important houses marked by the Tercentenary bears the name of another clergyman, the Reverend Mr. Noyes, who was his cousin and second in command of the landing party. The two were constant companions and protagonists in the theological warfare that took place among these contentious Puritans; yet neither is mentioned in the scene or text—only the name of young Nicholas Noyes, the immature son of the second leader, appears. The Yankee City histories carry long stories about both of these men. The local town and parish histories are filled with pages of references to the first leader; the *Dictionary of American Biography* has a long article on his life demonstrating his worth, power, and great influence on the development of the city. Samuel Eliot Morison also devotes an article to Mr. Parker and his theological activities.

A brief examination of the latter's influence and the

historic role he played will provide us with further
clues to the astonishing refusal to give him recognition
and identification in the float. Thomas Parker (1595–
1677) was born in Wiltshire, England and received his
advanced education at Magdalen College, Oxford, and
later on the Continent. [31] He obtained a grant to the
land which became the present township of Yankee
City and with his cousin, James Noyes—both properly
sponsored by the Puritan authorities—founded and
established Yankee City. Although trained as a Congregationalist, we are told, he believed in the Presbyterian doctrine of the clerical control of the laity. He
favored the theocratic principles of the rule of the few
over the many, of the sacred elect over the unredeemed.
He spent his life in controversy with various members
of his flock, trying to "restrain the democratic pre-
tensions" of the congregation. Historians of Yankee
City and New England tell us he "hounded the Quakers" with their individualistic doctrine of inner il-
lumination and grace. In short, in fact and sign he per-
sonified the masculine, authoritarian, theocratic, Calvinist values of the ascetic Puritan society that founded
New England. They had banished Ann Hutchinson
and her brother-in-law to the "wild country" across the
river for her belief in spiritual love. Parker belonged
to the conservative clergy who brought the strongest
pressure on Governor Winthrop and the magistrates to
protect the "New Jerusalem" from the forces of the
Devil and the promptings of the flesh and the "unredeemed."

The Quaker doctrine of the inner light, emphasizing
individual autonomy and love, struck at the very foundations of the Calvinist legal and absolutistic control of

the totalitarian state ruled by magistrate and clergy. Quakers accordingly were whipped, mutilated, and imprisoned at first (1656) and later sent to the gallows (1659). Although the more severe clergy and the magistrates approved such barbarities as well within the rights and duties of a government founded on the divine law of the Old Testament and the Hebraic code, many if not most of the laity did not. John Emery, the Tolerant Puritan, hero of our scene, was directly or indirectly opposing Parker, the unnamed villain in both scenes and the first father of Yankee City. The latter's symbolic emissaries in the Quaker scene, called "magistrates" in the official cast of characters—in fact the judges who enforced Puritanic, theocratic law—were the symbolic villains whose anonymity was substituted for the name of Parker. This was made abundantly clear by reference to the actual incident of Emery's arrest. The account comes from a respected local historian whose writings were used by those who composed the texts and prepared the floats, and was thus perfectly familiar to them.

> Two of the Quakers visited Yankee City on their way to Dover, and were then entertained by John Emery, as appears from the following statement: Edward and George Preston, and Mary Tompkins and Alice Ambrose, alias Gary, passed eastward to visit the seed of God in those parts, and in their way through Yankee City, they went into the house of one John Emery, (a friendly man,) who with his wife seemed glad to receive them, at whose house they found freedom to stay all night, and when the next morning came, the priest, Thomas

Parker, and many of his followers came to the man's house, and much reasoning and dispute there was about truth; but the priest's and many of the people's ears were shut against the truth. . . .

After a while the priest perceiving that the battle might be too hard for him, rose up and took the man of the house and his wife out of doors with him and began to deal with them for entertaining such dangerous people. They replied they were required to entertain strangers. The priest said it was dangerous entertaining such as had plague sores upon them. Which the woman hearing began to take the priest to do for saying such false, wicked and malicious words but he hasted away. Mary Tompkins called him to come back again and not to show himself to be one of those hirelings that flee and leave their flocks behind them, but he would not turn: and a while after most of the People departed: and when Ipswich Court came thither he was had and fined for Entertaining the Quakers.

Thus the symbol changes not only its meaning but its form as a sign. The Rev. Mr. Parker disappears as a visible form and the magistrates take his place before the audience. The highly respected and highly regarded Mr. Parker, an Early Father and leader of the founding fathers, becomes an anonymous sign on which contemporary hostilities are projected and by which derogatory meanings are evoked. The audience saw his substitutes less as magistrates than as persecutors. In fact, the local newspaper's full account of each scene in the parade, on the day following, refers to them as "two persecutors," thus indicating the meaning of the symbols of the Early Fathers to the audience of the Procession.

Other floats for this period express the same hostility to these founders of Puritan New England and to the authority and power of the seventeenth-century church and state. The "Trial of Goody Morse" was followed by a depiction of the famous confession of Judge Samuel Sewall, "who did penance for his part in the persecution," said the placard of the Procession, "by a confession." As a judge, Sewall was a hard, not to say cruel, person. As a man he was said to be gentle, warm, and kind. His famous diary and his love of the land of his youth in Yankee City seem to verify these statements about his humanness. [28]

The scene having to do with Sewall's confession, dated 1697, is the last presented for the seventeenth century and the time of the Early Fathers; it is not until about fifty years later (1745) that the next scene takes place. A whole new era, "The New Nation," had succeeded the old. This concluding scene of the Early Fathers, Sewall's confession, where one of the great men of Yankee City and New England "repents" and openly confesses his guilt in the socially approved auspices of the Old South Church of Boston, may well be symbolically the open confession of the ancestors put in the mouth of one of their most prominent representatives by the people of today. Through him, in the modern symbolism of the Procession, they are made to say that they felt and knew the deep guilt of their violence, hatred, and destruction of those who could love. The several scenes of the period of the Early Fathers, when examined as parts of a total symbolic

mosaic, clearly indicate that, while the fathers were respected and sometimes honored, there is beneath it all
a strong feeling of hostility. Contemporary Yankee City
is ambivalent in its feelings about them. The victims
who were attacked by these authorities—the Emerys,
the Goody Morses, and many others—and those who
gave shelter and comfort to the believers in the inner
light and a loving God, have superseded the stern
fathers in the affections and values of the community.

Perhaps even the stern elders of the tribe of Calvin,
among whom was Thomas Parker, felt this ever-present
and often suppressed antagonism and fought those
among their followers who expressed it. They who believed themselves to be the Moses and Aaron of the new
Canaan—these fathers of the new kingdom of God on
earth who banished, whipped, imprisoned, and occasionally killed their living sons and daughters—were
not unlike the harsh God they worshiped, who allowed
men to scourge and crucify His own Son that all might
benefit by His suffering. Cruelty sanctioned by sacred
authority can and must be forgiven; human cruelty,
whether sacred in New England or secular in other
totalitarian states, ultimately must find its judges who
condemn and repudiate it. Inevitably, no matter how
great their virtues otherwise, such men become candidates for the role of villain; or when grudgingly accepted, are given obscure places when the people gather
to celebrate their humanity.

In our search for villains we need to examine the relations of the early Puritans to the Indians. We have
noted elsewhere that in history the Indians were portrayed as bloodthirsty savages who wantonly killed the
innocent Puritans. There were four scenes in the Pro-

cession in which Indians appeared and several texts which defined what contemporary Yankee City thought and felt about the red and white men of earlier times and the outcome of their relations. In the second scene, "The First American," Indians were identified as part of the context of the "Wilderness." Here they are noble savages after the manner of Rousseau. In the scenes of Columbus and Captain John Smith they are friendly children of nature, young and attractive females more often than males. In "1695. The Indian Raid on Turkey Hill," a farmhouse is attacked and "the women and children were carried off." However, the placard insists that "all but one of them were subsequently found alive" and then, sympathetically, that "this was the only raid in Yankee City." This scene is the last in which Indians appear.

The texts for the several stories about Indians provide further insight. We learn from them that the Indians "lived a happy and idyllic life" and that they were "kind and hospitable to the first settlers." From these accounts it might be supposed that the relations of local whites and Indians were undisturbed by warfare. Yet a brief scrutiny of early histories indicates that, while peace sometimes characterized relations between the two races, many of the ancestors of Yankee City believed that the Indians were "children of evil and of outer darkness." Though little difficulty was experienced by the community itself, few Indians being in the close neighborhood, almost from the beginning members were engaged in hostilities on a broader field. We have seen that men from Yankee City fought in the Pequot and King Philip wars; money was also collected from heads of families in the town to support the

latter enterprise. In the Pequot Wars, four hundred
Pequots were burned. William Bradford's descriptions
of the massacre of the Pequots by the whites, quoted in
local documents, help us to understand some of the
present symbolic changes and re-evaluations of the
Indians and the white ancestors. He says, "It was a
fearful sight to see them [the Indians] thus frying in
the fire and the streams of blood quenching the sand,
and horrible was the stink and scent thereof." Bradford,
however, evaluates this "fearful sight," giving not only
the facts that went into the relation of whites and
Indians in which Yankee City was involved but the
feelings and beliefs that came from them and became
part of the collective life. "The victory," Bradford's
piety led him to believe, "seemed a sweet sacrifice and
they [the whites] gave praise thereof to God who
wrought so wonderfully for them, thus to enclose their
enemies in their hands, and give them so speedy a
victory over so proud and insulting an enemy."

The shifting images of the Puritan ancestors and
their relation to the men of today may also be illustrated
by brief quotes from the Tercentenary sermons
preached at the opening of the celebration. The pastor
of the First Church of Old City, whose history began
with the founders and whose pastorate went back to
the original Puritan divines and their theocracy, ob-
liquely protested against the rejection of the Early
Fathers and the rising secularism of the city. In his
sermon called "The Soul of History," printed in the
local paper, he told his congregation,

> History means absolutely nothing of any lasting
> worth save as it is interpreted in human life. And

not the lives of men, even the best of the race, as
they lived in the past, but of the immediate generation. *What good is there to be gained from a sort
of half-apologetic holding up of the life of the
Pilgrim or the Puritan?* [Italics mine.] For example,
acknowledging their cold, repellant, conceited, self-
righteous bigotry, but pointing to some praise-
worthy acts and a few principles that might be
worthy of emulation, when the truth is that his life
was but the interpretation of a man's conception
of the Divine revelation. His character was the
soul of the religious life of his day; and its true
worth all depended upon his, and his generation's
ability to read the story of the past aright.

This is the great Book of Life that lies open
before our generation today. All the stirring events
which we may crowd into the next few days; the
scenes we may try to reproduce, and notable characters who shall again seem to walk our streets,
will leave nothing of lasting worth for us to build
into our lives, save as we find their contribution
to the great revelation of God, as through the succeeding generations of men.

The minister of St. Paul's Episcopal Church, where
many of those in charge of the Procession were parishioners, fashioned quite a different image of Puritan
ancestors for the members of his congregation, whose
forebears once listened to the elegant Bishop Bass. He
emphasized the original unity and oneness of the Puritans with the Anglican Church from which the present
Episcopal Church emerged.

While yet in the harbor of Yarmouth, England, the Puritans who left England in 1630 wrote an affectionate letter directed "to the rest of our brethren in and of the Church of England" themselves avowing their continued attachment to "our dear Mother Church." The realization that their convictions would lead them out of the arms of their "dear Mother Church" came over them very gradually. In fact it was not until after a conference with members of the Pilgrim colony that they saw their destiny at the time to be that of separation from the church by the founding of a new one.

The pastor of the fashionable Unitarian Church, present product of the early nineteenth century revolt against the rigid asceticism of the earlier Puritan theocracy, in a sermon likewise printed in the local paper spoke of the "outward lack of grace in the speech, manners and religion of our ancestors, and the much greater and proper sense of joy in life and beauty that we have today. The reason for the difference is that the Puritans were specialists, and, like all specialists, hard and narrow, able to see only the things with which they were preoccupied. The life of God is properly held by us as something meant to permeate all existence."

The first of the nine floats in the period of greatness carried the announcement, "Bishop Bass." With it was the explanation, "In 1797, made first Bishop of Massachusetts; minister of St. Paul's Church, Yankee City, in 1752." Its sponsor was the Episcopal Church itself. The present membership of the church is still one of the most aristocratic in Yankee City, leading all others in the number of parishioners belonging to the old-family class.

From the histories of the time it appears that the bishop, a lineal descendant of the daughter of John and Priscilla Alden, started his ambitious career as a Congregationalist, but soon found the aristocratic Anglican Church more in keeping with his spiritual needs and earthly ambitions. After he graduated from Harvard, followed by a period in England where he was ordained to the priesthood by the Bishop of London, he returned to Yankee City and was installed as the pastor of St. Paul's. During the Revolution, historical reports inform us, he was at best "lukewarm" to the American cause, being in constant touch with those in the church who maintained allegiance to the throne. Following the troublesome times that came after the defeat of the British, when the Anglican church was in the greatest disorder, its leaders reorganized and strengthened it to make it a purely American institution. When the Constitution became the fundamental law of the land and Yankee City began to prosper, at the time when the great houses were being constructed on Hill Street, all those who had once been British Anglican became American Episcopalian, and many others among the wealthy upper class, then laying the foundations for its later acceptance as the old-family status, moved over to what a noted local writer has called "the aristocratic Anglican church of St. Paul." Most of their descendants are still there.

The mitred bishop, splendid and at the very pinnacle of the sophisticated church whose elaborate rituals offered spiritual and aesthetic grace to the worldly elegance of the families of Hill Street, was in his time their *man.* The splendor which surrounded his office and the very structure of his church's organization were in every way contrary to the Puritan and pietistic simplicity which motivated the spiritual life of the early fathers who had founded Yankee City. Yet it was in turning against these very aristocratic, hierarchic forms and their outward symbols that the early fathers had migrated and come to found New England. But in the Procession the bishop and his mitre were symbols which expressed the aristocratic values not only of his contemporaries but of their descendants who now trace their origins and legitimacy to the period in which this class established itself. Bishop Bass, as a symbol, is not the sacred representation of a saint often found in the community processions of Catholic Europe and Latin America, where they are offered to the faithful for their adoration and spiritual respect, but the image of a community ancestor whose presence today speaks of the power and glory of the period of greatness when the mercantile economic class and the social old-family class became the functional leaders and models for the whole society.

Eight floats later, ending this historical period in the Procession which started with Bishop Bass, came Bishop Cheverus, first Catholic bishop in Massachusetts. The text tells us, "He often visited Yankee City," later returned to France "and was made a Cardinal." In this same text Bishop Cheverus is closely linked with the superior Protestant society of the time.

> In Boston, a Protestant and Puritan city, his noble character and winning manners, his learning and his eagerness to be a good citizen of the community where he lived, soon made him friends of all creeds. When the little Catholic chapel became too small

for the growing congregation, there were as many
Protestant as Catholic names on the subscription list
for a new church, and at the head stood that of
John Adams of Boston, then President of the
United States. Father Cheverus often spoke in Protestant churches, often addressed learned societies
and helped found the Boston Athenaeum.

The Holy Name Society of the Immaculate Conception
Church in Yankee City—the "Irish church" in popular
parlance—sponsored the float which displayed the bishop's image. All the sponsoring committee had Irish
names. Only the designer, a functionary of the central
committee, had an old Yankee name. When the bishop
rode forth among the people he must be regarded not
as one immersed in the close and intimate sacred
mysteries that unite God and man and celebrate His
eternal timelessness, but as a *man* who wore the proud
regalia of a bishop and later the red robes of a cardinal
—a dignitary whose high position at the time of greatness was recognized not only by the Church but by the
superior Protestant society which he frequented. To
those who sponsored him and to those who designed
and fitted the symbol of the bishop into the Procession,
his first duty as a sign was to give secular status and
high place in the community to the Irish, primarily,
but also to other and later Catholic Americans whose
cultural traditions, like the Irish, were not sufficiently
anchored in the early tradition of the town. From the
point of view of both the Yankees who designed the
Procession and those who accepted and sponsored the
design, this superior symbol nicely fitted their needs
and was most convenient to have. The bishop had been
around at the right time.

Benedict Arnold and the Image of the Ethnic

From the earliest stages of their planning, those responsible for the success of the Yankee City Tercentenary were conscious of the need for obtaining the
wholehearted collaboration of the organizations and
churches of ethnic and religious groups. Since almost
half the community was of ethnic origin and consciously
participated in groups which identified their members
with minority subsystems, and since it was hoped to in-
duce the whole community to participate, the leaders
of the celebration, recognizing their problem, were
anxious to do everything possible to obtain full co-
operation from the various cultural and religious mi-
norities.

Since these groups, including Jews, Poles, Greeks,
French Canadians, and others, were all of comparatively
recent origin, none being older than about the fourth
decade of the nineteenth century, when the Catholic
Irish first appeared, to select appropriate symbols for
sponsoring ethnic groups and to make assignment of
them was a difficult problem for the central committee.
Since the interest and main emphasis of those responsible for the subjects chosen was upon periods before
the arrival of the new immigrant groups, the problem
was even more thorny. The conception of the celebration and the pageant had to do with the Puritan ancestors and the flowering of New England culture; the
themes of the great ethnic migrations and their assimila-
tion—the melting pot, the Promised Land, and the
goddess of Liberty welcoming them—democracy for all
and every kind of race and creed—such themes were nowhere present. Indeed, those who conceived and pre-

sented the pageant saw themselves as teachers initiating the new peoples into the true significance of the nation.

Symbols such as Bishop Cheverus, first Catholic Bishop of Massachusetts, present at the end of the eighteenth century; the Marquis de Lafayette, heir of the American Revolution; the aristocratic French Catholic refugees; and Columbus and others provided symbolic representations from which many of the groups could choose. The problem of sponsorship progressed smoothly until the leaders of the Jewish community selected (and were granted by the central committee) Benedict Arnold to be their group's symbol in the Procession. This was publicly announced by the local paper. The next day the chairman of the central committee issued a statement to the effect that there had been a mistake and the Jewish group had yet to choose their symbol.

How could such a situation have arisen? Why did it occur? And what is its significance symbolically?

We shall attempt to provide probable answers. To understand the immediate problem, we must first take up the whole question of symbolic congruence, the identification of the symbol with its sponsor, not only in the case of the Jews and other ethnic and religious groups, but with all the symbols developed in the pageant and their corresponding sponsoring groups.

The problem of sponsorship, of a collective symbol— the rejection of all other representations and the selection and acceptance of one to stand for the meaning of the group before the community—of course involves the question of the degree of identification with the symbol, what the group's aspirations are, and what the symbol means to the larger collectivity. Such identification with the meaning of a sign to members of the group and to those outside it depends on several factors: the group's structural place in the community, its status and rank, and the symbolic congruences of its own meanings to itself and to others. The identification also involves historical factors: the present and past historical significance of the object or event that has become a collective symbol, the historical significance of the group which selects it for sponsorship, and the historical meanings which the larger group, in this case Yankee City, attributes to itself.

We will examine the problem of sign and group identification by first reviewing a few of the more obvious sponsorships and analyzing them in the terms just given. The float for Columbus, a Catholic, was sponsored by the Catholic Knights of Columbus; the "First Class at Harvard" by the local Harvard Club; the landing of the first settlers by an historical association composed of lineal descendants; old-time shoemaking and early silversmiths, by those industries.

The choice of the Knights of Columbus was multidetermined by several identifications. The identity of name, of group and hero, and the Catholic religion as well as other factors were primarily involved. But there was no direct connection of the local association with the person for which the symbol stood, such as descendants of the first settlers had with the "Landing of the Founders." Still, Columbus was the "first" European to land in America and is credited by history with the beginnings of this society, even preceding the Puritans and the Founders; as such his symbol had prestige and was popular and clothed its sponsors with a great variety of significant meanings. The criteria of structural place, symbolic congruence of group, and the meaning of a symbol to the sponsor and others, were well cared for by this choice. The prestige of this highly rated Catholic club and the prestige of the Catholic discoverer took care of problems of the group's status and all those having to do with history.

But although of probable significance in the meaning of the community, Columbus was not of the group that was celebrating its *own* history; his activities were but a distant aspect of the settlement of a huge continent. He and his sponsoring group—highly valued and respected—were identified, but not completely, with the whole life of the community. The symbol of Columbus in the pageant conveyed among other meanings that old and new Americans were integral parts of a larger whole; that they were inextricably intertwined, yet that differences were present and distinguishable. In terms of ultimate identifications and belongingness, the Sons and Daughters of the First Settlers of Old Yankee City who sponsored their own ancestors, the first founders, had a collective symbol to represent them to the whole collectivity which satisfied all the criteria. It said—and they and the community said—that they completely belonged, and they were so identified.

Coming now to the problem of selecting an appropriate symbol for the Jewish group; this proved more difficult and awkward. "The Chairman of the Tercentenary Committee," a brief paragraph in the Yankee City *Herald* said, "wishes to state that an error was made in the announcement of the assignment of the float to the Jewish citizens. The design of the historical event their citizens will portray has as yet not been made by the artist." The "error" was of major

magnitude, the only apparent one committed by the
committee in planning and arranging the delicate matter of "fitting" the themes of the floats to the sponsoring groups. The event apparently first assigned to the
Jewish community, or requested by it, was the encamp-
ment of Arnold's troops in Yankee City before embark-
ing for his Quebec expedition. The official announcement on the previous afternoon had said that "the
Jewish citizens of the city have notified the Tercentenary Committee that they will enter a float in the parade
which will be a feature of the celebration. The subject
assigned to them is the expedition of Benedict Arnold
to Quebec." Following was a description of the event.

> On September 15 and 16, 1775, nearly 1000
> soldiers under the command of Arnold arrived
> in Yankee City on their way to Quebec. . . . In
> this regiment was one company composed largely
> of Yankee City men commanded by Captain Ward.
> Rev. Samuel Spring was chaplain of this regiment.
> He preached to a large congregation at the First
> Presbyterian church on Sunday, September 17 and
> he later became pastor of the North Congregational
> Church.

How this embarrassing public situation could have
happened under such carefully controlled conditions
clearly has much to do with symbolism. Benedict Arnold, the great villain for Americans, is consciously and
unconsciously identified with Judas Iscariot, the betrayer of Christ. The Jews in the minds of the ordinary,
or higher, classes of Yankee City are not fully and completely identified with the rest of the community. They
are a people who are not Christian, often believed to

be hostile, or worse, by those who are anti-Semitic; thought of as the betrayers of Christ and responsible, through Judas, for his crucifixion. It was the Jews who were publicly accepting the symbol of the traitor and betrayer of the republic, Benedict Arnold.

The problem becomes more perplexing when it is realized that one of the active members of the committee which decided upon the historical events and heroes to be depicted, and how each event would be shown by the sponsor, was a member of a highly aristocratic family which in cultural background had once been Jewish. She and her friends, all of the upper-upper class, had been responsible for preparing the Tercentenary story which placed Benedict Arnold and his expedition in the symbolic showcase of historic personages from which the sponsors chose their symbols.

An analysis of this occasion and its outcome will permit us to understand something of the symbolic position of this ethnic people and their position in American life. It was established that the agreement which became an "error" had taken place, but since the field research started some time after the occurrence, we were unable to elicit reliable evidence about all the circumstances. Such possible factors as initial ignorance of Arnold's full significance could not be ascertained. In general we were told by everyone, still with embarrassment, "It was a mistake." Everyone preferred to remember that the Jews had sponsored "that wonderful float" of Captain John Smith "which came almost at the beginning of the parade."

Since it is abundantly clear that the members of the committee had every reason to avoid unpleasantness and were anxious for the ethnic groups to be smoothly in-

corporated into their enterprise, and since it is equally
certain the Jews did not want to be identified with
disloyalty and the symbol of a traitor, how was it possible for this event to occur?

Interviewing after the event clearly indicated that the
selection and assignment had indeed been made and
that the "error" announced was but a face-saving polite-
ness. This is further validated by the later selection,
with no further awkwardness, of the symbol of Captain
John Smith.

For our first approach an examination of the larger
symbolic context is helpful. We have been asking the
question, why did the Jews select, or why were they
given, Arnold? But the more general and significant
question, which goes to the fundamentals of the symbol system of the collective rite and on which the Jewish
selection is merely dependent, is this: Why was the
symbol of Arnold included at all by those who planned
the floats to which the religious, civic, and other social
groups were limited? Three hundred years of history
made the problem of selecting historic episodes difficult;
why, then, was the theme of Arnold, awkward to handle
and to sponsor, included among the select and significant few? The question now is not why the Jews first
sponsored him, but why the committee itself should
put the mark of approval on him and sponsor him as
a fitting hero of its history.

Liberal quotes of the text are necessary to understand its significance to those who wrote it and to anyone, including the members of the Jewish community,
who selected it.

September 15, 1775 was one of Yankee City's
great days. War had been declared between Eng-

land and America. The Battle of Bunker Hill had
been fought, and now General Washington was
besieging Boston which was occupied by British
soldiers.

Canada was called the back door of America,
and Washington feared the British might attack
our frontier settlements from the North, or even
march upon Boston or New York. He decided to
make the first move himself, and so on this September day Yankee City saw Colonel Benedict Arnold
at the head of eleven hundred troops, march
briskly into town, ready to embark on a campaign
against Quebec.

In this account Colonel Arnold, the trusted representative of George Washington, is a hero. There is no
mention of his villainy. He was leading a powerful
group of men, many of whom were Yankee City soldiers,
on the famous Quebec expedition. He was an officer
and a gentleman, entertained by the Tracy family in
the mansion that still stands as a monument to them.
Many can trace their ancestry to the men who were in
his expedition. A prominent historical spot on the Old
Town Green is a monument to them and to the event.

To the upper-class committee he was a hero, and he
was presented as such, later historical and symbolic
events notwithstanding. The importance of the expedition to Quebec, its identification with the birth
of the nation and with Washington, the land and sea
aspects of it, all identified with Yankee City, made it
for that city the most important military event of the
war. Arnold was its leader.

Had one of the old Yankee organizations or one from
the old-family upper class sponsored the float, the mean-

ing of the *expedition* would have become paramount in
the symbol and the meaning of Arnold, while prominent, would have been absorbed in the larger context.
His villainy would not have been forgotten, but its
significance in the pageant would have been unimportant. The congruence of sponsor and sign would
have emphasized the story's text.

But when the Jewish connection was made, the
ambiguous history of the relation between the Jewish
and Christian groups and the present secular group's
separation from full integration into the larger community were brought into focus. All the deep anxieties
and concerns of both groups about their relations to
each other and among themselves were mobilized. The
Jews could not really afford to sponsor such a symbol;
their own self-regard and the respect and esteem they
needed from others would not permit it. Whoever may
have been responsible for the suggestion, the success of
the celebration itself made it impossible for either of the
parties involved in the sponsorship to allow it.

Symbolic congruence is here something more than
the fit of a symbol, along with others, into an approved
form; it also includes the relation of the group to the
symbol and other groups' relations to the sponsoring
one and to their own symbols. The Jewish community
and the central committee in seeking to represent the
power and prestige of a great event failed to realize that
one person in the event had his own—and the most
powerful—symbolic significance, deeply involved in the
connotations of betrayal. They failed to see this soon
enough. From one point of view it speaks well for the
place of this ethnic group in the community that the
committee regarded their place in the city as being such

that they could afford the sponsorship, heedless of any symbolic risk.

When the last of the scenes of the Period of Climax passed the reviewing stand closing the eighteenth century, eleven more followed, spread through the whole nineteenth century and thirty years of the twentieth. These ended the Procession. Instead of an average of one float a year, as for the great period, there was only one for every twelve. Perhaps less happened in this hundred-odd years; yet four wars were fought in which Yankee City men participated, the industrial revolution came to the city and to America, large industries grew on the eastern seaboard and in the city, America became a world power, and the great migrations westward took Yankee City people as far as San Francisco, where a street was named in its honor. The exciting clipper ship era came and quickly departed; the tremendous migrations of the peoples of Europe—Irish, Jews, Poles, and many others—poured into America and radically changed the cultural and religious composition of Yankee City. The great surge of technological invention and application—railroads, canals, the telegraph, the automobile, the airplane, radio, and hundreds of others—grew and accelerated.

The symbols of the Procession also said that while our Protestant fathers created a new kingdom of God conceived in liberty, it was soon dedicated to a stern sectarian autocracy brought forth by a Protestant theocracy. In the years that moved toward social distinction and economic achievement and the ones thereafter when power and glory went elsewhere, secular necessity and technological science destroyed the collectivity's conviction of knowing and holding the one absolute Truth. Now secular rites of legitimation are necessary to create in the minds of the participants the spiritual power of the Protestant past.

None of these statements is consciously or explicitly made, yet the symbols of the pageant, it seems possible to discern, express such feelings. The evidence at very best is no more than suggestive and any conclusions must be pushed beyond induction and inference to speculation. Yet such feelings and thoughts are present in the non-rational world of the groups and individuals of Yankee City, proud of its own past—proud, too, of the advances of a nation that grew to greatness as the moving frontier went on to the Pacific and to world power, leaving Yankee City and her glory far back in time and far distant from present world events. Only the rational ordering of the symbols of place and time could here loosen non-rational feelings about today and tomorrow to make a distant yesterday come true today and continental distances shrink to the limits of a city.

Part III

The Living and the Dead

Introduction

Symbol systems function in part to organize individual and group memories of the immediate and distant past and their expectancies of the future, and by so doing strengthen and unify the persistent life of each. Those symbols which evoke memories of past events for the individual or the group are greatly contracted and condensed, often modified beyond the power of the individual or group to recognize what their full references are. Such condensed systems arouse the emotions of individuals and the sentiments of the group; the emotions and sentiments aroused range from overwhelming intensity to slight feelings with only minimal significance to those who have them. They may range from the indifference of an onlooker passing a highway sign in a swiftly moving car to the devoted involvement of the initiate holding the Communion cup.

Generally speaking, living symbols which direct the attention of the individual or group to the past and relate him to it tend to be non-rational and evocative rather than rational and referential. Symbols which evoke *sentiments* proper for contemporary ritual recognition of the memories of an occasion often have little to do with recreating the beliefs and ideas involved in the actual event. They become condensed versions of much that we have felt and thought about ourselves and the experiences we have in living together. But the *effect* of what has been forgotten remains a powerful part of the collective life of the group.

Such basic groupings as the family order transform and store traditional meanings as part of the physical conditioning of the organisms which are members of the interactive group. The conscious and "unconscious" symbols we retain are present expressions of past experiences, related and adapted to the ongoing life of the species, the society, and each individual.

From one point of view, human culture is a symbolic organization of the remembered experiences of the dead past as newly felt and understood by the living members of the collectivity. The human condition of individual mortality and the comparative immortality of our species make most of our communication and collective activities in the larger sense a vast exchange of understanding between the living and the dead. Language, religion, art, science, morality, and our knowledge of ourselves and the world around us, being parts of our culture, are meaningful symbol systems which the living generations have inherited from those now gone. We use these symbols briefly, modify them or not, and then pass them on to those who succeed us. Thus, in fact, communication between living and dead individuals maintains continuity of culture for the species. Secular symbols probably more often emphasize the living present; sacred symbols appear to be more concerned with death, with the past of the species and the future of the individual.

The symbolic diversity of the collectivity and its symbolic unification are treated in the next two chapters, one on the cemetery as a sacred symbol system, and the other on Memorial Day as a cult of the dead which unifies the living through their discourse with their cherished dead. The evidence comes from field studies of

the ceremonials and systematic mapping of the burials
and family plots in several graveyards.

The relations of several professions, notably doctors,
ministers, priests, and undertakers, to death and the
transition of the living toward death are examined and
their significance interpreted.

CHAPTER 5

The City of the Dead

The Cemetery

Yankee City cemeteries are collective representations which reflect and express many of the community's basic beliefs and values about what kind of society it is, what the persons of men are, and where each fits into the secular world of the living and the spiritual society of the dead. [35a] Whenever the living think about the deaths of others they necessarily express some of their own concern about their own extinction. The cemetery provides them with enduring, visible symbols which help them to contemplate man's fate and their own separate destinies. The cemetery and its gravestones are the hard, enduring signs which anchor each man's projections of his innermost fantasies and private fears about the certainty of his own death—and the uncertainty of his ultimate future—on an external symbolic object made safe by tradition and the sanctions of religion.

The social boundaries of the sacred dead and the secular world of the profane living are set apart and joined *materially* in Yankee City by clearly defined physical limits marked by ordinary walls, fences, and hedges. The living and the dead are *spiritually* joined

and divided by ceremonies for the dead—among them
funerals which occur daily, Memorial Day rites, and
the dedication and consecration of burial ground—
which separate the sacred and profane realms by use of
these symbolic methods. All are founded on, and give
expression to, the feelings and beliefs of the people of
Yankee City. Rituals of consecration have transformed
a small part of the common soil of the town into a
sacred place and dedicated this land of the dead to God,
to the sacred souls of the departed, and to the souls of
the living whose bodies are destined for such an end.
The rituals which establish graveyards tacitly imply
formal rules and precepts which define the relations of
the profane and sacred worlds of the living and the dead.
The funeral—a formal rite of separation of the recently
dead from the living—is, broadly speaking, an unending
ritual, for although funerals are separate rites, they occur
with such continuing frequency that they maintain a
constant stream of ritual connection between the dead
and the living. Once a year the cult of the dead in the
Memorial Day rites for the whole community strengthens and re-expresses what the chain of separate funerals
accomplishes throughout the year.

The funeral symbolically removes the *time*-bound individual from control by the forward direction of human time. He no longer moves from the past towards
the future, for now (in the minds of the living) he is in
the unmoving, sanctified stillness of an ever-present
eternity. At death the ageing process, conceptually a
form of human time existing in the nature of things,
loses its control of the individual. The march of events
no longer has meaning for what he has become. His
timeless ("eternal") soul is in a sacred realm where hu-

man and social time lose most of their meanings; his
dead, ephemeral body becomes part of a process where
human time has little significance. The time of the
living as the society conceives it cannot be understood
without knowledge of "dead" time. In many ways the
two are contrary to each other. As opposites, dead and
live time express the duality of existence, the sacred
and the profane, the "controlled" and the "uncontrol-
lable." The ephemeral and the eternal, activity and in-
ertness, are all part of the meaning of the duality of live
and dead time. The popularity of the play and motion
picture "Death Takes a Holiday" was built largely on
the symbolic point that human time no longer had control over human destiny; events were timeless because
the *time of death* was no longer in opposition to the
time of life. Rather the "holiday" of death meant that
the sacred time of eternity had been substituted for the
secular time of man. Holidays and holy days are moments in the calendar where ordinary time is flouted.
The author of the play, however, also made another
point when he used the term "holiday" (rather than
"holy day"); he allowed his audience to gratify their
longing to translate into the sacred, eternal time of the
dead the pleasant, sensuous world of the living.

The cemetery, separate and distinct from the living,
yet forever a material part of Yankee City's cultural
equipment, bridges these two times, ending the one and
beginning the other. As man changes physically, the
"conveyor belt" of social time redefines his changing
place in the community and moves him onward until
finally, at death, it ceremonially dumps him into a new
set of meanings where human time no longer defines his
existence. The cemetery's several material symbols

play their part in relating the time of eternity to human time. Man's fate, as Yankee City conceives it, can be found in these signs. Let us examine them.

The cemeteries in Yankee City are divided into lots of varying sizes which are ordinarily the property of particular families, occasionally of associations. The burial plots are referred to by the surnames of the families who own them. The individual graves, with their individual stone markers, are arranged within the limits of the lots —more often than not according to the status of the dead individuals within the family and the dictates of mortuary style prevailing at the time of their deaths.

The emotions and thoughts of the living about their dead always express the antithetical elements that enter into the placement of the dead. Human time continually makes its demands for controlling eternity; maintenance of the identity of the dead is partly dependent on placing them in living time and space. Human space concepts continue to be used to locate the dead. Location of the dead in time and space helps to maintain their reality to those who wish to continue their relations with them. The cemetery contributes its material signs to help maintain this system of meanings and feelings.

The cemetery as a collective representation is both a city and a garden of the dead. The two symbols fuse and merge in the collective thinking of the people of Yankee City. The most modern cemetery in the community, well over a hundred years in age, accents its natural surroundings and emphasizes the symbols of nature, but only as they are fashioned and expressed within the limits and control of men and society in the design of a formal garden. It is a miniature, symbolic replica of the gardenlike dwelling area of a better-class suburb, or an elaboration of the formal gardens of aristocratic families. It is a symbolic city built in the form of a garden of the dead.

"Garden" and "city" are both feminine images in our culture, the former a dependent symbol of the more ancient Mother Earth. The garden is also a symbol of both life and death. As a *place* it symbolizes life, vitality, growth, and the fertility of the earth. As a symbol of the *processes* occurring there it expresses feelings about man's involvement in the eternal cycle of life and death, its shrubs and flowers come and go and are born again, its life dies, decays, and enriches the soil where new plants and shrubs are reborn and flower again. Summer and winter, life and death, eternally repeat themselves in the processes of the garden—an artifact formed by, and subject to, the will of man.

Elm Highlands, the most modern cemetery of Yankee City, was consecrated in the first half of the last century as a "rural burial place" where landscape gardening united "the beautiful in nature with sculptural art, thereby creating a garden cemetery." The citizens composed two original hymns for its consecration. Both explicitly use maternal and female symbols to refer to the cemetery and the return of the living to a maternal and female resting place. The one from which the following quote was taken also recognizes the cemetery as a "City of Our Dead" and refers to the common fate of the living and the dead and their mutual hope for immortality through their relations with the supernatural power of Christ.

. . .

> We here appoint, by solemn rite,
> On this sequestered, peaceful site,
> With flowery grass and shadowy tree,
> The City of Our Dead to be.
>
> Though this now sacred turf must break
> Our dearest forms of life to take;
> On Nature's calm, maternal breast
> 'Tis meet her weary children rest.
>
> May He, who, pitying, "touched the bier,"
> Console each future mourner here;
> And all the dead at last arise
> With joy to meet Him in the skies!

The author of the hymn explicitly speaks of the return of the "weary children" to the "maternal breast"
of Nature where they find eternal "rest." The more
obvious female symbolism involved with the insertion
of the body into the open grave which then encloses it
in the "body of Mother Earth" is not acceptable at the
conscious level to members of our culture. Unconsciously, the open grave and the uterus are compatible;
they also fit the social assumptions of our rites of passage. The rite and facts of birth separate the new individual from the womb of the mother and, following the
events between the rites and facts of death, complete
the life cycle by returning the human body to the maternal body of Nature. The Christian rites of baptism
and those surrounding death symbolically recognize the
meanings assigned to these facts. In the Catholic Church,
for example, the liturgy of Holy Saturday explicitly
views baptism as both a birth and a death rite while

bringing to the manifest level of understanding the vaginal significance of the "immersion" in the water of the font. On the other hand, Extreme Unction and Christian funerals non-logically—but with great effectiveness—symbolically state the meanings of death as both an ending and a beginning, as a rite of death and a rite of birth.

The author of the sacred poem, in speaking of the "weary children" finding "rest," puts the fixed eternal world of sacred time in opposition to the wariness of those *moving* through human time. The return of the "children" to the breast of the mother, back to the beginning of time for them where the beginning and the ending are one, touches and may evoke powerful yet unsatisfied human feelings and use them positively to reduce anxiety about death. Whether the "peaceful" equilibrium and quiet of prenatal existence influence the postnatal meaning of experience is debatable, but the strong desire to maintain close and unchanging relations with the mother and the infantile need to possess her are well documented human longings. These feelings, morally stated in the sacred symbols of consecration, non-morally felt in the unconscious longings of men, are bound to the female symbol of Nature, the beginning and ending of human time. The cemetery as an object dedicated to God and man and consecrated to "our dead to be," its graves, and the cemetery as a city and garden, are all culturally controlled female symbols. One must suspect that their significance not only derives from the logical and non-logical meanings of culture but lies deeply rooted in the life of the human animal.

The fundamental *sacred* problem of the graveyard is

to provide suitable symbols to refer to and express man's hope of immortality through the sacred belief and ritual of Christianity, and to reduce his anxiety and fear about death as marking the obliteration of his personality— the end of life for himself and for those he loves. The assurance of life hereafter for the dead already in the cemetery and for those being buried is an assurance of life hereafter for the living. Maintaining the dead as members of society maintains the continuing life of the living. The living's assurance of life everlasting is dependent on their keeping the dead alive. Should the dead really die, in the belief of those who put them to rest, then they, too, must die. The cemetery is an enduring physical emblem, a substantial and visible symbol of this agreement among men that they will not let each other die. For a very few, it is a sacred or sometimes an open admission that the power of tradition and convention is greater than the strength of their own rational convictions.

The fundamental *secular* problem the graveyard solves is to rid the living of the decaying corpse, thus freeing them from the nauseous smells of corruption and from the horror of seeing the natural decomposition of a human body, thereby helping to maintain the satisfying images of themselves as persistent and immortal beings. Another social function of the graveyard is to provide a firm and fixed social place, ritually consecrated for this purpose, where the disturbed sentiments of human beings about their loved dead can settle and find peace and certainty. Death destroys the equilibrium of the family and other intimate groups in which the deceased participated during his life. When it comes, the interaction and exchange of intimate gestures and symbols, resulting in each individual's personality internalizing part of the person of the other with whom he intimately interacts, ceases. This process no longer provides a mirror, however opaque and distorted, in which the individual may feel he sees his own reflection and thus realize himself as a social being. The belief in immortality, strengthened and reinforced by the funeral rite, helps correct some of the feeling in the survivor of loss of self. For the survivor to continue to see and feel himself still living in, and related to, the dead life of the other it is necessary for him to reconstruct his image of the other; but in doing this he must also rethink who he himself is, at least in so far as he relates himself to the dead person. This constitutes an essential part of the social-psychological processes of the living during the transition of death.

The cemetery provides the living with a sacred realm they have created by means of their social control of divine power, a function of sacred symbolism, in which they can deposit the impure and unclean corpse in a grave that belongs to it not so much as a corpse but as a sacred person, in a grave which also belongs to them, the living. The grave with its markings is a place where the living can symbolically maintain and express their intimate relations with the dead. There is a kinship of kind, too; today's dead are yesterday's living, and today's living are tomorrow's dead. Each is identified with the other's fate. No one escapes.

The grave is marked so that the living can approach it as something that belongs to a separate personality; it is not merely a symbol that refers generally and abstractly to all the dead. The cemetery is a symbolic meeting place for the dead and the living, for the realms of the sacred and profane, for the natural and for the supernatural. It is a social emblem, whole and entire, yet composed of many autonomous and separate individual symbols which give visible expression to our social relations to the supernatural and to the pure realm of the spirit. It is a meeting place which faces out to death and the sacred absolute and back to the secular realities of the finite and the living. In it the time of man and the time of God are united. It is a "final resting place" where the disturbed and bruised sentiments of the living members of the society mark the natural death and ultimate disposition of an individual organism and its detachment from the species, thus fixing a place in time where the living can relate themselves in human, understandable, emotional terms to the spiritualized personality now in the timeless realm of the supernatural other world. The members of the societies of the living and the dead meet here as "God's children" and are accordingly one people. The cemetery as a collective representation repeats and expresses the social structure of the living as a symbolic replica; a city of the dead, it is a symbolic replica of the living community. The spiritual part of the city of the Christian dead, often thought of as part of the City of God, is sometimes equated with the Invisible Body of Christ. For many Christians, each is an integral part of a greater mystery.

The social and status structures which organize the living community of Yankee City are vividly and impressively reflected and expressed in the outward forms and internal arrangements of the several cemeteries of the city. Just as cemeteries reflect in miniature the past life and historic eras through which the community has passed, so contemporary graveyards symbolically express the present social structure. This memorial of the living for the dead has been created in their own image.

During the field research we observed and described all the city's graveyards in Yankee City; several were studied intensively and systematically.[1] Their grounds and burial lots were plotted, an inventory was taken of the ownership of the various burial lots, and listings were made of the individuals and families buried in them. By interviews and through the collection of official cemetery documents, we were able to reconstruct their history and study the ongoing social processes. For obvious reasons all names of people, places, and particular cemeteries are fictional. To increase anonymity, the evidence from several of them has been combined into one composite statement.

The great importance of the elementary family organization as a fundamental and primary unit of our social structure is everywhere present in the collective representations of the cemetery. The configuration of the personalities in the family is reflected in the relative positions of burial of the various kin. The father is often in the center of the burial plot, but the mother occasionally occupies this position; father and mother sometimes hold an equal position in the center.

The use of stone borders to outline and define the separate character of the family plot emphasizes the basic unity and primary importance of the elementary family. Thus the live facts of birth and procreation are reflected in their graveyard symbols. The conflict be-

1. I am very much indebted to Leo Srole and Buford Junker for their field studies of the several cemeteries. I am also in the debt of other members of the research staff for their observations.

tween the individual's family of orientation, into which
he was born, and his family of procreation, which he
has helped to create by marriage and producing children, are also clearly marked in the cemetery. By interview and by the disposition of the body, we were able to
demonstrate that this competition between two families
for its possession is clearly reflected in what happens
in the graveyard. If the family of orientation is stronger,
it is likely that there will be a large family plot with
the father and mother occupying a more or less central
position, with the male children and wives placed on
each side of them and the grandchildren on the
periphery. This is more often the pattern for upper-
class position. If the family of procreation is stronger,
or there is conflict between the families of birth and
marriage, this family unit tends to break off by itself
and the burial plot then may contain its male head, his
wife, and their unmarried children. Although not confined to one class, this type of burial is most characteristic, as far as we could discover, of the middle classes,
particularly those who have been upward mobile.

These two types of burial—the large, extended family
and the small, limited one—represent the extreme differences in burial as they are related to the families of
orientation and procreation. There are intermediate
forms showing the variations that necessarily must occur in a society where there are differences among the
several classes and there is opposition between the
families of birth and marriage. When the family organization of extended kindred is as powerful as usual in
the upper-upper class, it is likely that the family plots
will record this class difference. When the lineage principle is powerful and the patronym is of real significance

to a class, this too is likely to be reflected in the recognition of each in the arrangement of the dead and the
inscriptions on the tombstones. Sometimes the lineage
of the mother may be expressed by the inclusion of
her maiden name on the stone. This may appear in any
class, but it is more frequent with the upper class, where
the patronym of the mother is of special significance
to the social position of the family. As far as we could
determine, it rarely appears in the inscriptions of the
lower classes.

A Vacancy in Elm Highlands Cemetery

The symbolism of the graveyard, marking and expressing family conflict and solidarity, is well illustrated
by the graves of the Worthington family. Jonathan
Worthington, the son of an old Hill Street family, is
no longer buried in the family burial ground, but in
a small lot by himself on one of the low-rising knolls
on the other side of the cemetery, a long distance from
the family plot on the high hill where he was buried
at the time of his death. His father had purchased the
family lot when the children were young. Places were
provided for his wife and all the children and their
children's children. The family gravestone, a modest
yet imposing shaft, was erected before Mr. Worthington's death. The graves of two of his children who had
died when quite young were at one side of the plot,
the small stones fittingly inscribed. Jonathan's older
brother and his wife, the victims of an accident, were
buried side by side within the family lot, near the
father and the place that Mrs. Worthington would occupy beside him. She often said it was a source of
satisfaction and comfort to her to know that some day

she would be there beside her husband, with their children all around them. Once—but only once—she had said more literally, to the delight of the malicious and the vulgar, "I feel better when I realize my body will always be there beside my husband's." [2]

Jonathan had never been like the other sons. He disliked business and wanted to be a painter. Because of his delicate health as a youth his parents, after brief disapproval, had relented and allowed him to have his wish. After a period of study in Paris he had lived in New York. There he met and married a beautiful Polish girl who was earning her way through art school by modeling for artists. Although Theodora was American born, it had displeased his mother; she had hoped he would marry a daughter of one of the old families whom he had courted during prep school days.

The fact that Theodora had lost her religious faith and no longer belonged or went to the Catholic Church was of some comfort to Johnnie's mother. When she agreed to Mrs. Worthington's suggestion that they have something more than a justice-of-the-peace wedding, and she and Johnnie were married again in an Episcopal church in New York, the event filled Mrs. Worthington with great hopes everything in time might work out all right.

When Johnnie and Theodora moved to Yankee City and refused to live with the mother in the old family house, but "took an old barn of a house" down on the river, remodeled it to provide studios for both, and

2. The evidence comes from members of the immediate family. Before his death Jonathan had told us personally much about himself, his family, and the conflict between his wife and mother. Close friends of the family, as well as enemies, told the rest.

lived a quiet life, refusing invitations to dinner and declining to be a part of the social world his family knew, Johnnie's mother's increasing hostility to his wife became a topic of gossip along Hill Street and among their friends on the "North Shore."

Only a few years later Johnnie's frailness turned into real illness demanding the attention of the family doctor. After a quiet visit from his mother the doctor urged them to give up their place on the river and move into the old Hill Street home where he could have better attention. To this he finally agreed. Here he and Theodora had a bedroom and sitting room in a small suite upstairs that could be separated from the rest of the house. The senior Mrs. Worthington, despite her anxiety about his illness, felt almost happy again because she had her son back under the family roof. She and Theodora were formally polite and, with a little effort, were able most of the time to avoid each other and to maintain a semblance of cordiality.

Johnnie and his wife had been at the old home only a few months when he became much worse. Suspecting that his health was poorer than anyone admitted, he finally persuaded the doctor to give him a frank report on his condition and was informed that he was likely to die within a short time. The mother and wife each had several tearful conversations with him, but neither was able to talk fully and frankly about what she felt or to speak of what might happen when he died.

One afternoon, shortly before his death, he asked to see his mother and wife together. When the two Mrs. Worthingtons had come in and the nurse had left, closing the door behind her, he said to them, "I want to say to both of you that you have been simply grand.

I have been able to talk about everything to you. Some of it has been rough and tough for you to take. You both love me and I love you. My having to die now just when I think life is beginning to be something doesn't make sense to you or to me, but that's the way it is and that's the way it's going to be. But I suppose if I lived to be a hundred I would think I was too young to die right away. Anyway, we've been all over that one.

"There is something else that's bothering me. It seems a little silly for me, being the kind of man I am, to talk about it, but I've been thinking that I don't know for sure where I am going to be buried, and somehow I need to know where that's going to be."

The senior Mrs. Worthington moved her rocking chair back just a little and began rocking herself tentatively, as if she wanted to substitute movement for speech. She cleared her throat. Johnnie's wife looked down at her hands and then at him. Finally, she turned her face towards Mrs. Worthington. Mrs. Worthington spoke:

"Why, Johnnie, there has always been a place in the family plot for all of you children. Surely you know that." Johnnie looked at her anxiously and asked, "And that means that there will be a place for Theodora, too?" There was a brief pause before Mrs. Worthington said, "Yes, your father provided places for all the husbands and wives of our children."

When Jonathan died, Theodora was so overcome with emotion and uncertain of what was happening that many things perceived during the funeral and the burial did not have meaning to her until after several weeks had passed and she began to rearrange her experiences and think about them more rationally. During periods of weeping at the burial, she had noticed that Johnnie had been put in one corner of the burial ground and that his older brother was buried next to him. Later reflection made her realize that the traditional pattern of husband and wife being side by side was impossible unless the body of the brother was disinterred. In the springtime and after further thought about the matter, Theodora took some flowers down to Johnnie's grave. During this visit, after thinking about where the other members of the family would be buried, she realized that there seemed to be no place provided for her. She waited until an appropriate moment and faced Mrs. Worthington with the question as to what provision had been made for her own burial place.

Mrs. Worthington said she had not wanted to distress Johnnie at the time of his mortal illness, so had told him a "little white lie" about there being a place beside him for Theodora. No place was provided for her, because "no one would ever have believed Johnnie would ever marry." She informed Theodora that she would be very glad to make arrangements for a plot of ground as near to the family burial ground as possible. The conversation became more heated. Finally, when Theodora left Mrs. Worthington's room she rushed to her own, packed her bags, and made arrangements to have her personal effects moved to a hotel in Boston. Here, sitting in her room, she felt more lonely and isolated than since the early days of her adolescence, when she had realized that her outlook on life was different from that of other children her own age. She felt that she had lost not only the living Johnnie but the dead one and even the symbol referring to his burial. She finally decided to call a lawyer and discovered that she was within her rights to have her husband's body removed to another burial place.

Theodora purchased a small lot on the knoll far from the family burial ground and made the necessary arrangements at the cemetery for the disinterment. The lot had room for two graves; one is now occupied by Johnnie.

Johnnie died a number of years ago. Since that time Theodora has occupied herself once more with her profession and has been absorbed back into the art world. Here she has met men who have occasionally attracted her. At the present time it seems likely that she will marry a successful New York artist. She has told her friends that, although she still loves Johnnie, the new man interests her and life seems very lonely without a husband to share it with.

Meanwhile, there is a vacant place in the family lot of the Worthingtons which was once filled by Johnnie's casket, and there is also a vacant place in the new family lot which was to have been Theodora's when she died. The meaning of the separate burial places and the vacancy in each is not lost on those who know the Worthingtons. Just as family solidarity and the status of each member are usually marked by burial customs and their permanent symbols in the cemetery, so can deep conflict and hostility leave their own meaningful marks. Where the body of a man is placed when he dies tells much about his meaning as an individual, but it may tell even more about his social place and significance to those who survive him. The gossips of Yankee

City do not use scientific terms to state what they think, but what they say expresses even more effectively what such terms should mean.

Collective Representations of the Sexes, the Several Ages, and the Institutions of Yankee City

Most institutions or associations leave their impress on the symbolism of Elm Highlands and the sign system of the cemetery. They are not merely imprints but meaningful sets of diverse symbols to which members of the various groups can repair at least once a year. The symbolic marks around which organized actions occur, and to which the mental attention of the members is given throughout the year, are placed there by the members themselves. The living mark the places of the dead with meaningful signs that refer to what the living want them to be, thus strengthening and freshening their memories about the dead past and maintaining it as a living reality in their thoughts and feeling. Such marks perform their share in maintaining the life of the social heritage.

The basic recognition of the superior and inferior statuses of males and females in our society is clearly reflected in the graveyard. The superordinate males are often given preference with larger and more prominent headstones, and their funerals give them greater ritual recognition. The eulogy, for example, when the corpse is a male, is likely to be more elaborate and the positive points in the life career of the person more fully developed. This is perhaps to be expected since the man of the family is more likely to have a recognizable public experience and record. But although the symbols of the graveyard—position, type of headstone, treatment at burial, etc.—formally give the adult male a superordinate recognition commensurate with his former status as head of the family and as father and breadwinner and the one whose patronym all members of the family carry, women are more fully recognized informally. The inscriptions on their tombstones are likely to be filled with deeper sentiments of attachment than those for males. The male inscriptions more often express the sense of respect and duty, whereas those for women speak of love and tender affection.

Age grading is clearly involved in the symbolism of all the graveyards. Those unfortunates who die as children have secondary places within the family plot. Their stones are small, commensurate with the "length" of their lives and the size of their small bodies. The inscriptions for subadult males as well as females are likely to be filled with expressions of love similar to those on the gravestones of females. The purity and innocence of the child are stressed, implying the young person's supposed freedom from the ultimate moral and supernatural responsibility for his acts.

The symbols of age in the graveyard unconsciously express the subordinate role of the child and subadult and the superordinate role of the adult; the social personality of young people and women is less developed and less important that the social personality of male adults. The overwhelming majority of the people of Yankee City would deny these statements, declaring that the souls of all are equal in the sight of God and in man's sight, too, when he faces God during the crisis of death. Yet our listing of the place and size of gravestones in the several cemeteries, as well the evidence from the sentiments of the inscriptions, overwhelmingly indicates that the simple and subordinate social positions of females and children are clearly reflected in the mortuary symbolism.

The elaborate associational structure of Yankee City also becomes a symbolic part of the community of the dead and influences the cemetery as a collective representation. It does so in a variety of ways. Sometimes an association, such as the Masons, conducts the funeral. Symbolic plaques of a more or less permanent nature are placed on the graves of members. Yearly these plaques are refurbished—particularly for Memorial Day —to recognize the relation of the dead and living members of the organization. Emblems of such organizations as the American Legion, the Spanish War Veterans, the Women's Relief Corps, the Firemen's Association, Elks, Knights of Pythias, Moose, and many similar organizations are permanent parts of many graves. Many of these associations play a prominent role in the Memorial Day rites. Several associations have purchased burial plots where some of their members are buried; either because the member did not have sufficient funds or because his devotion to the organization was so strong that he wished to identify himself permanently with it. There are also associations which care for aged men and women of former good circumstances and superior class, which not only give them care while living but bury them in the association's burial plot.

The place of the church in the community is symbolized in the cemetery by a variety of usages. The church, the organization primarily responsible for maintaining and fostering the Christian religion, whose principle purpose is to help its members to achieve immortality through belief in the divinity of Jesus Christ, plays the most important institutional role in relating the city of the living to the city of the dead. The communicants of all the Protestant churches have common burial grounds. Catholics and Orthodox Jews usually have separate graveyards hallowed by their own rituals of consecration. The present inclusion of all Protestants in one cemetery provides a common sacred place where all sects can disregard their doctrinal differences. The funeral rites in which they participate without regard to their church affiliation also symbolically unite them. Moreover, the Christian afterworld to which such mortuary rites assign the souls of the departed is one place. For Protestants, the cemetery is increasingly a symbol which is helping to break down sectarian differences and unite them in one group. The sectarian holy ground once attached to each church now remains largely a memorial to a distant, respected past, though burials occasionally still take place in God's half-acre.

All the gravestones and most of the mortuary art of Christian cemeteries use Christian symbols, the principal ones being the Cross, the Lamb (either as Christ or as the Christian member of Christ's flock), and many other Christian representations found in most cemeteries. Some of the inscriptions on the stones clearly express the relation of the living to the dead and of the dead to the supernatural world. Among them are "Blessed are the dead which die in the Lord," "Sleep and take thy rest," "Asleep in Jesus," "More light, more love, more life beyond." In other words, they emphasize the wish and the belief that the dead still live.

The several ethnic groups in Yankee City have left definite marks on the cemeteries. There is, first, the dual cultural character of the several communities. Inscriptions often appear both in English and in the ethnic language. There are wooden crosses made in a form characteristic of the ethnic background as well as headstones on the same grave. Sometimes there are indications that the ethnic wooden cross has been removed and replaced by an American headstone—clear evidence that the new generation of American children of ethnic families are exerting their influence on the family plot. Ritual objects having ethnic connotations are on some of the graves, often appearing rather incongruous to the eyes of native Americans. For example, on one such grave there was an American flag beside a small replica of a house within which could be seen wax flowers and a candle. The whole of it was overhung with a trestle. The more recent the ethnic group the greater the likelihood that such objects and ethnic variations will appear in the mortuary art; the older the ethnic group the less difference is likely to appear between its graves and those in the Yankee part of the cemetery.

Perhaps one of the more significant symbolic variations is a greater use of the American flag on all ethnic graves. Whereas American tradition is likely to assign the use of the flag to the graves of soldiers, recent ethnic groups often make no such distinction. The flag seems to imply for many of them that the deceased was a citizen, or the family believes he wanted to be. Some ethnic associations are particularly active in making sure that the American flag appears on the graves of their members. There also seems to be some feeling that burials of members "in American soil" gives the living a greater claim to being American nationals. At some funerals it was stated that the person had ceased to be only part

American; his body was now one with America itself. A few of the ethnic groups have separate sections set apart from the rest of the cemetery, which are then redivided according to the family or extended family groups. Some do not use formal arrangements but informally place their dead near each other and in a separate part of the cemetery.

Autonomy, Ambivalence, and Social Mobility

Perhaps one of the most interesting and significant activities found in the cemeteries of Yankee City is the removal of bodies from one part of the cemetery to another or their transfer from the cemetery where they were first buried to another. Such disinterments are not infrequent. They occur every year in most of the cemeteries. One caretaker informed us that he moved several bodies every year from his cemetery to Elm Highlands. When we examined the evidence to determine why these removals took place we learned that in some cases they were made because of changes in religious faith. Some occurred because the living members of the family had been socially mobile and had moved from the lower status the family occupied at the time of the person's death to a higher position. Motivated by embarrassment or strong love of parents and a wish to treat the dead as they might have done had opportunity offered earlier, the socially mobile living members of the family sometimes disinter their dead and place them in the "better" locations commensurate with their present social position. The values and beliefs which motivate such people and the reaction of some of the community to this behavior are perhaps best portrayed in the composite characterization I have called "These Bones Shall

Rise Again" (the whole profile, here considerably shortened, is given in Volume I of this series).

Mr. Charles Watson (lower-middle class), the superintendent of the cemetery, squatted on his haunches while he supervised the pick-and-shovel activities of his two workmen. It was hot. He had removed his blue serge coat and laid it carefully over a gravestone. He loosened his tie and opened the collar of his white shirt. Dust rose from the dry earth. While Sam Jones (lower-lower class) broke the soil on one side of a burial plot, Tom Green (lower-lower class) shoveled the already loosened earth from the opposite side of the plot.

The burial lot where these operations were proceeding was down on the flat ground in one corner of the cemetery. The headpieces were stone and rather small. Next to and just below this flat part of the cemetery was the area of wooden headpieces. Many had fallen and lay rotting on the ground. On the other side of the cemetery the stone headpieces were larger and increased in size until they reached the hill section, where there were some elaborate funeral urns. In this area a whole burial lot was often bordered with white marble.

The shoveler stopped his work and lit a cigarette.

"I can't understand that guy," he said. "Why the hell can't Phil Starr leave his old man and old lady rest in peace? Why, they been down in this here grave for thirty years, and now, by God, he's digging them up and running all over town with them. I say, once they're buried, let them stay buried. The dead ought to be left alone—they ought to rest in peace."

The pickman stopped and wiped his hands on his overalls.

"What makes me sore is it ain't because the old bastard had to get them out because of something else, like a new road being put through or city improvements, but he's doing it on purpose because he's got to be a big shot. Why, my own mother is buried right over there by that rosebush. It's good enough for her and there wasn't a better woman ever lived than she was."

The other picked up the conversation.

"Why, I remember the time before he made his dough in the Neway Shoe Factory when he didn't have a red cent. Why, that guy——"

"I think you men," said the superintendent, "aren't seeing this thing right. Mr. Starr is only showing his love for his father and mother. When they were alive he still had to make his money, and he couldn't do the things for them he would have liked. If he had had the money when they were alive, he told me, he would have moved them out of that little shack they had down there in the flats and up to his house on Hill Street. That's natural. Anyone who's worth his salt would want to do that for his pa and ma, especially when he's able to do it. But, you see, they died too soon.

"He told me just the other day he wanted to give them the best place to rest in that could be found in the cemeteries in this town. I tried to show him one of our better lots up on the hill but, 'No,' he said, 'only Elm Highlands will do.' He's putting them in a grave up there on the highest hill next to the Breckenridges and the Wentworths and all of those other old families. It's going to be his own lot. He's a-doing this for his pa and ma. Just what any decent American would do for his."

"Oh, yeah?" said the shoveler.

"That sounds okay," said the pickman, "but he ain't worried about this place not bein' good enough for his pa and ma. He's worried about it not bein' good enough for him. I bet that son and daughter of his don't like to come down here with him to decorate their grandpa's and grandma's grave."

"Sure," the shovelman continued. "It makes those kids remember that their old man is just one jump from the clam flats."

"I think you men are wrong," said Mr. Watson. "I sometimes see Mr. Starr at the Elks. He always stops and speaks. Last time he saw me he said, 'Charlie, how are you?' And I said, 'I'm fine.' 'How's your missus?' says he, and I said, 'She's okay, too.' "

The two workmen said nothing. They resumed their work. Mr. Watson went back to his small office. After he had gone, Jones spoke:

"Christ, Charlie'd kiss anybody's ass for a quarter."

They went on digging.

The efforts of Mr. Starr to assemble "all" of his family in a place favorably located to give effective expression to his recently acquired position in the class system of Yankee City portray some of the social and psychological conflicts in the family and status structures of Yankee City. The successful climb of a man from the low status of his birth to a superior position, which results in his family of procreation, including his wife and children, occupying a higher class level than that of his parents and the family of his birth, inevitably puts severe strain on the relations between the members of the two families. Customary usages of the parents and children and other members of the family no longer fit all situations that arise. The funeral and burial rites, as well as other rites of transition during periods of crisis and stress, when experienced by families involved in mobility, accentuate the strain sometimes to the point of open conflict. On such occasions some of the deepest and most irrational feelings that possess men dominate and harass their lives.

At a time of death, the ambivalent feelings of hostility and love which ordinarily exist in all families between such kindred as parents and their children, brothers and sisters, as well as the parents- and children-in-law, are carefully and smoothly handled by our conventions and the traditional symbolic behavior of the death rites. In many societies the ambivalent love and hostility of the living for the dead are expressed and controlled by beliefs that the sacred soul of the departed is hostile to the living. Consequently, the mourning ceremonies allow both the grief of love and the aggression of hostility to be symbolically expressed. Among Australian aborigines and many other peoples, the dead are believed to have two souls: a friendly good one and an unfriendly bad one. The funeral and mourning rites express affection for, and carefully guide, the good soul to the sacred totem well while frightening the evil one with hostile threats away from the group.

The feeling in Yankee City is not that the soul is hostile to the living; a sense of guilt felt by the living about some of their hostility to the dead person is often expressed by regret as to inadequate treatment of the person while he was alive. Whereas the Australian aborigines use sacred symbols to control the souls of the dead in order to eliminate them and be sure they are transferred to a place safely away from the living, the people of Yankee City turn their graveyards into sacred realms of love and respect, where only positive and affectionate sentiments are expressed for the deceased. [114a] The dead are kept, as it were, intimately close to the love of the living. They are carefully protected and the cemetery is a familiar part of the town.

Often relatives appear at funerals, express their grief, and confess their "unwarranted" enmity for the dead man whom, while he was alive, they strongly disliked and avoided. Formal and informal behavior during funerals sometimes results in old feuds being settled and rebellious members reintegrated into the family. This is accomplished by the hostility of the secular living members of the family for the dead man being translated into a feeling of guilt during the crisis and rites of death. Meanwhile, the once ordinary living man, now dead, is transformed in their thoughts and feelings into a sacred person. The ordinary living with their hostile thoughts feel inadequate before the dead; external aggression is often turned inward on the (guilty) self.

Families which have not been disturbed by the social mobility of some of their members find the crisis and its transformations easier than those where mobility has existed. The man who has striven successfully to realize his ambitions to reach the top, and in effect, consciously or not, has rejected his parents, their values and way of life, is particularly vulnerable. When they die and guilt assails him he must have strong inner armament to protect his ego from yielding to the self-condemnation of his conscience. His moral self turns traitor and attacks what he is and what he has done to himself. Since much of his moral life lies deep within his unconscious and has its being there, surviving as such from the time of his childhood when he internalized many of the moral values and beliefs of his parents and made them part of himself, he is nakedly vulnerable and defenseless. What he has now become must be alien to what he once was. Despite the tough-minded internal controls he may have established, which permitted him to "leave home," in fact and emotionally he still feels the exaggerated guilt of a mobile man.

During life, while in competition for the success for which many Americans try, he may have defied his father and sometimes humiliated and shamed him; by his marriage to, and life with, a woman from a superior level he often made it heartbreakingly clear to his mother that for him she was inadequate. No matter how successfully they free themselves from maternal ties, few mobile men can guard themselves from the overwhelming sense of guilt which normal people feel in less violent form as the result of their ambivalent feelings for a loved person. The disinterment of the mother and father from their lowly graves and the removal of their bones to the mortuary splendor of "a burial on the hills of Elm Highlands" not only allows the guilty son to act out and sometimes free himself from his guilt, but also permits conspicuous display of his wealth before his less well-placed kindred, while placing his parents where they symbolically belong according to his present status needs.

Another painful factor operating during the crisis of death is accentuated in the feelings of the mobile man. Our society has always emphasized the values of individualism; the freedom and rights of an independent conscience and intellect are fundamental parts of our basic democratic dogmas. We train our children, particularly in the middle class, to be self-directed autonomous persons, yet deep within our moral and religious life there is strong condemnation of anyone who disobeys the traditional communal rules of the group. If a sense of sin is a result of the infractions of the sacred rules which are believed to unite man, society, and God, and such rules are believed to be formulated by, and an expression of, God, then the autonomous man during his early development must either internalize the social world about him in such a way that a personality is produced which is never at variance with God and society—an impossible task—or he must constantly face the pain of internal and external conflict. He will not find a place of harmony, for what he is as a moral and intellectual self and what he must be as a person withstanding the pressure exerted on him by the rules of his secular and sacred worlds cannot come to terms. The pain and guilt felt by the "sinful man" whose autonomy has directed him from the traditional moral rules are the inevitable results of the conflicting values our society has about him and his kind. We encourage autonomy and train the young for it, but we covertly and sometimes openly condemn those who make themselves into autonomous persons. The strong, successfully mobile man develops defenses against it, but his armor can never be quite sufficient to save him from a feeling of guilt "for doing and having done what he needed to do." When his parents or other loved ones die, he inevitably feels a deeper sense of egoistic guilt than the non-mobile person who has obeyed the rules, reduced his internal decision-making to a minimum, maximized his obedience to external social directions, and thereby fitted himself into the conventional places provided for his kind by the social traditions.

Transition Technicians—the Funeral and Other Rites of Transition and the Power and Prestige of the Professions

From the above considerations it is clear that the symbolic significance of the cemetery as a material artifact reflecting the community life of Yankee City and the private worlds of its members cannot be fully comprehended by an examination limited to the grave itself. The symbolic rites which relate the living to the dead are integral parts of the whole life situation.

The movement of a man through his lifetime, from a fixed placental placement within his mother's womb to his death and the ultimate fixed point of his tombstone and final containment in his grave as a dead organism, is punctuated by a number of critical moments of transition which all societies ritualize and publicly mark with suitable observances to impress the significance of the individual and the group on living members of the community. These are the important times of birth, puberty, marriage, and death. The usual progress of all such rites of transition, as Van Gennep has demonstrated, are characterized by three phases: separation, margin, and aggregation. The first period of separation consists of symbolic behavior signifying the detachment of the individual from an earlier fixed point in the social structure; during the intermediate period of margin the status of the individual is ambiguous— it is not fixed for him or his society—he moves in a world where he is no longer what he was nor has attained what he is to be; in the last phase, of aggregation, the passage is made complete. The individual is again in a fixed status and reintegrated into his society. He is in a new status—new for him, but a traditional one for the society, a status which the society defines as the end and goal of a particular transition rite. The society recognizes and consecrates the successful achievement of the passage of the individual. [44]

At the same time his change of status and the reordering of his relations with other members of the society are recognized and sanctioned. The transition phases of separation, margin, and aggregation always involve others who are in direct relation with the individual during this time. They, too, are in positions of uneasiness and confusion which are expressed in their feelings and actions. The different societies have developed traditional symbols which express the varying feelings of other members of the society, usually the family of the person concerned, and direct their actions to an attainment of the ultimate goal of each transition.

The informal and non-official behavior which is always a part of all transition rites is often a channel of expression for paradoxical emotions and sentiments which are not altogether inappropriate. The "tears of joy" at a wedding, symbolically a time of joy, may express feelings of loss, deprivation, and even hostility felt by members of the two families; the informal gatherings of friends and relatives after the funeral for bread and drink among peoples where wakes are not sanctioned, when laughter and tears are intermingled, often allow feelings to be expressed publicly and relations established which the official funeral has not permitted. In our society the unofficial behavior of fathers during the period of birth and confinement of the expectant mother, often a source of amusement and a target for the satirist, is an informal expression of the social sentiments formalized by the *couvade* in "primitive" societies. These sentiments of anxiety about themselves in the crisis are not provided for in our symbolic usage at the birth transition.

The symbols of our *rites de passage* of birth, death, and the others occurring between them always operate at four levels of behavior and consequently involve sentiments, emotions, and values which are of the deepest significance to the whole social system and powerfully affect the participating individuals. The levels of behavior are: species activity, technological and social action, and the action system which relates men to the supernatural.

Throughout the life span and in all rites, the social personality of the living—the product of the individual's interaction with other members of the society and the sum of the social positions he has occupied while living in the social structure—influences, and is influenced directly and indirectly by, the rest of the society. This means that the effects of the social personality of each individual are felt by other members of the group and retained as part of their memories. Consequently, when a member of a community dies, his social personality is not immediately extinguished. His physical lifetime is ended, but social existence continues. It exists so long as memory of it is felt by the living members of the group.

As Chart 2 indicates, death does not destroy the social personality, for in the memory of others it continues to exist, and only disappears when all trace of it is

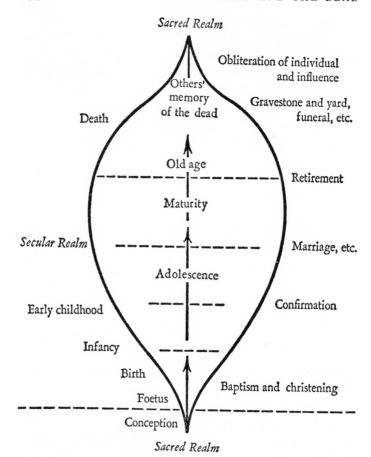

Sacred Realm

Obliteration of individual
and influence

Others'
memory
of the dead

Death

Gravestone and yard,
funeral, etc.

Old age

Retirement

Maturity

Secular Realm

Marriage, etc.

Adolescence

Early childhood

Confirmation

Infancy

Birth

Baptism and christening

Foetus

Conception

Sacred Realm

Chart 2. The Expansion and Contraction of the Social Personality
(during the Passage of the Individual through Life)

obliterated from the memory of the living and it no
longer exerts any influence upon them. Thus the social
personality starts in the sacred realm, passes through a
secular existence, and returns to the sacred world of
the dead. Birthdays and anniversaries of marriage are

symbolic recognitions of the original events. They usually function within the realm of the family, contribute to its solidarity by allowing its members to reassert their own values and beliefs about themselves, and allow the social value of the person and the occasion to be reasserted in symbolic form by the group. The flowers given to a mother on her birthday or to a wife on a wedding anniversary, or placed on a parent's grave, revive and restate by yearly ritual the changing yet continuing meaning of an individual's life to him and his society.

Our complex western European society, during the long periods of its increasing differentiation, has developed a number of occupational statuses closely related to the several rites of passage which mark and define the passage of social time from birth to death. They are largely the older and more honored professions, which possess extraordinary positions of privilege, power, and prestige. Very early in the development of this culture they assumed functions in the rites and crises of transition that once were the duties and obligations of the families involved. Since the families of the changing individual are primarily concerned with his crises of change, it would be expected that their members might conduct the several rites. Although at such times family members are very active, professional men are called in to take charge: doctors, lawyers, ministers, priests, and, to a lesser extent, teachers assume leading roles in one or more of the several crises. They are the transition technicians standing by as the time conveyor belt transports and transforms those who compose its traffic. They manipulate the highly valued symbols and play their part in defining and establishing what is happening to the lifetime of each individual and what this means within the social time of the group.

The activities between death and burial are filled with tension, grief, and disorder in the social world which immediately surrounds the deceased. During mortal illnesses, fear mingled with hope in the thoughts of the dying person, his family, and the friends who surround him, has created strong anxiety and tension in the relations of all those intimately involved. For some, the sacrament of Extreme Unction provides a rite of transition which effectively separates and removes the soul of the living from the ordinary secular world, transports it, and places it in a position where it can be integrated into the spiritual world. Only a minority of Protestants now summon the spiritual aid of the minister to help them through the period of the death crisis. The feelings of fear and guilt which fill the emotions and thinking of family and friends often prevent them from calling in the minister, since his extraordinary visit might be interpreted as a sign that the techniques of science are no longer effective—that the minister as a representative of the sacred world is assuming the dominant place until then occupied by the doctor. His appearance could signify the certainty of approaching death.

There are significant differences between the relative status of priests and ministers in the community. The priest is of significance to the less as well as the extremely devout Catholics in all rites of transition. The fundamental human crises have been ritualized by the Catholic Church to the point where all the principal ones are raised to the ritual importance of sacraments. Five of the seven sacraments are directly related to times of crisis and transition in human life. The other two are also used in transition rites. Baptism for birth; confirmation for the child's passage from early immaturity to the beginnings of maturity—from the exclusive dominance of the family to a more responsible and larger participation in the society; the sacrament of marriage for sexual cohabitation and the passage of the individual from the family of his birth to his family of reproduction; and Extreme Unction for death: all are associated with transitions and life crises. For one devoted to a celibate existence, ordination is essentially a substitute for the marriage rite; it transforms the secular man of the world, living in the larger profane realm of the flesh, into a member of an adult spiritual order—a member of the sacred realm of the Church. Only the sacraments of the Eucharist and penance are not directly symbolic expressions of critical transition periods in which there is a marked change of the individual's status in the structure of the community.

The symbolic role and ecclesiastic authority of the priest in all these rituals are very great. The part he plays and the symbols he manipulates are of the very greatest supernatural significance, for they invest the transitional crises and the *rite de passage* occasioned by each of them with the absolute power of the Divine presence. Through the priest, the eternal Divine elements become part of, and are directly related to, a secular, mundane, transitory moment in one individual's life. The symbolic role and activity of the priest, backed by the authority of the Church and confirmed by the faith of the communicant, raise him to a position of highest professional rank.

The position of the priest in the Irish community as well as in the French Canadian group in Yankee City is very high. Since they belong to ethnic groups which rank below the old Americans and since their religion is considered inferior to that of the Protestants, they do not enjoy a status in the larger community commensurate with that held in the several Catholic communities of French Canada or southern Ireland.

Protestant ministers occupy a variable position in professional status and in class levels. They rank in social class from upper-lower to upper class, most of them being upper-middle. Despite the fact that the status of Protestantism is high (particularly certain indigenous forms of New England Protestantism) and the ministers largely of old American background and New England heritage, they cannot be sure of the secure place held by the priest within his own immediate community. Compared with priests, doctors, and lawyers, their position is weak. The reasons for this, although complex, are fairly clear. The role of the minister since the Reformation has been increasingly secularized. Many of the sacred symbols largely centered in *rites de passage* celebrating events of importance in the lives of the people have been destroyed, and those that remain are often weak and not of great importance. When the great system of sacred symbols was broken or destroyed by the forces that produced Protestantism and the absolute power largely removed from those which remained, much of the authority inherent to the cloth disappeared. God's vicars need his signs to make manifest what it is that they and he are. Words are important symbols, but the mysteries of the Word need other symbolic usages to manifest the full power of God.

Most of the symbols visible and perceptible to the senses have been removed by the hostility of Protestant reform. Vivid and sensuous ceremonies that capture the inner world of the individual, colorful images that elicit and contain the fantasies of his private life, have been abandoned and condemned. The Protestant minister, weakly armed with an anemic liturgical apparatus and devitalized spiritual imagery, has had his spiritual power reduced; the reinforcement of visual drama often needed to make his words significant to his congregation has been taken from him. He is often reduced to the use of verbal symbols, now impoverished by the debilitating effect of two centuries of science. Their potency with a Protestant audience, now highly secularized, is dependent not only on supernatural sanction but on their scientific and rational validity. He is in the awkward position of having to make sense with the symbols he uses, not only to the sacred but to the most secular part of the profane world. In the various times of transition the minister is often humiliated by having to compete with undertakers for the central role in burying the dead, with justices of the peace for the marriage rite, and with a varied assortment of speakers representing all parts of society at high school and college graduation exercises.

Although the liturgical life of the Protestant church has not disappeared but is still alive and in many ways vital, even in the Evangelical churches it does not possess the symbolic strength nor the validity of faith that it has among the Catholic faithful. Although verbal symbols are significant and necessary parts of any great liturgy, they are not by themselves as effective as those

which depend on visual symbols as well as those appealing to the other senses.

For most Protestants, funeral orations and sermons
by the minister are still believed necessary and important. An analysis of a number of them indicates that
the primary function of the eulogy is to translate the
profane person in the feelings of those who mourn from
secular living into the sacred world of the dead and of
Deity.

The funeral oration must reassure the living that
immortality is a fact, that the personality of the dead
has not ceased to exist, and that spiritual life has no
ending, since death is only the transition from life in
the present to eternal life in a spiritual world. The
establishment of these spiritual truths in the minds and
emotions of the audience prepares them for the next
important step: the transformation of the total person,
once a living combination of good and bad and of spiritual and profane elements, into a spiritual person who
is a certain, or at least very likely, candidate for immortality. Thus his lifetime, bound by ideas of transition,
is transposed into the eternal time of death. Essentially,
from the point of view of what is being done to the
dead person, the whole is an initiation rite and com-
pares very closely with the initiation rites which many
pass through in life.

Since at most funerals the whole group of mourners
is composed of individuals who have considerable
knowledge of the habits and activities of the deceased,
each individual if questioned could often mention traits
of the deceased which as evidence might cause an entirely just—not to say harsh—judge to refuse the candidate admittance to a happier life. The task of the

minister is a delicate one. He must touch lightly on the earthly traits of the dead and then move gracefully over to his positive virtues and his spiritual qualities. Since he possesses an immortal soul given him by God, and since those most lacking in spiritual grace and moral competence are never categorically evil, these small and often insignificant positive traits of the personality are easily substituted in the words of a skillful speaker for the whole person, and the transfiguration takes place. The symbolic functions of the eulogy are to transform what are memories of the secular living into ideas of the sacred dead, and to re-form recollection of the personality sufficiently to make it possible for everyone to believe that entrance into heaven or any of its contemporary vague substitutes is not blocked or impossible.

The symbolic activities of the audience are minor but sufficient to allow them some participation, at least to the point of permitting them to affirm informally what the speaker asserts. The accompaniment of the casket in a funeral procession to the cemetery and the brief ceremonies there allow the living to demonstrate their love and respect to the end.

The doctor plays one of the more sympathetic roles of modern science. He is able to personify its optimism and insistence that all problems must be solved, for the public believes that science has its own miracles which can effectively pull back dying men from the edge of the grave. As long as the doctor continues to function as the central figure during a serious illness, everyone concerned can continue to believe that the sick person has his chance to live.

The role of the physician at the death of a patient

who is a beloved member of a family is very complex and often difficult. Ordinarily he functions as a friend and an expertly trained professional who, with life and death in his hands, solves all problems and keeps human beings alive; but at death this role must be relinquished. His own conception of his role and his professional oath demand that under the most pessimistic circumstances, where death seems certain, he try to keep the patient alive and "hope for the best." His dominant position in the death crisis makes it difficult for him to shift openly from the role of the protector of life to one who prepares the family for approaching death by predicting its likelihood. Yet in many instances this is what he must somehow do. The tremendous pressure placed on him by those who transform their hope for the recovery of their loved ones into a firm belief that a hopelessly ill person will not die often makes it impossible to prepare the family for the imminence of dissolution. The doctor, to function in the combined role of scientist, friend, and citizen, must be a symbol of life rather than of death.

Despite the doctor's being the scientist and the "man in white" who brings new miracles to the sick to make them well and who, as the family physician, is friend and confessor, with intimate and privileged knowledge about family members and the relations among them, his role is not entirely positive. Although the formal symbols which surround him are positive and life-giving, the informal ones are negative. There is often a feeling of ambivalence, hostility, and distrust mixed with the faith, trust, pride, and genuine affection among members of a family for the profession. In Yankee City the grim jokes about the undertakers being beneficiaries of the doctors' mistakes, the stories about various instruments being left in the body after the operation or excessive charges and pink pills and bottles of highly colored liquids being no more than chalk and colored water, as well as the sexual jokes about the doctor shifting from his professional, bedside manner to an all too human masculine one, all testify to this feeling of ambivalence about doctors.

The gossip about various doctors which appeared in our interviews again testified to themes of fear and hostility about them—tempered, it must be remembered, by willing submission to their "fatherly authority" and by genuine trust in their skill and love and respect for them as persons. The ambivalence towards doctors is usually divided symbolically into two types of concept, one being "my doctor" in whom I take pride and the other the "sawbones" who is suspected of varying infractions of the moral code, professional incompetence, and exclusive interest in his fees, as well as malpractice. Doctors in the intermediate position between these two types, when known by the informant, are likely to be well thought of or treated with indifference.

When a patient dies, a doctor must be sure that the family and other members of the community do not saddle him with responsibility for the death. In one sense, the physician is in a strong position because he is the professional expert who alone can make final judgment of the causes of the event. Professional ethics and mutual protection demand that his colleagues speak approvingly, keep quiet, or defend him, should gossip and rumor attack him. The surgeon, because of his central role in a dramatic situation, is particularly subject to threats of unpleasant criticism.

The doctor can announce the cause of death, sign the death certificate, and usually depend on the community and its officials to accept his pronouncement. But, given the various types of personality among those who grieve and feel guilty about their covert or open hostility to the deceased, the doctor must play his role carefully and well to make sure he will not be blamed and possibly have his reputation and career destroyed. His professional reputation must be reinforced by moral authority. Should there be doubts about his private moral life there may also arise questions as to his professional competence. Since doctors receive little or no training in problems of human relations, it is clear that each learns informally and by trial and error how to handle this difficult problem; sometimes by the quiet, sardonic advice of other doctors. Moreover, the society itself helps to protect the doctor, for, after all, its members believe —and must believe—that the profession is necessary to heal the sick and prevent death. Individual faith and trust are needed by all who use doctors to reduce their anxiety and conquer fear. It is not strange that most members of the community have a personal interest in protecting their faith in their own doctors by helping to protect the community's faith in the medical profession.

The doctor, particularly the surgeon, must take care of his own internal psychological problems. He must learn how to convince himself most of the time that he has done everything to save the patient or he may find it impossible to cope with the moral pressure of a succession of unpleasant outcomes. Self-confidence is often attained by allowing the role he plays for his patients to convince him that he is what they believe him to be.

Since any doctor must always play a positive public role for his clients and act out beliefs and sentiments he may not feel, but which he knows are expected by his patients and their families, whose fear and anxiety demand constant reassurance from his deportment, he often learns to allow his experiences with his patients to convince him that he is what they think he is. His conception of himself in time largely corresponds with the role in which the public sees him. If he cannot achieve this he pays an intolerable and sometimes tragic price internally for his efforts to manage his own self-evaluations.

The authority and significance of a doctor for his patients and their families is clearly related to the class position of each. We made a careful statistical study of the clientele of each doctor in Yankee City. It demonstrated that patients, largely unconsciously, tended to select doctors who belonged to the class just above them. As such, the doctor was sufficiently superior to have superordinate value to the patient and yet near enough to allow the patient and his family to have confidence that he understood their needs. In Yankee City there were fifteen doctors; four were in the upper-upper, three in the lower-upper, and eight in the upper-middle class. The ethnic factor, while operating to some extent among the lower classes, did not seem to be of great importance in the middle and upper classes in their choice of doctors, whereas social class was of great importance.

The lawyer, the doctor's principal competitor for status, plays an important but usually not a central and crucial symbolic role in any of the important rites of passage. His symbolic activities at times of birth, marriage, and death are of secondary significance when compared to those of the doctor, but still his role is of great secular importance during these various crises.

Of crucial importance in understanding a lifetime from the point of birth to the point of death is the exact place where the professional role fits into the social system itself. Doctor and lawyer are usually private enterprisers. They relate themselves "voluntarily and freely" to their clients through such institutions as the hospital, their offices, and other business enterprises. In Yankee City they are independent and free, whereas minister, priest, and teacher are functionaries within organized hierarchies. The positions of the latter are dependent on the prestige and power of the structure to which they belong and to the status assigned to them within the structure's hierarchy. When the prestige of a church is very high and the minister is the powerful and active head of his organization, his position in the community is likely to be high, but when the sacred symbols of religion are not fully trusted or highly regarded, and when in addition the church itself ranks low in the community, his position must be correspondingly low. In Yankee City the Episcopalian and Unitarian churches ranked higher by a notch or two than did other Protestant churches. Although they had parishioners from all levels of the society, they were considered the upperclass churches, whereas the Presbyterians and Congregationalists were somewhat less highly ranked and Baptists and Methodists were well below. The social position of ministers generally corresponded to the prestige of the church. This is so partly because of the church's reputation and its social place within the community and partly because its members select their ministers and are likely to choose men who fit their own criteria for suitability.

The Undertaker

The role of the undertaker, as everyone knows, has developed very rapidly in the last few generations and is likely to continue to increase the social area it controls. Whereas it was once customary for the family with the help of friends to "lay out the dead" and prepare the corpse for burial as well as to "sit up" with it to show respect and indicate that duty, honor, and love were being bestowed upon the dead person's memory, the undertaker is now called immediately after death to take charge. At death the second phase of the general period of crisis begins, the first being the period of the last illness and the second the time between death and burial. The mortician has developed his place by satisfying a need for which those in distress were willing to pay. Basically he is a private enterpriser who will do the ritually unclean and physically distasteful work of disposing of the dead in a manner satisfying to the living, at a price which they can pay. He sells his goods and services for a profit. His salesmen, applying the sound logics of business enterprise, attempt to sell his goods—coffins and other mortuary paraphernalia—at the highest price possible, and he buys at a price low enough to maximize profit. As a businessman he advertises, enters into civic life, and engages in other activities businessmen use to increase business and compete successfully with their rivals. As enterpriser he hires employees—drivers and other skilled workers—and by steadily increasing the size of his work force and the effectiveness of his sales organization, enlarges his business, profits, and importance in the community. [47]

As a skilled artisan he uses the expertness of the embalmer, thereby drawing upon some medical knowledge. He must also be proficient in the art of the beauty shop and the cosmetician to perform the last toilette of the corpse. This, of course, includes washing, powdering, painting, the use of paraffin, and other devices of the beauty shop. He must see to it that the corpse is properly clothed and that it conforms to the expectations of its audience, particularly the bereaved family. In this he functions to save responsible members of the family and their friends from performing the menial and unpleasant tasks necessary to prepare a body for burial. He does the physical work of taking the ritually unclean, usually diseased, corpse with its unpleasant appearance and transforming it from a lifeless object to the sculptured image of a living human being who is resting in sleep. The contemporary image of the corpse is that of a human being temporarily resting with his eyes closed, or perhaps someone who has but recently gone to sleep and will soon waken.

The corpse, although a dead human being, is supposed to "look well." Those who pass by in procession to look upon the deceased want a glorified, or at least peaceful, image of the live person they knew and loved. The undertaker closes the staring eyes, the gaping mouth, strengthens the sagging muscles, and with the aid of cosmetics and the help of soft silks and satins in the coffin's interior provides the central character of the tragic ritual with the proper appearance. Some of the favorite expressions of those who pass by "to pay their last tribute" are: "He looked very well—" "He looked just like he did when he was well—" or "You would think he was taking a nap or was resting his eyes for a minute." The people of Yankee City do not use formal death masks to look at what they want to see in death. But the skill of the undertaker provides an informal one which says that the dead who wear it look like life, that they are only asleep and will soon awaken. The art of the undertaker, despite its extreme secularity and its traffic with the impure things of this world, provides a symbolic product which fits very neatly into the needs of the symbolic life of Yankee City.

In performing these ritually unclean tasks the undertaker reduces the horror the living feel when in contact with the cold and "unnatural" remains of a loved person, particularly during the uncertain in-between stage of the funeral rites of passage, when anxieties are greatest. The undertaker helps to remove the pollution and corruption of death at less emotional cost to the living. In the language concerned with rites of transition, he allows the living to pass through the phases of separation and margin with less pain than if he were not present.

The staging and arrangements for the funeral ritual are largely in the undertaker's hands. He must place the coffin and arrange the flowers so that their dramatic effect is most easily brought out. He must be unobtrusively responsible for making certain that during the moments of intense emotion and sorrow no awkward situations arise. He must be sure that family, near kindred, and friends are properly placed in the audience, that pall-bearers are chosen who are symbolically correct and physically capable. He must be certain that all arrangements have been made with the proper officials at the cemetery and with the police escort for the funeral procession. Above all, he must be the competent stage manager and impresario who conducts the ritual of the tragic drama, beginning with the mortuary chapel, church, or home, that continues and coheres as a tragic procession across the crowded streets of the city to the open grave in the cemetery. In one sense he is the producer who fashions the whole enterprise so that other performers, including the minister, the eulogist, the organist, the vocalist, family, and mourners, can act becomingly and get the approval and praise for the funeral's success and receive the sensuous satisfaction that the funeral's symbolism evokes. At the same time all this must be performed in such a way that the uncontrolled grief and random behavior of the living when they face the dead will not destroy the form of the ritual.

Despite the fact that the undertaker performs a necessary, useful service and provides necessary goods for an inevitable event, that the skills and services he brings to bear are of a high order, and that he is usually well paid and very often successful as an entrepreneur, there is considerable evidence that neither he nor his customers are content with his present symbols and status within the occupational and social hierarchy of Yankee City. There is an increasing tendency on the part of the undertaker to borrow the ritual and sacred symbols of the minister and other professional men to provide an outward cover for what he is and does.

His place of business is not a factory or an office but a "chapel" or a "home." Its furniture and arrangement often suggest the altar and auditorium of a church. He frequently dresses in ritual clothes reserved for roles of extreme formality, high etiquette, and prestige. His advertisements, while cautious and careful not to use symbols indicating a particular sect (unless specialized for that purpose), tend to borrow from the language of religion. The brochures and other attendant literature used to advertise the functions of the enterprise skillfully draw on the traditional symbols of the church.

Although the social processes continue to turn the role of the undertaker from that of businessman into professional mortician, there is a considerable hostility to it. It cannot be forgotten that he handles the unclean aspects of death while the minister controls the clean and spiritual phases of it. The undertaker makes a business profit, whereas the minister is given a professional fee. The deep hostilities and fears men have for death, unless very carefully controlled and phrased, can turn the undertaker into a scapegoat, the ritual uncleanliness of his task being identified with his role and person. The thousands of undertaker jokes that appear on the radio and in other mass media as well as in informal gossip, which relate him to the more despised and feared features of death, are ample testimony to this fact. To hold this hostility in check it is necessary for him to surround his functions with sacred symbols and to profess a very high code of ethics. These uplifting efforts are often successfully attacked. For example, in Yankee City an undertaker was the principal sponsor of a non-denominational Easter service on one of the historic hills of the community. Although popular, the service met with considerable ambivalent "kidding" and comment about his skill in advertising his business and putting himself right with everyone so that he would get their trade. This despite the fact that he was known as a conscientious Christian. Undertakers have become the modern target of many of the same jokes as were once directed at grave-diggers.

Unless the place of the church and its supernatural symbols increases in importance, it seems likely that the professional role of the undertaker and his use of sacred symbols will continue to grow. His present prominence demands that his business enterprise receive the protection of professional ethics as well as the social form of sacred symbols. It is even possible that in the more remote future the church may incorporate the mortician into its system of functionaries or perhaps take over his functions as part of its own duties; in some sects the custom of referring members to an undertaker of the membership, presumably holding harmonious and trustworthy religious views, already approaches this. Death being at the very center of the sacred life of any society, the functionary who plays a prominent role in its rites is likely to become heavily ritualized and develop a sacred role.

The Life Span of a Cemetery and the Continuing Life of a Community

As long as the cemetery is being filled with a fresh stream of the recently dead it stays symbolically a live and vital emblem, telling the living of the meaning of life and death. But when the family, the kindred, and other members of the community gradually discontinue burying their loved ones there, the cemetery, in a manner of speaking, dies its own death as a meaningful symbol of life and death, for it ceases to exist as a living sacred emblem and, through time, becomes an historical monument. As a symbolic object it, too, is subject to

the meaning of time. Its spirituality then resides in a
different context, for it becomes an object of historical
value in stable communities rather than a sacred collective representation effectively relating the dead to the
living.

The active cemetery, funerals, and mourning symbols
ritually look to the sacred life of the future while marking the secular end of the lifetime of the individual,
while the "dead" cemeteries look backward to the life
of the past. Their gravestones are not so much symbols
of a man's death as the fact that he and the others once
lived and constituted in their aggregate a way of life
and a society. If a cemetery holds no future for *our own*
deaths to mark our passage from the living to the dead
—if we cannot project the life of our time into it—
then its dead belong to the *life* of the past. The gravestones become artifacts that refer to the past; the cemetery becomes a symbol speaking of the people of the past
to those of the present and stands for the regard of the
present for its own past. But man's hope for immortality, his hope for the future, cannot be evoked by such
historical symbols. They must be projected into cemeteries and into other symbols which represent man's
beliefs and feelings about himself.

There are eleven cemeteries in Yankee City. Each has
been filled with the city's dead for part or all of the
period from the 1600's until the present. Only six were
decorated on Memorial Day. The others were neither
repaired nor decorated and were no longer being used
as burial grounds. The graves were filled with the ancient dead. Their living descendants did not recognize
them for a number of reasons: the family had moved
west or gone elsewhere; the intermediate kindred con-

necting them with the living were buried in more recently established cemeteries, which did not extend to the earlier generations, but received the homage of the living; the dead had no living representatives, or the living representatives had no interest in, or knowledge of, their ancestors. The last two reasons are really one, for connections with the dead are always present but the knowledge or interest to trace these relations may not be.

Although these graveyards did not receive family recognition, it might be supposed that the associations would decorate them, but none did. Yet these same graveyards had been the objects of considerable attention and much ritual only a few months previous to the Memorial Day exercises we first studied. The answer to this paradox has already been suggested in the chapter on historical rituals, in the transforming symbolism of present and past. It is sufficient to say here that the very old graveyards lose their sacred character and become objects of historical significance and are accordingly recognized.

Two semi-active graveyards were in this process of change. They were the oldest cemeteries in use. Large areas were filled with undecorated graves which, except for Memorial Day, were not cared for by the cemetery authorities. They were becoming less sacred and most of the sections involved were not sufficiently "historical" to have fully acquired a new set of values. In a stable community such as Yankee City there is little chance that they face an ultimate loss of all value and that their land will be captured for business enterprise. Such seems to be the fate of many cemeteries in rapidly changing and growing communities where the social structure and population are unstable, this instability in the social system being reflected in the people's disregard of the cemetery as a collective representation to express either their sentiments for the dead or their feelings about the past. In an unstable community, where the changing social structure is reflected in disregard of the cemetery as a collective representation and it no longer has sacred value, the sentiments attached by social groupings such as the family and association disappear. The community loses its values for itself as a totality. Without traditions and a feeling for social continuity, the living lose their feelings for the social character of the graveyard.

When cemeteries no longer receive fresh burials which continue to tie the emotions of the living to the recently dead and thereby connect the living in a chain of generations to an early ancestry, the graveyards must lose their sacred quality and become objects of historical ritual. The lifetime of individuals and the living meanings of cemeteries are curiously interdependent, for both are dependent on an ascription of sacred meaning bestowed upon them by those who live. The symbols of death say what life is and those of life define what death must be. The meanings of man's fate are forever what he makes them.

CHAPTER 6

Cult of the Dead

"The Crosses, Row on Row . . ."

Every year in the springtime the citizens of Yankee City
celebrate Memorial Day. Over most of the United States
it is a legal holiday. Being a holy day as well as a holiday, it is celebrated accordingly. For some it is part of
a long weekend of pleasure, extended outings, and athletic events; for others it is a hallowed day when the
dead are mourned and religious ceremonies held to express sorrow. But for most Americans, especially in the
smaller cities, it is both sacred and secular. They feel
the sacred importance of the day when they, or members of their family, participate in the ceremonies, but
they also enjoy going for an automobile trip or seeing or
reading about some important athletic event staged on
Memorial Day weekend. This chapter will be devoted
to the symbolic analysis and interpretation of Memorial Day to learn its meanings as an American sacred
ceremony: a rite that evolved in this country and is
indigenous to it.

It is the thesis of this chapter that the Memorial Day
ceremonies, and subsidiary rites such as those of Armis-
tice (or Veterans') Day, are rituals comprising a sacred
symbol system which functions periodically to integrate

the whole community with its conflicting symbols and its opposing, autonomous churches and associations. It is contended here that in the Memorial Day ceremonies the anxieties man has about death are confronted with a system of sacred beliefs about death which give the individuals involved and the collectivity of individuals a feeling of well-being. Further, the feeling of triumph over death by collective action is made possible in the Memorial Day parade by recreating the feeling of euphoria and the sense of group strength and individual strength in the group power which is felt so intensely in time of war, when the veterans' associations are created and the feeling so necessary for the Memorial Day's symbol system is originally experienced.

Memorial Day is a cult of the dead which organizes and integrates the various faiths and ethnic and class groups into a sacred unity. It is a cult of the dead organized around the community cemeteries. Its principal themes are those of the sacrifice of the soldier dead for the living and the obligation of the living to sacrifice their individual purposes for the good of the group so that they, too, can perform their spiritual obligations.

Before proceeding to our analysis, let us say that the material for it was obtained by careful observation of the Memorial Day celebrations in Yankee City. A number of field people covered all aspects of the first ceremony studied. Participants were interviewed before, during, and after the ceremonies. What was said and done was observed and written down at the time the observations were made. Documents, including manuals of ritual, announcements of proceedings, and newspaper accounts were gathered.

The field work of the second year needed fewer ob-

servers, since it was used to check on the first year, fill
in gaps, and determine how much the ceremony and the
separate rites varied. While there were minor differences, they were of no significance—even the scores of
speeches made during the two ceremonies varied so little
that it would be difficult to distinguish parts of them.
In other words, the form of the ritual was standardized
and set for both the dramatic and oral rites.

World War II materials on Memorial Day have since
been collected on several occasions and show little difference. New names have been added, minor changes
in the procedure occur, the organizations vary slightly,
but the basic form is the same. The same sentiments,
values, beliefs, and rituals are presented. Perhaps the
brief inclusion of women as *objects* of the ritual is the
most marked difference. They, too, have their place in
contemporary warfare.

The sacred symbolic behavior of Memorial Day in
Yankee City, in which the whole town and scores of its
organizations are involved, is ordinarily divided into
four periods. During the year, in the first phase separate
rituals are held by many of the associations for their
dead, and many of these activities are connected with
later Memorial Day events. In the second phase preparations are made during the last three or four weeks for
the ceremony itself, and some of the associations perform public rituals. The third phase consists of the
scores of rituals held in all the cemeteries, churches, and
the halls of the various associations just before the final
joint celebration of the entire city. These rituals consist
of speeches and highly ceremonialized behavior. They
last for two days and are climaxed by the fourth and last
phase, in which all the celebrants gather in the center

of the business district on the afternoon of Memorial Day. The separate organizations, with their members in uniform or with fitting insignia, march through the town, visit the shrines and monuments of the hero dead, and finally enter the cemetery. Here numbers of ceremonies are held, most of them highly symbolic and formalized.

The two or three weeks before the Memorial Day ceremonies are filled with elaborate preparations by each participating group. Meetings are held and patriotic pronouncements are sent to the local paper by the various organizations which announce what part the organization is to play in the total celebration. Some of the associations have Memorial Day processions, memorial services are conducted, the schools have patriotic programs, and the cemeteries are cleaned and repaired, graves are decorated by families and associations, and new gravestones erected. The merchants put up flags before their establishments and residents raise flags above their houses. Advertisements for wreaths, flowers, flags, and gravestones are prominently displayed in the paper. Some of the shop windows are filled with war relics connected with the experiences of local men and their families.

All these events are recorded in the local paper and most of them discussed by the town. The preparation of public opinion for an awareness of the importance of Memorial Day and the rehearsal of what is expected from each section of the community is carried out fully and in great detail. The latent sentiments of each individual, each family, each church, school, and association for its own dead are thereby stimulated and related to the sentiments for the dead of the nation.

A number of important events in all the ceremonies observed occurred shortly before the Memorial Day ceremony. The John Cabot–Antony Cellini Post of the Veterans of Foreign Fields met to prepare for the ceremony. This organization, named for two Yankee City men killed in action, was composed of soldiers of World War I. Next day the local paper published an announcement by the officers to the men of this organization: "Veterans of Foreign Fields: The time has again come when every veteran should pause for a day to pay tribute to those men who, in serving our great republic, gave their lives in her defense. To this end you will assemble . . ." There followed instructions for the Memorial Day activities of the association's members. When the commander of the John Lathrop camp of the Sons of Union Veterans, an organization which also had a name of a local here, issued "orders of the day" he said, "Brothers, you may neglect your duties to your organization for ordinary meetings, but Memorial Day is a holy day."

Meanwhile "six out of thirteen surviving members of the W. L. Robinson Post, 94, Grand Army of the Republic, were given a rousing welcome by the Rotarians at the customary pre-Memorial Day luncheon." The G.A.R. were symbols of a past and a crisis of the United States which everyone knew and felt, but no member of the audience had experienced. The chairman of the day told how Yankee City responded to Lincoln's call and of the "hundreds of thousands who had died as a living sacrifice for their country." He appealed to the members of Rotary to do their share "to make Memorial Day a holy day given over to things patriotic."

The members of the G.A.R., the youngest eighty-five and the oldest ninety-six, replied. One of them, Comrade Smith, spoke of "the stirring times following the firing upon Fort Sumter." He said he became acquainted with President Lincoln while stationed in Arlington as a colonel's orderly. "When the President called on the colonel it was my duty as orderly to escort the President inside. Lincoln was very democratic and did not think it beneath his dignity to shake hands with an ordinary private. I often shook the hand of the President."

The greatest symbol of the solidarity of the American Union, "the martyred President of that great crisis in American life," was thus made to seem near to Mr. Smith's listeners. The old man and his words were living symbols connecting the Rotarians to the dead past.

Another veteran of the Grand Army declared that it "would be a good thing if children in the schools today could be taught to remember love of country and obedience to law." He praised organizations such as the Rotary Club and said "it would be ideal if a committee was appointed to interview the school authorities with the view of stressing the need of patriotic teachings."

Meanwhile members of the American Legion had anticipated this suggestion, for they had made arrangements for members of their organization to give patriotic addresses the day before Poppy Day to all the public and parochial schools "to instruct the children in the principles of patriotism and to indoctrinate them with Good Americanism." Their speeches, too, referred to "our sacred dead and their sacrifice."

Numerous "memorial services" were conducted by men's and women's associations. The Yankee City *News* announced a few days previous to Poppy Day that "the annual memorial services of Michael Collins Circle, Daughters of Isabella, were held yesterday afternoon at three o'clock at St. Mary's cemetery. After the names of twenty-six deceased members were called by the chancellor a wreath was placed on each grave. Reverend John O'Malley, chaplain of the circle, offered prayer. There was a large gathering of members present at the services."

Several days before Poppy Day the former war mayor wrote to the *News*. He had a city-wide reputation for patriotism and for his unselfish services to the city and its soldiers in 1917–18. The letter, addressed to the commander of the local American Legion Post, was printed in the most prominent part of the front page:

Dear Commander:

The approaching Poppy Day brings to my mind a visit to the war zone in France on Memorial Day, 1925, reaching Belleau Wood at about eleven o'clock. On this sacred spot we left floral tributes in memory of our Yankee City boys—Jonathan Dexter and John Smith, who here had made the supreme sacrifice, that the principle that "might makes right" should not prevail.

At Hill 108 we picked the poppy I am sending you. At this scene of desolation, poppies were growing as plentifully as daisies in New England and one could feel with McCrea the inspiration that caused him to write his famous lines.

With the memory of this visit, each recurring Poppy Day has a deeper significance to us.

I feel sure that our citizens will purchase poppies freely on Saturday of this week and that many will make generous cash contributions to the welfare fund of the post.

Three days later the newspaper in a front page editorial told its readers, "Next Saturday is the annual Poppy Day of the American Legion. Everybody responds cheerfully to this appeal . . . We ask for a generous response to this appeal." The editor concluded:

Everybody should wear a poppy on Poppy Day. Think back to those terrible days when the red poppy on Flanders fields symbolized the blood of our boys slaughtered for democracy. Remember Dexter and Smith killed at Belleau Wood. Remember O'Flaherty killed near Chateau Thierry, Stulavitz killed in the Bois d'Ormont, Kelley killed at Hill 288, Cote de Chatillon, Jones near the Bois de Montrebeaux, Kolnikap in the St. Mihiel offensive and the other brave boys who died in camp or on stricken fields. Remember the living boys of the Legion on Saturday.

The names of those killed represented most of the ethnic and religious groups of the community and all class levels. They included Polish, Russian, Irish, French Canadian, Italian, and Yankee names. The use of such names in this context emphasized the fact that the voluntary sacrifice of a citizen's life was equalitarian. They covered the top, middle, and bottom of the several classes. A front page appeal on the day following, signed by a committee of citizens, included names from all six classes, from all religious faiths, and from nine ethnic groups. Again no explicit reference was made to the selection of names, but the names were felt to be "representative," which meant that they represented the segmentary ethnic groups, all creeds and status levels of the community. The people were appealed to as "citizens," the most equalitarian of Yankee City terms—the democratic status from which men are taken to be transformed to the equally democratic status of soldier.

Poppy Day came the day after this appeal, on the Saturday preceding Memorial Day Sunday. At that time red poppies are sold to the citizens by the American Legion. As everyone knows, the red poppy symbol is taken from John McCrea's poem, "In Flanders Fields." In this poem the author, a Canadian soldier who lost his life on the western front, first made the red poppy a symbol of the "blood sacrifice" made by the Allied soldiers in France. The poem, first published in *Punch,* gained immediate popularity. Now every Yankee City boy knows it and many have memorized it. It appears in most patriotic exercises in the schools.

The patriotic societies have taken over the symbol of the poppy for their own uses, but its significance is still dependent upon the poem. The cluster of contemporary meanings deeply embedded in the life of this society is found.

> In Flanders fields [where] the poppies blow
>   Between the crosses, row on row,
>   That mark our place . . .
>
> We are the Dead. Short days ago
> We lived, felt dawn, saw sunset glow,
>   Loved and were loved, and now we lie,
>   In Flanders fields.
>
> Take up our quarrel with the foe:
> To you from failing hands we throw

The torch; be yours to hold it high.
If ye break faith with us who die
We shall not sleep, though poppies grow
                    In Flanders fields.

Many of the Legion in uniform, assisted by Boy
Scouts and a corps of women aids, sold artificial poppies on the streets and in the business houses of the
town. When interviewed, some of the Legionnaires expressed strong feelings of self-sacrifice and of obligation
to help less fortunate comrades; some revived memories
of former days; others regretted that the people too
quickly forget their responsibilities to their soldiers.
Unconsciously they all complained that the Yankee City
people failed to respect them as soldiers as they once did
during the war.

Significant selections from two interviews follow:
"Sure, these poppies are for a very fine cause," one said,
"you know all the money will be used for Yankee City
disabled veterans. Why, I've been here since 5:30 this
morning. Last year wasn't so good as the year before.
People are beginning to forget, the public doesn't remember things very long. They ought to go into one of
them hospitals and then they wouldn't forget so quick."

In the next interview we see the same emphasis on
sacrifice expressed somewhat differently. "You see that
big fellow across the street with all the medals on?"
another inquired. "Well, he was hurt during the war,
and he's in pretty bad state; he ought to be in a hospital
himself. Last year in the parade he refused to stay at
home and insisted on coming out and carrying the
colors. In the middle of the parade he just fell down flat
from sheer exhaustion. Luckily someone rushed out

and just got the colors in time before they touched the ground, but you can't keep that fellow back."

About half the people purchased poppies, and almost all those who did wore them. Each thereby symbolically reminded all who passed of the impending Memorial Day ceremony and of its reference to the dead of the last and previous wars.

The Church and the Military Altars of Sacrifice

The topic for Sunday morning services was the meaning of Memorial Day to the people of Yankee City, as citizens and Christians. We can present excerpts from the sermons of only one Memorial Day to show their main themes, but recorded observations of sermons and other Memorial Day behavior before and since World War II show no differences in the principal themes expressed. Indeed, although twenty years have passed some of these words seem interchangeable. The Reverend Hugh McKellar chose as his text "Be thou faithful until death."

He said,

> Memorial Day is a day of sentiment, and when it loses that it loses all its value. We are all conscious of the danger of losing that sentiment. It was that spirit which led the Pilgrims to suffer that a nation might be born, and it led the boys in blue and gray to suffer that a nation might be kept together.
>
> What we need today is more sacrifice, for there can be no progress or achievement without sacrifice. There are too many out today preaching selfishness. The boys of '61 and '65 had the spirit of sacrifice, sacrifice is necessary to a noble living. In

the words of Our Lord, "Whosover shall save his life shall lose it and whosoever shall lose his life in My name, shall save it." It is only those who sacrifice personal gain and will to power and personal ambition who ever accomplish anything for their nation. Those who expect to save the nation will not get wealth and power for themselves.

Memorial Day is a religious day, the day of sweetest memories. It is a day when we get a vision of the unbreakable brotherhood and unity of spirit which exists and still exists no matter what race or creed or color, in a country where all men have equal rights.

It is better to let the soldiers' graves go unnoticed rather than scatter them with flowers of hypocrisy, for the only way to venerate them is to imitate them. [Here he quoted from the end of the Gettysburg Address.] We too must rededicate ourselves to the high ideals for which they died; that is the spiritual test for us today. Memorial Day is above all a spiritual day. We must acquire the devotion of the boys of the Blue and the boys of the Gray.[1]

The field worker filed out with the rest of the congregation. An old gentleman told him that attendance at church was falling off. "Yes," he said, "there are not so many of the old New Englanders. It's these new foreigners who have come in that have spoiled it. That's what cuts down our church attendance. But there are some good foreigners. It's good once in a while to get a mixture of good fine stock, especially from northern

1. Quotations of sermons and speeches in this section are from notes taken on the scene by a field staff of seventeen persons, also written materials supplied in some instances by the participants.

Europe, especially from Scotland. You know Scotland is the place where John Knox came from, who started Presbyterianism."

The minister of the Congregational Church spoke with the voice of the Unknown Soldier to emphasize his message of sacrifice. After the congregation sang "Faith of Our Fathers Living Still" the minister preached his sermon, entitled "The Voice of the Unknown Soldier."

It brings tears to our eyes when we see the groups of the Grand Army of the Republic as they decorate the graves of their comrades for it brings to our memory those who gave full measure of life as a sacrifice to preserve the Union. All those who died for liberty and democracy in '61 and '17 speak to us on this day of memory, and of all these nothing speaks as loud as the voice of the Unknown Soldier.

If the spirit of the Unknown Soldier should speak, what would be his message? What would be the message of a youth I knew myself who might be one of the unknown dead? He didn't want to go. He had a home and family, good position, happy prospects, and a sweetheart. I married him on the day he left. A few weeks later he was sent to France. No news for months and then a returned officer told how the youth had just delivered a message under fire and had not stopped to rest when he was struck by a shell. If he could be that Unknown Soldier in Arlington Cemetery I wonder what he would say. I believe he would speak as follows: "It is well to remember us today, who gave our lives that democracy might live. We know something of the sacrifice." If we, the living, only knew the meaning of that blood-washed word "sacrifice" we would use it less freely.

A quotation from the Unitarian minister will be sufficient to introduce the other theme stressed in the Sunday church services. The subject, "Patriotism and Religion," was attacked in a scholarly manner. "The purpose of this sermon is to discover if religion and patriotism conflict. The text of the sermon is 'Render unto Caesar that which is Caesar's and unto God the things that are God's.' This minister concluded that "religion and patriotism do not conflict when there is real patriotism."

The first two ministers in different language express the same theme of sacrifice of the individual for national and democratic principles. One introduces Divine sanction for this sacrificial belief and thereby succeeds in emphasizing the theme that the loss of an individual's life rewards him with life eternal. The other uses one of our greatest and most hallowed symbols of democracy and the only very powerful one to come out of World War I: the Unknown Soldier. The American Unknown Soldier is Everyman of the mystery plays. He is the perfect symbol of equalitarianism. The third minister showed that there is no difference between true patriotism and true religion. There were many more Memorial Sunday sermons, most of which had these same themes. Many of them added the point that Christ had given his life for all (see Chapter 8, "Sacrifice: the Father and His Son").

That afternoon in the cemeteries, at the memorial stones named for Yankee City dead and in the lodge halls and churches, a large number of rites were celebrated. One was held at a memorial monument on

Newtown Common. It was supervised by the Sons of Union Veterans. Another, led by one of the Catholic orders, was in the Catholic cemetery. Two others were in the Homeville Graveyard, one held by the United Spanish War Veterans, the other by the Elks for their dead.

The Newtown monument consists of a gateway and two marble walls with the names of all the Union veterans from Yankee City written in bronze on the walls. Over the names is the legend, "Soldiers and Sailors of Yankee City." Near by is a statue of the "Returned Soldier." The speaker took his position in front of the gateway. To his right men in the uniforms of several associations stood with their guns at rest; to the speaker's left, facing the men, were uniformed women with the flags of their various women's organizations. At the extreme left and in the roadway in front of the tablet two G.A.R. veterans in uniform sat in a closed car with a son of a veteran as driver. The commander of the Sons of Union Veterans started the ceremony. He said, "This service here today is in memory of the G.A.R. We have it every year."

He was followed by a local minister.

> We are gathered at this shrine today in memory of the Grand Army. As we come here to these tablets with the quota from Yankee City inscribed upon them, it is a privilege and a fitting thing to do to recall the significance of the names here and what our forefathers did.
>
> There is one underlying principle more responsible for war than anything else. It was this that killed so many men, wounded so many others. It is in three letters, sin, an inevitable principle that

never can be evaded. Within sin lies its own punishment. Every sin must be atoned for. The nation
had been sinning. Since the nation had sinned it
was inevitable that sin must be atoned for.

Lincoln recognized the sin of the nation. Lincoln
was one of the greatest men who ever lived. He
said that if God so willed, if the war lasted until
every cent of money had been spent and every drop
of blood in the veins of the people within the nation were shed, yet the judgments of the Lord were
true and righteous altogether.

We come to these tablets with the names of the
men who went forth from Yankee City, those who
were with God and who believed in the sovereignty
of the nation. God intended the nation to be preserved for greater things, for the Spanish War, for
the World War.

If we could all visit the battlefields where men
died for their country, we would see for ourselves
the scenes of their great deeds. If, like me, you could
go to Gettysburg, where men have died and where
I went and where my father's battery smashed the
flower of the Confederacy, then as I did, you would
know about the carrying on of those men, how
they fought and bled and died. The deeds of our
forefathers are a legacy bequeathed to the community. Memorial Day commemorates what has
been done so that the peace of God and righteousness shall triumph.

A prayer addressed to "Our Father" followed: "We
thank thee for our fathers, for all they did and wrought.
We must accept the legacy from their bleeding hands,
not for war but for peace and so these organizations

gathered here dedicated to the service of those men will work together for love and country.

A squad of four with a man in charge stopped in front of the statue of the Civil War veteran and fired three volleys. The women placed wreaths and flowers over the tablets. Taps were blown by a Boy Scout and answered from the woods by another Boy Scout. The chaplain pronounced benediction.

The Elks' ceremony presents ample evidence that the Memorial Day ceremony has ceased to be Decoration Day to recognize the soldier dead of the Civil War and has become the sacred day for all the dead. The Elks' service clearly indicates the fear that death obliterates the individual. It also shows how some Yankee City people reassure themselves.

The Elks' memorial service was held at Elks Rest at the Homeville Cemetery. In the center of a group were two standards, one bearing a purple flag with the name and number of the Yankee City lodge and the other the lodge insignia. In line with these two standards stood a flag-bearer with the American flag. Attention was given to the graves of all deceased members.

The speaker was an Elk from a nearby town.

> Ladies and gentlemen, we are gathered here today at a hallowed spot in what has often been termed God's Acre. Elkdom, my friends, is the fairest flower that blooms in the gardens of fraternalism. The Elk who lives his Elkdom is bound to be a good man, he cannot be otherwise. Elks being human stumble along through life about like other folks, and when an Elk falls down he usually falls uphill. When he gets up he is on higher ground than before.

Savant and savage are equally dumb before the question: If a man die, shall he live again? No traveller has ever returned with maps or field notes of a life beyond the grave. The marvelous thing about it is that, despite the fact, all of us or almost all of us believe in the life hereafter. It is the universal belief of mankind, a belief that never had to be taught us, we just naturally believe it.

We have every reason to believe that we will see and know our dear dead brothers again. The extinction of the psychic entities is unthinkable, unbelievable, unnatural.

Wreaths were ceremoniously placed on the graves within the Elks Post enclosure.

While the Elks' ritual was being conducted, members of the Homeville United Spanish War Veterans gathered at the entrance of the cemetery waiting for the rest of their group to join them. They marched in parade from the gate of St. Joseph's Cemetery to a ceremonial grave where the veterans and women gathered. The ceremony that took place was in part read from the ritual book of the Spanish War Veterans. The speaker said,

The purpose of this ceremony is to honor those who preceded us to the land of the dead. This is the true patriotic day of the nation when the children of these men honor their fathers, the flag, and all for which the flag stands—bravery, glory, courage of people. It is fitting that the men who sleep beneath the flag of the Union should have graves decked with flowers in remembrance of this period of suffering and sorrow which molded this nation.

This was in the cause of liberty and of God. It is only right that we quicken the memories of the dead. It is our purpose to preserve and protect Memorial Day. In times of peace it is the duty of us as citizens to defend the flag and fulfill the patriotism of those who preceded us.

This was followed by an order from the post commander to stand at attention. Lincoln's Gettysburg Address was read. This rite and all others in the Memorial Day ceremonies seemed to strive for the perfection of feeling they believed Lincoln expressed when he dedicated the Gettysburg cemetery as a national monument. The speaker intoned Lincoln's words as if they were a religious chant.

After the ceremony this group joined others at the Baptist Church for the Vacant Chair ceremony, which took place late Sunday afternoon. The chief participants, including men of the G.A.R., the minister, and representatives of the Sons of Union Veterans, were on the platform, which was decorated with Memorial Day flowers. The commander of the G.A.R. was escorted to his place of honor.

There were four vacant chairs in a line at the front of the altar. Each had an American flag with a card on which was written the name of the G.A.R. veteran who had died during the year. Flags or banners of the several associations were displayed. At the center in front of the altar was a bivouac of four guns, each representing one of the dead. The pastor, as a son of a veteran, wore a medal. A woman played sacred music; the commander came forward and asked the women representatives of auxiliary organizations to rise and grasp their flags in their right hands. General John A. Logan's Gen-

eral Orders No. 11, which initiated Memorial Day, were
read.

> The 30th day of May, 1868, is designated for the
> purpose of strewing with flowers or otherwise deco-
> rating the graves of comrades who died in defense of
> their country during the late rebellion, and whose
> bodies now lie in almost every city, village, hamlet,
> and church-yard in the land. . . .
>
> We are organized, comrades, as our regulations
> tell us, for the purpose, among other things, "of
> preserving and strengthening those kind and fra-
> ternal feelings which have bound together the sol-
> diers, sailors, and marines who united together to
> suppress the late rebellion." What can aid more
> to assure this result than by cherishing tenderly the
> memory of our heroic dead. . . . We should
> guard their graves with sacred vigilance. . . .
>
> Let us, then, at the time appointed, gather
> around their sacred remains, and garland the pas-
> sionless mounds above them with the choicest flow-
> ers of spring-time; let us raise above them the dear
> old flag they saved from dishonor; let us, in this
> solemn presence, renew our pledges to aid and
> assist those whom they have left among us. . . .

The Vacant Chair ceremony was an imitation of
military exercises. When the minister prayed, both
hands were placed on the Bible, his eyes were closed,
and the audience lowered their heads in reverent attitudes. Everything was said in a ceremonial tone. A
woman cried quietly. The minister prayed,

> Father, we bow before Thee in this sacred place,
> sacred because of dedication and because Thou

art here. We come to this service not with cheer and joy but because chairs once occupied are now vacant. We come today honoring those who lived valiantly, to take notice of their service and now that the ranks are thinned by death, bless those that remain with us. Thy blessing on the remnants of the Grand Army of the Republic. Bless those organizations that tomorrow will be decorating the last resting-places of their comrades who have passed.

The commander announced the Gettysburg Address. The brother introduced his reading by saying, "We have present today here on the platform one who has seen and talked as a great friend with Lincoln. I wish I could bring to your minds a greater vision of that great man who saved the Union, as he stood on that battlefield and made that great though short speech, it was only 264 words." He quoted the Gettysburg Address in full ceremonial tone. His voice filled with emotion when he said,

It is for us the living, . . . to be here dedicated to the great task remaining before us—that from these honored dead we take increased devotion to that cause for which they gave the last full measure of devotion—that we here highly resolve that these dead shall not have died in vain—that this nation, under God, shall have a new birth of freedom— and that government of the people, by the people, for the people, shall not perish from the earth.

When the speaker reached the phrase "from these honored dead" he spread his arms out to include the four vacant chairs before him, making his words immediate and personal for the group. After completing Lincoln's address he asked, "Is patriotism dead? Why aren't these pews all filled?" He turned to the minister and said, "A few years ago there would have been crowds here and now there are few. Isn't that right, Mr. Commander? Is patriotism dead? No, it isn't dead, it is sleeping. May we promise Thee, our Country, that our youth will not be exposed to pernicious influences, that the present evils will be overcome. Grant, oh God, that we may perform our duty. Amen."

When he had finished, the commander addressed the adjutant and said, "Adjutant, for what purpose is this meeting called?" "For faith and to respect the honored dead." He was asked whether he had records of the men. The names and the complete records of the soldiers who had died were read. As soon as the name of a dead veteran was called a little girl put a wreath and a bouquet of white flowers over the flag on the chair. A Boy Scout "rolled" the drum three times after each record had been read. At the end the commander said, "The records are honorable and there is a place for the record in the archives of the Post."

Then the commander said, "We will now hear a few words from the Commander of the G.A.R." The old man was helped to the front of the stage. He grasped the pulpit firmly to support himself.

> I'm not much of a public speaker. I'm just a veteran. I consider Lincoln the greatest man the world has ever produced. I met him and became quite familiar with him, even shook hands with him. He was a very common man, not too proud to meet and know any one. Very plain, not what the ladies call a handsome man. I'm ninety-one, and I'm not

feeling very well. I lost two of my closest friends the last year. Ralph Aiken was a good friend of mine, he was the best natured man in town, always good natured, Tom Alison was a very old friend. I remember them. I have no more to say.

After a song entitled "The Vacant Chair" an address by the Reverend James was announced.

We come to pay tribute to these men whose chairs are vacant, not because they were eminent men, as many soldiers were not, but the tribute we pay is to their attachment to the great cause. We are living in the most magnificent country on the face of the globe, a country planted and fertilized by a Great Power, a power not political or economic but religious and educational, especially in the North. In the South they had settlers who were there in pursuit of gold, in search of El Dorado, but the North was settled by people seeking religious principles and education.

Our grandfathers held united and inviolate a great nation so our duty is to perpetuate the great religious forces of the world. Those who delve into the philosophy of history, as Lincoln did in the Gettysburg Address, discover that God has maintained this nation to be the prophet of the world.

Throughout all the ceremonies held in Yankee City on Memorial Day the survivors of the G.A.R. were treated as spiritual beings and there was definite pressure on them to fit into a spiritual setting as symbols, rather than representing their ordinary lives. When the commander of the G.A.R. spoke he was introduced, not so much as a G.A.R. man or the commander of the

Post, but as one who had known Lincoln, a man who
had a very high spiritual place because he was identified
with the great symbol, Lincoln; the relationship with
the "martyred President" was stressed rather than that
with the President or the man Lincoln.

On Monday morning, Memorial Day, further ceremonies were held in the graveyards, around war relics
and other symbols of death in war and battle. These
ceremonies took place in the cemeteries and before
monuments to the soldier dead.

At one of them the principal speaker, standing before
a tablet covered with the names of war dead, declared
that when "things are going to pieces, in these days
when the grafter is honored, it is heartening to know
that eternal values are still reverenced." He then talked
about Washington and Lincoln and their greatness.
"Our great institutions of learning would not have let
them in because they did not possess the proper quali-
fications, and yet we know now that Washington and
Lincoln had acquired something that made them great."
He said no character except the Carpenter of Nazareth
had ever been honored the way Washington had been
in New England. Virtue, freedom from sin, and righteousness were qualities possessed by Washington and
Lincoln, and in possessing these characteristics both
were true Americans, and "as Sons of Union Veterans
we would do well to emulate them. Let us first be true
Americans. From these our friends beneath the sod we
receive their message, 'Carry on.' Men may come and
go but the cause will live; though the speaker will die
the fire and spark will carry on. Thou are not conqueror, Death, and thy pale flag is not advancing."

In all the services of the third phase the same themes

were used in the speeches—most of them in ritualized, oratorical language—or in the ceremonials themselves. Washington, the father of his country, first in war and peace, had devoted his life not to himself but to his country. Lincoln (the most important symbol) had given his own life, sacrificed on the altar of his country. Most of the speeches implied or explicitly stated that Divine guidance was involved and that these mundane affairs had supernatural implications. They stated that the revered dead had given the last ounce of devotion in following the ideals of Lincoln and the Unknown Soldier. They declared these same principles must guide us, the living; that we too must sacrifice ourselves to these same ideals.

The beliefs and values of which they spoke referred to a world beyond the natural. Their references were to the supernatural.

The Parade: Ritual Link between the Dead and the Living

The parade, the fourth and final phase of the Memorial Day celebration, formed near the river in the business district. Hundreds of people gathered to watch the various uniformed groups march to their positions. They were dressed in their best. Crowds were along the whole route. The cemeteries were carefully prepared for the event.

The cemeteries had been repaired, cleaned, and decorated for Memorial Day. The grass was cut, the weeds burned, the hedges and bushes trimmed and shaped. Thousands of people had placed their flowers on "the graves of loved ones" and departed; others were continually coming and going to decorate the graves. Yellow flags with a green wreath had been placed on members' graves by the Yankee City Knights of Columbus. American flags with a star indicated the post of the Grand Army of the Republic. The Elks had blue and white flags in a round plaque. American flags in oval plaques had been placed by the Massachusetts State Guard. A St. Andrew's cross was on the graves of the Massachusetts Catholic Order of Foresters. The Yankee City Fire Department also had a St. Andrew's Cross, with an iron base. The Ladies of the G.A.R. had placed an American flag with a plaque; the Women's Relief Corps a St. Andrew's Cross with a bow of red, white, and blue ribbon. A gilt crown and cross marked the Daughters of Isabella. The American flag and a cross marked "U.S.A. and Cuba" with a red and yellow ribbon marked the graves of members of the camp of United Spanish War Veterans. The Moose had plaques; the American Legion had American flags with decorated plaques.

For one day the cemeteries were a place for all the living and all the dead, and for this one day the bright-colored flowers and gaudy flags gave them almost a gay appearance. Death declared a holiday, not for itself but for the living, when together they could experience it and momentarily challenge its ultimate power.

The people marched through the town to the cemeteries. The various organizations spread throughout the several sections of the graveyards and rites were performed. In the Greek quarter ceremonies were held; others were performed in the Polish and Russian sections; the Boy Scouts held a memorial rite for their departed; the Sons and Daughters of Union Veterans went through a ritual, as did the other men's and

women's organizations. All this was part of the parade
in which everyone from all parts of the community
could and did participate.

The Veterans of Foreign Fields, led by their drum
corps, marched through the cemetery to the farther end
to the "Greek quarter." The bands played until all the
organizations were in the cemetery; then the drum
beat. The Legion stood at attention by the grave of
"an unknown soldier" while it played "Nearer My
God to Thee." A large memorial stone said "The unknown of '61 and '65; W.R.C. of 1909."

Near the end of the day all the men's and women's
organizations assembled about the roped-off grave of
General Fredericks. The Legion band played. A minister prayed. The ceremonial leader of the Sons of Union
Veterans spoke.

> We meet to honor those who fought, but in so do-
> ing we honor ourselves. From them we learn a les-
> son of sacrifice and devotion and of accountability
> to God and honor. We have an inspiration for the
> future today—our character is strengthened—this
> day speaks of a better and greater devotion to our
> country and to all that our flag represents.
>
> Our flag, may we see thee, love thee, and live
> thee. Our country, may we see thee, love thee, and
> live thee. Let the flag be an inspiration that our
> youth may not be subject to pernicious influences.
> Washington and Betsy Ross created our flag out of
> a few strips of cloth. May we honor it as the em-
> blem of our country.

A member of the Ladies of the G.A.R. laid a wreath
on General Fredericks' grave, speaking of the "undying

devotion of General Fredericks, from the Ladies of the G.A.R." Directly after this she bent down and untied a basket she had been carrying and gave it to a child. The child recited a short poem about peace, beauty, and devotion. She opened the basket, releasing a snow-white dove which flew directly across the grave into a tall tree. This, according to the child speaker, symbolized peace and duty; others said it was the spirit of the dead. The band played and a benediction was given by a minister.

After the several ceremonies in the Elm Hill cemetery the parade re-formed and marched back to town, where it broke up. The firing squad of the Legion stopped at the front entrance of the cemetery and fired three salutes and a bugler blew taps. This was "a general salute for all the dead in the cemetery." The Auxiliary of the Legion gave a luncheon for the Legion and the W.R.C. and the Women of the G.A.R. had a lunch prepared for the G.A.R. and the Boy Scouts. At the luncheons the conversation was about "old times," and memories of men long dead were revived. The band played "old-time favorites."

A brief resume of the principal points stressed in the several phases of the ceremony brings out some basic facts to be remembered before we begin the interpretation.

The most widely used symbols, which appeared in many of the rites, were: Washington, Lincoln, his Gettysburg speech, McCrae's "Flanders Fields," the Unknown Soldier, the Gettysburg and Arlington cemeteries, the local cemeteries, and the dead themselves.

The dedication speech of the Gettysburg battlefield as a national cemetery supplies a prototype for all Me-

morial Day rites held throughout the country. Excerpts
from it occur in many of the addresses. Lincoln and
Washington have become national symbols which embody the values, virtues, and ideals of American democracy. The Unknown Soldier in Arlington Cemetery
is a symbol referring to all soldiers who are dead.
McCrae's poem states in symbolic language what the
people feel about the war deaths of 1917–18. As a
principal symbol of that war it bears many resemblances
to Lincoln's Gettysburg speech. Each was written by a
man who died for his country. Each stresses the sacrifice
of the dead for the living. Each declares that the living
must rededicate themselves to the principles for which
the dead gave their lives.

The symbolic acts and ceremonial speeches which
compose the ceremony have a number of fundamental
themes, chief of which is that the soldier dead sacrificed
their lives for their country. The dead are all one and
equal before the eyes of men and God. They voluntarily
offered their lives that their country might live, and in
so doing they did not lose their lives but saved them
forever. The principles for which they died must be
defended by those now living, and the sacrifices of the
soldiers oblige everyone to remember these sacred principles by embodying them in deed and thought and by
performing the Memorial Day rites as a visible testi-
monial of their significance to the living.

Throughout the Memorial Day rites we see people
who are religiously divided as Protestant, Catholic,
Jewish, and Greek Orthodox participating in a common ritual in a graveyard with their common dead.
Their sense of autonomy was present and expressed in
the separate ceremonies, but the parade and unity of

doing everything at one time emphasized the oneness of the total group.

The full significance of the unifying and integrative character of the Memorial Day ceremony and the increasing convergence of the multiple and diverse events through the several stages into a single unit, where the many become one and all the living participants unite in the one community of the dead, is best seen in Chart 5. It will be noticed at the top of the figure that the horizontal extension represents space and the vertical dimension time. The four stages of the ceremony are listed on the left side, the arrows at the bottom converging and ending in the cemetery. The longer and wider area at the top with the several well-scattered rectangles represents the time and space diversities of Stage I; the closely connected circles in Stage III show the greater integration achieved by this time.

During Stage I, in the earlier part of the year, it will be recalled that there is no synchronization of rituals. They occur in each association without reference to each other. All are separate and diverse in time and space. The symbolic references of the ceremonies emphasize their separateness. In general, this stage is characterized by high diversity and there is little unity in purpose, time, or space.

Although the ceremonies of the organizations in Stage II, shortly before Memorial Day, are still separate, they are felt to be within the bounds of the general community organization. There is still the symbolic expression of diversity, but now diversity in a larger unity (see chart). In Stage III there are still separate ceremonies but the time during which they are held is the same. Inspection of the chart will show that time

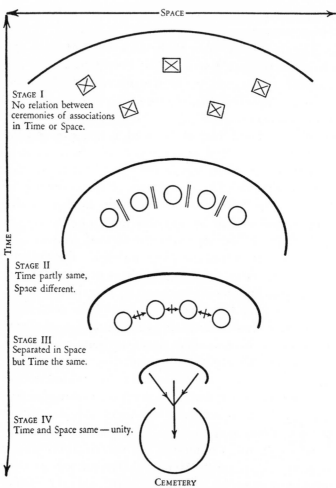

Chart 3. Progress of the Memorial Day Ceremony

and space have been greatly limited since the period of
Stage I.

The ceremonies in Stage IV become one in time and
in space. The representatives of all groups are unified

into one procession. Thereby organizational diversity is symbolically integrated into a unified whole. This is not necessarily realized in a conscious way by those who participate, but they certainly feel it. This period is the symbolic expression of diversity integrated into a unified whole. The chart is designed to symbolize the progressive integration and symbolic unification of the group.

Lincoln—an American Collective Representation
Made by and for the People

Throughout the Memorial Day ceremony there were continual references to Lincoln and his Gettysburg Address. The symbol of Lincoln obviously was of deep significance in the various rituals and to the participants. He loomed over the memorial rituals like some great demigod over the rites of classical antiquity. What is the meaning of the myth of Lincoln to Americans? Why does his life and death as conceived in the myth of Lincoln play such a prominent part in Memorial Day?

Some of the answers are obvious. He was a great war President. He was President of the United States and was assassinated at the close of the Civil War. Memorial Day grew out of this war. A number of other facts about his life might be added, but for our present purposes the meaning of Lincoln the myth is more important than the objective facts of his life career.

Lincoln, product of the American prairies, sacred symbol of idealism in the United States, myth more real than the man himself—symbol and fact—was formed in the flow of events which composed the changing cultures of the Middle West. He is the symbolic culmination of America. To understand him is to know much of what America means. [100]

In 1858, when Lincoln ran against Stephen Douglas for the United States Senate, he was Abraham Lincoln the successful lawyer, the railroad attorney noted throughout the State of Illinois as a man of above common ability and of more than common importance. He was an ex-congressman. He was earning a substantial income. He had married a daughter of the upper class from Kentucky. His friends were W. D. Green, the president of a railway, a man of wealth; David Davis, a representative of wealthy eastern investors in western property, who was on his way to becoming a millionaire; Jesse Fell, railway promoter; and other men of prominence and prestige in the state. Lincoln dressed like them; he had unlearned many of the habits acquired in childhood and had learned most of the ways of the highly placed men who were now his friends. After the Lincoln-Douglas debates his place as a man of prestige and power was as high as anyone's in the whole state.

Yet in 1860 when he was nominated on the Republican ticket for the presidency of the United States, he suddenly became "Abe Lincoln, the rail-splitter," "the rude man from the prairie and the river-bottoms." To this was soon added "Honest Abe," and finally in death "the martyred leader" who gave his life that "a nation dedicated to the proposition that all men are created equal" might long endure.

What can be the meaning of this strange transformation?

When Richard Oglesby arrived at the Republican

Convention in 1860 he cast about for a slogan that would bring his friend Lincoln favorable recognition from the shrewd politicians of New York, Pennsylvania, and Ohio. He heard from Jim Hanks, who knew Lincoln as a boy, that Lincoln had once split fence rails. Dick Oglesby, knowing what appeals were most potent in getting the support of politicians and in bringing out a favorable vote, dubbed Lincoln "the rail-splitter." Fence rails were prominently displayed at the convention to symbolize Lincoln's lowly beginnings. Politicians, remembering the great popular appeal of "Old Hickory," "Tippecanoe and Tyler too," and the "log cabin and cider jug" of former elections, realized this slogan would be enormously effective in a national election. Lincoln the rail-splitter was reborn in Chicago in 1860; and the Lincoln who had become the successful lawyer, intimate of wealthy men, husband of a well-born wife, and man of status was conveniently forgotten.

Three dominant symbolic themes compose the Lincoln image. The first, the theme of the common man, was fashioned in a form pre-established by the equalitarian ideals of a new democracy; to common men there could be no argument about what kind of a man a rail-splitter is.

"From log cabin to the White House" succinctly symbolizes the second theme of the triad which composes Lincoln, the most powerful of American collective representations. This phrase epitomizes the American success story, the rags-to-riches *motif,* and the ideals of the ambitious. As the equal of all men, Lincoln was the representative of the common man, both as his spokesman and his kind; now, as the man who had gone "from the log cabin to the White House," he became the superior man, who had not inherited but earned that superior status and thereby proved to everyone that all men could do as he had. Lincoln thereby symbolized the two great collective but antithetical ideals of American democracy.

When he was assassinated a third powerful theme of our Christian society was added to the symbol here being created by Americans to strengthen and adorn the keystone of their national symbol structure. Lincoln's life lay sacrificed on the altar of unity, climaxing a deadly war which by its successful termination pronounced that the country was one and that all men are created equal. From the day of his death thousands of sermons and speeches have demonstrated that Lincoln, like Christ, died that all men might live and be as one in the sight of God and man. Christ died that this might be true forever here and beyond the earth; Lincoln sacrificed his life that this might be true forever on this earth.

When Lincoln died, the imaginations of the people of the eastern seaboard cherished him as the man of the new West and translated him into their hopes for tomorrow—for to them the West was tomorrow. The defeated people of the South, during and after the Reconstruction period, fitted him into their dark reveries of what might have been, had this man lived who loved all men. In their bright fantasies, the people of the West, young and believing only in the tomorrow they meant to create, knew Lincoln for what they wanted themselves to be. Lincoln, symbol of equalitarianism, of the social striving of men who live in a social hierarchy—the human leader sacrificed for all men—expresses all the basic values and beliefs of Yankee City and of the United States of America.

Lincoln, the superior man, above all men, yet equal to each, is a mystery beyond the logic of individual calculators. He belongs to the culture and to the social logics of the people for whom contradiction is unimportant and for whom the ultimate tests of truth are in the social structure in which, and for which, they live. Through the passing generations of our Christian culture the Man of the Prairies, formed in the mold of the God-man of Galilee and apotheosized into the man-god of the American people, each year less profane and more sacred, moves securely toward identification with deity and ultimate godhood. In him Americans realize themselves.

A problem of even greater difficulty confronts us in why war provides such a powerful context for the creation of powerful national symbols such as Lincoln, Washington, or Memorial Day. Durkheim gives us a first important theoretical lead. He believes that the members of the tribe felt and became aware of their own group identity when they gathered periodically during times of plenty. It was then that social interaction was most intense and these feelings most stimulated.

In modern society interaction, social solidarity, and intensity of feeling ordinarily are greatest in times of war. It would seem likely that such periods might well produce new sacred forms built, of course, on the foundations of old beliefs. Let us examine the life of American communities in wartime as possible matrices for such developments.

The Effect of War on the Community

The most casual survey supplies ample evidence that the effects of war are most varied and diverse as reflected in the life of American towns. The immediate effect is very great on some towns and very minor on others.

In the average town the institutional life is modified, new experiences are felt by the people, and the townsmen repeatedly modify their behavior to adapt to new circumstances brought them by the events of a war. These modifications do not cause social breakdown; the contrary is true. War activities strengthen the integration of many small communities. The people are more systematically organized into groups where everyone is involved and in which there is an intense awareness of oneness. A town's unity and feeling of autonomy are strengthened by competition in war activities with neighboring communities.

It is in time of war that the average American living in small cities and towns gets his deepest satisfactions as a member of his society. Despite the disheartening events of 1917, the year when the United States entered World War I, the people derived deep satisfaction from it, just as they did from the last war. It is a mistake to believe that the American people, particularly small-towners, hate war to such an extent that they derive no satisfaction from it. Verbally and superficially they disapprove of war, but at best this only partly reveals their deeper feelings. In simpler terms, their observed behavior reveals that most of them had more real satisfaction out of World War II, just as in the previous one, than in any other period of their lives. The various men's and women's organizations, instead of inventing things to do to keep busy, could choose among activities which they knew were vital both to them and to others.

The small-towner then had a sense of significance about himself, about those around him, and about events, in a way that he never felt before (the same was true in 1917–18). The young man who quit high school during the depression to lounge on the street corner and who was known to be of no consequence to himself or to anyone else in the community became a seasoned veteran fighting somewhere in the South Pacific—a man obviously with the qualities of a hero (it was believed), willing to give up his life for his country, since he was in its military forces. He and everyone else were playing, and knew they were playing, a significant role in the crisis. Everyone was in it. There was a feeling of unconscious well-being—a euphoria—because everyone was doing something to help in the common desperate enterprise in a cooperative rather than in a private spirit. This feeling is often the unconscious equivalent of what people mean when they gather to celebrate and sing "Hail, Hail, the Gang's All Here." It also has something of the deep significance that enters into people's lives only in moments of tragedy.

The strong belief that everyone must sacrifice to win a war greatly strengthens people's sense of their significance. Everyone gives up something for the common good—money, food, tires, scrap, automobiles, or blood for blood banks. All is contributed under the basic ideology of common sacrifice for the good of the country. These simple acts of giving by all individuals in the town, by all families, associations, schools, churches, and factories, are given strong additional emotional support by the common knowledge that some of the local young men are representing the town in the military forces of the country. It is known that some of them may be killed. They are sacrificing their lives, it is believed, that their country may live. Therefore, all acts of individual giving to help win the war, no matter how small, are made socially significant and add to the strength of the social structure by being treated as sacrifices. The collective effect of these small renunciations, in general belief, is to lessen the number of those who must die on the altars of their country.

Another very strong integrative factor that strengthens the social structure of the small town and city is that petty internal antagonisms are drained out of the group onto the common enemy. The local antagonisms which customarily divide and separate people are largely suppressed. The feelings and psychic energies involved, normally expended in local feuds, are vented on the hated symbols of the enemy. The local ethnic groups, often excluded from participation in community affairs, are given an honored place in the war effort, and symbols of unity are stressed rather than separating differences. The religious groups and churches tend to emphasize the oneness of the common striving rather than allowing their differing theologies and competitive financing to keep them in opposing groups. The strongest pressure to compose their differences is applied to management and labor (the small number of strikes is eloquent proof of the effectiveness of such pressure). A common hate of a common enemy, when organized in community activities to express this basic emotion, provides the most powerful mechanism to energize the lives of the towns and to strengthen their feelings of unity. Those who believe that a war's hatreds can bring only evil to psychic life might well ponder the therapeutic and satisfying effects on the minds of people who turn their once private hatreds into social ones and join their townsmen and countrymen in the feeling of sharing this basic emotion in common symbols. Enemies as well as friends should be well chosen, for they must serve as objects for the expression of two emotions basic to man and his social system—hatred and love.

The American Legion and other patriotic organizations give form to the effort to recapture the feelings of well-being when the society was most integrated and feelings of unity most intense. The membership comes from every class, creed, and nationality, for the soldiers came from all of them.

Only an infinitesimal number of associations is sufficiently large and democratic in action to include in their membership men or women from all class levels, all religious faiths, and most, if not all, ethnic groups. Their number could easily be counted on the fingers of one hand. Most prominent among them are the patriotic associations, all of them structural developments from wars which involved the United States. The American Legion is a typical example of the patriotic type. Less than 6 per cent of the several hundred associations include members from all classes. Of the remaining 94 per cent, approximately half have representatives from only three classes or less than three. Although the associations which include members from all levels of the community are surprisingly few, those which stress in action as well as in words such other principles of democracy as the equality of races, nationalities, and religions are even fewer. Only 5 per cent of the associations are composed of members from the four religious faiths—Protestant, Catholic, Jewish, and Greek Orthodox—and most of their members came from the lower ranks of the society.

Most prominent among them was the American Legion. Why should this organization, sometimes accused of being intolerant and hostile to the opinions of variant groups, occupy this democratic position? The answer lies in the social context in which it was created. The American Legion, born of the experiences of the soldiers of World War I, is an organized effort to maintain "for all time" the values experienced by those who have participated in war. The G.A.R., the Sons of Union Veterans, and the Spanish War Veterans are similar products of earlier wars. The Sons of Union Veterans, a non-military group, testifies to the fact that war experiences are not just those of soldiers but of everyone in the community.

Furthermore, in functioning to maintain the values of a war experienced in battle by very few of its members, the Legion demonstrates, as does the whole system of the cult, that something more is involved than the formation of an organization of soldiers.

The intense feeling of belonging, the satisfaction of facing death collectively and conquering its fear, and the sense of well-being and euphoria which war engenders contribute to the wish to maintain its effects in peacetime. In our efforts to accomplish this we organize associations which emphasize the democratic dogmas and create cults which dramatically re-express the feeling of past wars.

Just as the totemic symbol system of the Australians

represents the idealized clan, and the African ancestral worship symbolizes the family and state, so Memorial Day rites symbolize and express the sentiments of the people for the total community and the state. But in so doing, the separate values and ideas of various parts of the community are also portrayed. The ideas and values of several religions, ethnic groups, classes, associations, and other groupings are symbolically expressed and their place within the social structure of the community clearly indicated.

Lincoln and Washington and lesser ritual figures, and ceremonies such as those of Memorial Day, are the symbolic equivalent of such social institutions as our patriotic societies. They express the same values, satisfy the same social needs, and perform similar functions. All increase the social solidarity of a complex and heterogeneous society.

The Function of Memorial Day

The Memorial Day rites of Yankee City and hundreds of other American towns, we said earlier, are a modern cult of the dead and conform to Durkheim's definition of sacred collective representations. They are a cult because they consist of a system of sacred beliefs and dramatic rituals held by a group of people who, when they congregate, represent the whole community. They are sacred because they ritually relate the living to sacred things. They are a cult because the members have not been formally organized into an institutionalized church with a defined theology, but depend on informal organization to order their sacred activities. They are called a cult here because this term, though more narrowly used in common parlance, accurately places them in a class of social phenomena clearly identified in the sacred behavior of other societies.

The cult system of sacred belief conceptualizes in organized form sentiments common to everyone in the community about death. These sentiments are composed of fears of death which conflict with the social reassurances our culture provides us to combat such anxieties. These assurances, usually acquired in childhood and thereby carrying some of the authority of the adults who provided them, are a composite of theology and folk belief. The deep anxieties to which we refer include anticipation of our own deaths, of the deaths or possible deaths of loved ones, and—less powerfully— of the deaths or possible deaths of the wise of our generation—those who have taught us—and of men in general.

Each man's church provides him and those of his faith with a set of beliefs and a mode of action to face these problems, but his church and those of other men do not equip their respective members with a common set of social beliefs and rituals which permit them to unite with all their fellows to confront this common and most feared of all enemies. The Memorial Day rite and other subsidiary rituals connected with it form a cult which partially satisfies this need for common action on a common problem. It dramatically expresses the sentiments of unity of all the living among themselves, of all the living with all the dead, and of all the living and dead as a group with God. God, as worshiped by Catholic, Protestant, and Jew, loses sectarian definition, limitations, and foreignness as between different customs and becomes the common object of worship for the whole group and the protector of everyone.

The unifying and integrating symbols of this cult are the dead. The graves of the dead are the most powerful of the visible emblems which unify all the activities of the separate groups of the community. The cemetery and its graves become the objects of sacred rituals which permit opposing organizations, often in conflict, to subordinate their ordinary opposition and cooperate in collectively expressing the larger unity of the total community. The rites show extraordinary respect for all the dead, but they pay particular honor to those who were killed in battle "fighting for their country." The death of a soldier in battle is believed to be a "voluntary sacrifice" by him on the altar of his country. To be understood, this belief in the sacrifice of a man's life for his country must be judged first with our general scientific knowledge on the nature of all forms of sacrifice. It must then be subjected to the principles which explain human sacrifice whenever and wherever found. More particularly, this belief must be examined with the realization that these sacrifices occur in a society whose Deity was once incarnate as a man who voluntarily sacrificed his life for all men.

The Memorial Day rite is a cult of the dead but not just of the dead as such, since by symbolically elaborating sacrifice of human life for the country through, or identifying it with, the Christian Church's sacred sacrifice of the incarnate God, the deaths of such men also become powerful sacred symbols which organize, direct, and constantly revive the collective ideals of the community and the nation.

Part IV

The Family of God

Introduction

The evidence for the chapters on sacred family symbols, as the references and footnotes indicate, are from officially sanctioned sources; the books which embody them are primarily symbolic products of traditional Catholic and other liturgical churches, but the public worship of other Protestant churches is part of the evidence. All are significant and important parts of our religious culture. The first chapter is directed mostly at the Mother and Her Child; the second, the Father and His Son. These two chapters and the sections on age rites and holy coitus are the core of family and species influence on traditional Christian symbolism.

Perhaps we should re-emphasize sacred symbols. Sacred symbols are largely non-logical, evocative, and expressive. They speak of feelings and mythic beliefs, not necessarily true or false, which lie deeply imbedded in the ongoing emotional life of the species. The words and concepts of a religion may be logically organized and systematically arranged according to the tenets of some of the greatest of the logicians, yet all such sacred systems are ultimately based on the non-logical feelings of man. Ultimately, proof and validity are not to be found in any kind of empirical testing, for the ultimate meaning of such mythic symbols lies beyond ordinary experience.

They tell of older and more fundamental facts of man's poor existence. Science is not equipped to test the truth of their meanings. The basic "truths" our species has learned and transmitted through living millions of years on earth, expressed in an infinite variety of sacred signs and reified symbols, belong to an order of reality beyond the concepts and methods of contemporary science. Science can only know them in its own terms and imperfectly translate them into a symbol system often contrary to their nature. But for the scientist their natural meanings can be discovered only in what they represent, what they evoke, and how they function in the social and species life of man. Sacred collective representations are symbol systems which for the members of the group express and refer to their collective life. They reflect and evoke what people feel and think themselves to be in times of social action. They symbolize what the values and beliefs of the group are. The group being a social and species system, such collective representations symbolize for men what they feel and think about themselves as animals and persons.

CHAPTER 7

*Sacred Sexuality—the Mother, the Father, and
Their Family*

The Family and Christian Symbolism

Although the sacred order must be rationally defended
by rational men who are believers, its ultimate validity
is forever founded on a non-rational base where men
know what is true and real because they *feel* they know
what is true. In those cultures which prize rationality,
each religion must have its St. Thomas Aquinas, its
Scotch theologians or their equivalents, who belatedly
prune and domesticate the ancient beliefs and primitive
practices of believing men to conform to the rational
norms of civilized men. Thus rational men make what
is essentially a non-rational matter "rationally" acceptable to them. They are often not so much apologists as
translators, yet for St. Thomas, as for all believers, the
central facts of his own beliefs were mystical and non-
rational.

If religious symbols are collective representations, reflecting at the supernatural level the collective realities
of the group, most of those present in the sacred world
to which Christians ritually relate themselves are formed
by, express, and reinforce the family structure. What
the Church is, Protestant or Catholic—its own self-

conception—the image in which its members conceive themselves, as well as the sacred way of life which orders their relations to the Church and to God—in short, the supernatural order of Christianity—is formed in, and nourished by, all or part of the family as a social and biological system. The Church, its rites, beliefs, and practices, would not exist if the family failed to survive. The Church, forever dependent on the family for its existence, expresses more concern about, and exercises greater moral influence on, the family than on any other human institution. The sanctions exercised against extramarital sexual life, the breaking of the marriage tie, birth control, and the deeper incest cravings are more than sacred interdicts of disapproved conduct; they are also expressions of the anxiety of the Church about its own sacred symbolic life. Should the present form of the family disappear, the Christian Church would necessarily undergo revolutionary changes. The hostility of contemporary revolutionary movements against both family and religion is not happenstance. The values and beliefs of the two institutions energize and strengthen each other. Religion and family are at the center of the eternal, ongoing group life of man. They conserve and cherish the indwelling unity and human identity of a thousand generations and a multiplicity of institutions of the most diverse peoples. It will be one of the tasks of this chapter to show why this is true.

The concern of the Church with the control and regulation of sexuality and the family is not simply because its symbols reflect and reinforce the morality of the group. The mental life of the Church is also deeply dependent on the feelings and actions of the

mated pair, of parents and children, of brothers and
their sisters, both as models and factors in the processes
of reification which transfigure the beliefs and values
and feelings these persons have about themselves and
their mundane life into the sacred symbols of Christian
belief. The negative and positive beliefs and values surrounding the sexual act, with its pleasures and satisfactions, including the identification of such behavior with
sin and the ambivalent acceptance of it under the mari-
tal control of the family, are expressed by and permeate
some of the most important Christian symbols. Mary,
the Mother and Virgin with no sexual experience;
Joseph, her human husband, many believe without sexual contact with his wife; Jesus, their son, unmarried
and with no sexual experience, the human offspring of
a sacred impregnation in which there was no sin or male
physical contact—all are, paradoxically, part of a family
symbol system. A mother whose own conception is held
by many to have been without the stain of original sin
is part of this sacred system. Mortal man could not understand this immortal society or feel its significance
were he not a mental and physical creature of his own
family. The meaning of a mother who is a virgin may
be difficult for rational men to comprehend, but it is
easily felt and non-rationally understood by them as
sons of mothers who are wives of all-too-human husbands. The struggle to control their animal emotions
in a moral order is reflected in the symbolism of the
Church and in its basic theology.

Christian doctrine recognizes many sacred as well as
secular forms of the family. They are all interrelated
and interdependent, moving from the physical through
the social to the sacred levels. Even the mysteries of the

abstract and abstruse Holy Trinity through its three
Persons are involved in the family order and are felt by
Catholics and others to be more clearly understood by
the one human who had the closest family relations
with the three, the Virgin Mary. "The ineffable mystery of the Holy Trinity," Cardinal Mindszenty declares, "was unlocked to her [the Virgin Mary] more
than to all other human beings. The first tie binds her
to God the Father whose eternal Son became her son.
. . . The second heavenly tie binds her to the Son who
is in truth her child. . . . The third heavenly tie binds
her to the Holy Spirit, Whose espoused and pure bride
she is. Hence, she was created as a most pure and untouched virgin." [1]

For Christians the most significant fact in the relation
of the sacred and profane realms is the birth, life, and
death of the Son. The Word is made flesh—a *spiritual*
God is made *incarnate* in the symbolic form of his
human birth as a son to a human family. His Father
so loved all men that he gave his only begotten Son to
them, that those among them who could believe would
live forever. His only Son was born to a woman who
was a virgin, who had been impregnated by him through
the power of the Holy Spirit. The Son (in human form)
lived, suffered, and died, slain by those he came to save
from suffering and death, his spiritual kindred as po-
tential sons of God, though far from kin in spiritual
development. The depths of human depravity could not
be more powerfully represented. Yet all men can be
saved from death because by their evil actions and his
spiritual ones Christ "redeemed" them and showed them
the way to Heaven and eternal life.

1. Mindszenty [76], p. 72.

The ultimate, most perfect conduct man can imagine —this in sharp contrast with his own depravity—is achieved when his brother-god, whom he has slain, rescues him from his own degradation and from the power of death. Furthermore, his gentle "older" brother intercedes with the stern father for him and by his atonement establishes a new order which for all time and for all men guarantees them the chance of redemption, salvation, and eternal life. It is significant that it is believed that man's greatest evil act, when he crucified his brother-god, was also the greatest act of God's goodness. Sacred evil and sacred good derive from the same horrible deed; the ultimates of human understanding are thus founded on family sentiments.

Distinctions are sometimes drawn by theologians between Christian concepts of love. The love they attribute to God often shows the unlimited love of a parent who can love his children unheedful of their deserts and yet remain "sovereign" with (parental) authority. The love of his children is "dependent" and filled with a "desire of good for the self." Dr. Anders Nygren, in his book *Agape and Eros, A Study of the Christian Idea of Love,*" which distinguishes between love as Agape and love as Eros, declares that "Agape is God's way to man —Eros is man's way to God." [2] Agape does not recognize value but creates it. On the other hand, "Eros is determined by and dependent on the quality of its object—Eros recognizes value in its object and therefore loves it." The Loving God, like loving parents, can love and bestow value on wayward children.[3] [84]

For Christians, life is dually conceived, the sacred and

2. Nygren [84], pp. 81, 87.
3. See *ibid.*, "The Content and Idea of Agape," pp. 75–81.

profane realms are separate and distinct, their forces opposed and antithetical, yet one. Simply put, the more traditionally minded Christians believe that far *above* profane, mortal man is the sacred, immortal, supernatural world. Such lesser spiritual beings as the saints, the angels, and the souls of the born and unborn are members of this higher order of existence and subordinate to, and ruled by, the three great male personae of Christian Deity, the austere Father, the gentle Son, and their everpresent and always active Holy Spirit. They are the Three who are also the One. Beneath all of them in the ordinary secular realm of human beings, it is believed, the eternal struggle of good with evil for supremacy over flesh and matter is fought within the moral world of each man. In Yankee City and elsewhere in human society, it is a conflict that is never won, yet never lost.

Despite the hostility between the spirit and the profane flesh, the two are, and must be, in Christian thought mutually dependent and interrelated halves of a larger physical and cultural unity. Much of the meaning of the "flesh" in Christian belief has to do with the bodily actions and human emotions of males and females, the moral beliefs and values related to the two sexes and their acts and emotions, and the implications of sexuality for the spiritual order. We will first examine Christian thought about the relation of the church to the moral order of the family, and to the family as a species order consisting of the procreative pair and their offspring.

The faith of many of the Christian churches of Yankee City asserts, explicitly or implicitly, that men and women should be sanctioned by God "to enter the sexual domain." While some Protestants believe that marriage is no more than a civil and legal act, which a church wedding may celebrate, most hold with all Catholics either that God enters as the third party to the marriage rite or that the vows themselves are sanctioned by God through the rites of the church. The marriage rite may not be a sacrament, but for most Protestants it is a holy ceremony involving God. The rules of the moral order and the species life system are thus reinforced by supernatural sanctions.

Biological survival in such a system is thus made dependent on the approval of a father-son God, a single symbol combining the procreating and procreated life process and the actions of his human surrogates. In the past, and present, he and they have disapproved of a large variety of sexual unions because of the biological and spiritual nearness of the pair or for various social and spiritual disabilities.

For man to survive the two sexes must come together, copulate, produce, and protect their offspring. The social institutions which directly control this vital nexus of species life—the relation of the copulating pair and of this same procreative pair and their dependent offspring—control the source of human life. They give social form to, and are charged with, the vital energies which actuate human existence and dominate the basic forms of interaction in which human animals become human beings and emerge as moral, reasoning members of the social order. [12]

The customs and conventions of Yankee City, expressed in the formal and informal rules which regulate marriage, surround the "sexual domain" with a wall of negative values, symbols, and sanctions forbidding and interdicting every other form of sexual experience except those reached by the marriage gate and the domain into which it opens. The rules are often broken, yet their spirit is a powerful, coercive force in the life of everyone. Perhaps the most powerful repressive rule regulating sexual contact is the family incest taboo which forbids sexual relations between such kindred as mothers and sons, fathers and daughters, and brothers and sisters. The incest interdictions are the most important social inhibitions established on man's physical conduct, setting up immeasurably powerful broad controls over the sexual and procreative life of the species which greatly modify natural species organization and make harsh and rigid demands on the early learning experiences of each individual. The fact that many able scientists until Freud believed the feelings expressed by the incest taboo to be instinctive and not learned or socially derived indicates how quickly and effectively the human family system trains its young to obey automatically the taboos of incest. The sources of their power and efficacy lie far below human consciousness and contribute to the reduction of competition and open conflict within the family. They channel internal aggression into the larger society, thus protecting the social foundations of human moral existence. These feelings and attitudes, which are continuing, integral parts of the family structure, are necessarily given expression in the sacred symbols of the Christian faith.

Sexuality, Procreation, and Marriage in Christian Symbolism

The bond between the several secular and sacred forms of family life is clearly recognized in Catholic

doctrine. We shall examine the beliefs to establish the
symbolic form of the believed relations. The meaning
and function of the social and biological family in Christian symbolism will become apparent. The biological
family, hard, enduring, and central to all life, is the
matrix from which the basic beliefs of Christianity
emerge. On it are founded the eternal symbols of the
truths of Christian faith.

Sexual intercourse, unsanctioned by marriage, according to church doctrine is of flesh and matter and
as such (it is believed) evil and sinful, belonging to the
realm of the profane. Wedlock, sanctioned by church
and society, controls and disciplines man's species relations and places them within the moral *forms* of the
social group. Here the basic moral order, sanctioned
and in Christian faith instituted by God, justifies and
sanctions the sexual act. The reciprocal exchange of
rights and duties, obligations and privileges, between
the husband and wife is initiated by the marriage rites
through the mutual surrender of self, the sharing of
each by the other, and the completion of each sex by
the two becoming one in a marriage relation which controls the sexual act.

Marriage in Catholic thought—less so in Protestant
—has three purposes: offspring, mutuality of the two
persons, and the recognition of God. "The Church,"
says Von Hildebrand, "assigns three ends to marriage
which St. Augustine sums up by the words *proles, fides,*
and *sacramentum.*" [4] The marriage act, sexual intercourse, is not only for the generation of children, but
significant for man as a human being because it is the

4. Von Hildebrand [49], p. 16. The quotations on the following three
pages are from the same source, pp. 16–42.

expression and fulfillment of wedded love and community life and therefore belongs to the moral order. It is also involved in the sacred because the utilitarian function of producing a new generation of men *in quantum animal* has been combined with the function of the sexual act as an expression of wedded love (*in quantum homo*) "because the two elements have been organically united by God." The bodily function of the marriage act, being for the generation of children, its continual focus is on the relation of the older and younger generations in the parent and child relation. For this purpose the copulating pair "in their mutual gift of self" submit to the moral control and social usages of human marriage. The family and the family systems are thereby integrated into and controlled by the moral order of the whole community. The species relations of the sexes too are ordered, disciplined, and confined to the rules and sanctions of the culture, and transformed and invested with the moral values of the society.

These Christian beliefs and values presuppose the possible emergence from the sexual act of new human beings, a new generation of men who will insure the persistence of the culture and the continuity of the group. The bodies of the infants resulting from sexual intercourse are the products of semen and ovum, but their souls are God's own creation. The sexual act is therefore a spiritual mystery in Catholic belief and among many Protestants because it means the mysterious creation of a body and a soul—"a body that receives its *form* from the soul and transforms it from mere matter into a human being . . . the parents procreate a human body destined for the most intimate union with an immortal soul and from which it actually receives its form." (*Anima forma corporis;* the soul is the form of the body.)

Some Protestants view the sex act as secular, subject only to moral control, unless conception takes place. Conception having occurred, the problem of the soul, and the new body and soul as God's child, is the same sacred problem for these believers as for other Christians. The more extreme rationalists among them reject its significance by taking a "scientific" explanation of personality (and the soul), but most face it or tacitly agree to it as a sacred event in which God is involved.

The second end of Christian marriage is mutual assistance, meaning that rights and privileges are mutually exchanged and duties and obligations reciprocally assumed by the procreative pair. This bond is founded on love, and wedded love is separated from other forms of physical love because the relation of the husband and wife lies within a moral order established, or recognized, by God. "The church sees in married love," declares Franz Walter in *The Body and Its Rights in Christianity* (quoted by Von Hildebrand), "the mutual attraction of the two sexes, implanted by the creator in human nature and the foundation and indispensable condition for the most intimate and indissoluble community of life between human beings of different sexes and as such it gives it her blessing."

Between the social bond and the bodily union there is "a profound organic unity" because sex is unique and central within the individuals involved in the act. "The sexual gift of one person to another signifies an incomparably close union with the other and a self surrender to him or her. . . . The sex union is a concrete ex-

pression of wedded love which intends the mutual gift
of self."

Sex (it is believed) belongs to the innermost being of
each person and is entirely private. When two individuals reveal themselves to each other in a sex relation
they surrender their selves to each other and initiate
each into the other's secret. From this moral fact the
bonds of matrimony are created, and within them the
human quality of sex is created. When the sexual act
takes on human quality it takes on *form,* and "form is
the soul and spiritual quality." This is the relation of
sex to the soul and of flesh to the spirit and God; this
is the essence of the sacrament, the third purpose of
marriage and the Christian element.

It is also significant that an essential part of marriage for the church and the secular order is that sexual
intercourse must take place, and semen must be deposited in the uterus. Thus signifying that marriage, in
being a "will to unite" and a benevolent feeling for the
beloved, is also for the purpose of generating children.
A bride is not a wife and a bridegroom is not a husband
until they have completed the sexual act.

The three levels of the sexual act—physical, moral,
and symbolic, and the equation of each to the several
levels of adaptation later described—are illustrated by
Chart 4. The upward pointing arrows indicate that the
sexual act influences the bond of wedded love and the
moral order; the downward-pointing ones show that the
animal act is controlled and formed by the moral order.
The downward-pointing arrow between circles *B* and
C indicates that the "quality of wedded love" is under
the control of "the pre-established harmony of Christian
rites."

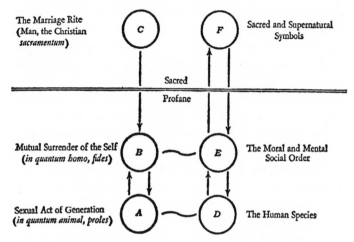

The Marriage Rite
(Man, the Christian
sacramentum)

C

F

Sacred and Supernatural
Symbols

Sacred

Profane

Mutual Surrender of the Self
(*in quantum homo, fides*)

B

E

The Moral and Mental
Social Order

Sexual Act of Generation
(*in quantum animal, proles*)

A

D

The Human Species

Chart 4. The Three Levels of the Sexual Act (according to Catholic Dogma and Its Scientific Equivalents)

The interconnected circles on the right represent the several levels of human adaptation to which the different parts of the sexual life are equated. The horizontal double lines on the left separate the Christian from the moral and animal realms, and the ones on the right remove the sacred and supernatural symbols from those of the secular and profane world. Furthermore, the arrows connecting the circles *E* and *F* indicate that the sacred symbol system is directly under the influence of the moral order which helps control the secular life of the family.

The marriage ceremony which sanctions and consecrates the relations of the sexual pair and symbolically marks the relation's inception as one ritual act is not sufficient to maintain the relation's spiritual quality throughout its existence, for sexual activity within the marriage bed ranges from mere sensuality to behavior

which transcends the flesh and approaches the spirituality of its divine model. Such variation ranges from the
impure to the pure, from flesh and matter to the spiritual activity of a being capable of participating in the
divine life. But the pure man or woman is not lacking
in sexual desire. On the contrary, it is officially held that
the man or woman who is insensible to sex is not favorable to purity. Men and women who do not feel sexual
desire are merely weak sexually. Pure men and women
control and transcend the demands of the flesh; they
recognize the spiritual and human qualities of sexual
desire and relate themselves to each other sexually as
persons within the spiritual and benevolent bonds of
marriage. The sensual man indulges his animal desires
for themselves and experiences an animal pleasure in
the use of another person. The weak man or woman
lacks an essential element of purity: the will to unite.
Impurity consists in the abuse of sex. It is both a desecration and a degradation, a desecration partly because
it abuses the sanctity of one of God's children, and a
degradation of the person who desecrates another. In
such a relation the soul is made captive of the flesh, particularly in any unsanctioned union, and accordingly is
lost to God. Under these conditions it is literally submerged in matter.

Although sex implicates the higher nature of man, it
has within it intrinsic dangers which threaten man's
spiritual existence. The orgasm, with its violence and
fury, tends to overpower the spirit and swamp it, for,
with the exception of death, the orgasm is the most profound physical expression of which man is capable.

The pure man understands that sex belongs in a special manner to God and that man can only make use of

it as explicitly sanctioned by Him. In the rite of marriage, man is given "divine permission to lift the veil of the mystery," and he cannot directly abandon himself without restraint to the pleasures of sex. Throughout the sexual period of each marriage, in every marriage act, men and women must be forever aware that they are moral beings in wedded relations with another person. Such sexual relations are pure, removed from the control of the flesh, and formed on supernatural foundations. Their mutual concern about the welfare of the other, the knowledge that they participate in the mystery of the possible creation of a new human being, and the benevolent love of the husband and wife ennoble sex.[5]

The family of souls created by the rite of human marriage is believed to be founded on, and an expression of, the Mystical Body and, as it were, "a mystical body in miniature." For the Catholic Church "Christian marriage is a sign or symbol of the Mystical Body of Christ. In origin they both come from God, in structure, both are one and indissoluble . . ." "By marriage there is established in each family, as it were, a mystical body in miniature." [6] For St. Paul, marriage is not so much a fact in its own right as a symbol of the union of Christ with the Church.

> "Husbands, love your wives, as Christ also loved the Church and delivered himself up for her, that he might sanctify her, purifying her in the bath of water by means of the word, and that he might present her to himself a glorious Church, not hav-

5. *Ibid.*, pp. 97–105.
6. Ellard [38], p. 309.

ing spot or wrinkle or any such thing, but holy and
without blemish." [7]

The Mystical Body, the Bride of Christ, some theologians declare, was formed at the time of the crucifixion "when She came forth from the wound made by
the lance when he was crucified." Like the first woman,
Eve, who was taken from the side of her husband, Adam,
so the church came from the side of the New Adam,
Christ.

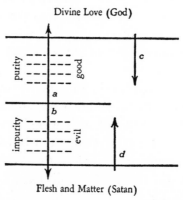

Chart 5. The Relation of Marriage to the Sacred and Profane

Let us recapitulate and analyze what has been said by
use of a chart (see Chart 5). The moral world of man
extends from the inferior realm of flesh and matter to
the superior world of God and the supernatural. There
are varying degrees of purity and impurity, of good and
evil, in the sexual act; the increasing purity approaches
the supernatural (arrows a and b pointing up and down).
Divine love, the foundation of purity, extends into the

7. Ephesians 5:25–28 [8e].

moral world (arrow *c*) and can and should become part
of man's wedded life, or man can degrade himself to
such a degree of impurity that his moral world is submerged into flesh and matter (arrow *d*). Thus, we see
that the moral life of man as a sexual creature is a
constant struggle between the spirit and the flesh, the
moral rules sanctioned by sacred belief and the pleasurable satisfaction of uncontrolled sexual appetite—in
brief, between the forces of good and those of evil.

The family as a moral system is an arena where the
forces of God and Satan meet in an endless struggle.
Within their sexual relations men and women carry on
a moral struggle to conquer impurity and transform
themselves into pure beings who participate in divine
love. A moral universe is made out of the treatment of
the sex relation; it is dualistically conceived in terms of
purity and impurity, the first being joined with the
forces of good and ultimately with the Christian God,
and the other with the powers of evil and, for some,
with Satan. Sexual intercourse, the basic bond and
creator of the links of species life, for the Christian
occupies a central point of incalculable importance in
the moral and spiritual life of man. Only in marriage,
as *one* of the social relations which compose the family
structure, is it permitted to take place. And the family
of the wedded pair is firmly placed in the larger moral
context of a family system of parents and children, and
this larger family unity under the moral control of
society and God.

We have presented the traditional Christian (particularly Catholic) ideology of the relations between the
sexes and of human marriage and its place in the human

family. There are several other forms of marriage which exist beyond the limits of ordinary life in the symbols of the supernatural world, and which are of crucial importance for understanding the sacred life of Christianity and the relation of the Christian to his God. The two principal officially recognized ones are the marriage of the soul, as bride, to Christ the sacred bridegroom; and the marriage of the Church (as bride) to Christ her sacred spouse. We shall see that these two symbolic forms are closely related to sacredly sanctioned human marriage and that these supernatural forms are not understandable without knowledge of, and experience with, human marriage and sexuality.

The Bride and Christ: Symbols of a Symbol

The soul of each man and woman in Church doctrine has a twofold, direct relation with Christ, as an autonomous soul and as an integral part of the mystical body of the Church. The souls belonging to human males and human females, being alike and feminine in form, are receptive to God, the giver, very much as women are open and receptive to men. The souls of men and women are therefore female, open and ready to contain the masculine creative sacred principle. "In the natural order woman represents, in contrast to man, the receptive principle," says Von Hildebrand, ". . . In relation to God, however, this characteristic of predominant receptivity is not confined to the female sex. Here, . . . where God and man meet, the man as an individual soul is as purely receptive as the woman. Here God [the male procreator] alone is the giver, the creative and fertilizing principle . . . And this is preeminently true in the supernatural order of the soul as the bride of Christ, the God-man." [8]

The soul, as a sacred Christian being intimately related to Christ, as we have said, is feminine. Its relation to Christ is further defined as that of the wife to her Divine husband or, more particularly, as the passionate young bride yearning for the love of her bridegroom. The singing of the love of the new bride for her husband and of the bridegroom for his beloved in the Song of Songs, once a poetic folk drama, is symbolic of the emotions that exist in supernatural marriage. Most Protestant and all Catholic Bibles as well as their sectarian interpreters identify the bride as the Church or the soul, and their bridegroom as Christ.

Just as the soul is feminine and in a nuptial relation with Christ, so the Church is also feminine and also the bride of Christ. "Like the church herself, every member of Christ's mystical body is a bride of Jesus. Jesus is the bridegroom," Von Hildebrand declares, "of every soul which is a member of his mystical body," which means of every soul that has been baptized into the Church. However, the Church as the spouse of Christ is at the same time a virgin. An examination of this factual contradiction but symbolically congruent belief in which "virginity and wedlock are united with Christ" will lead still deeper into the meaning and significance of Christian symbols.

The female church is controlled by males, priests who are created in the masculine image, in effect the other Christs who are the husbands of the church as well as the heads of the family whose worshipers are its

8. Von Hildebrand [49], p. 124.

children. Finally, in the Catholic Church, the pope, the ultimate head of the hierarchy, is the "papa" for the entire church on earth. Meanwhile, the Church eternal in heaven is the spouse of the bridegroom, Christ, and their relationship is that of the bride and groom where her feelings for her husband are most effectively stated officially in the Song of Songs. On earth the Church contains, and is comforted by, the masculine Holy Ghost.

The relation of the Church to Christ as founded on human marriage and the husband-wife relation is clearly established by St. Paul:

> For the husband is the head of the wife as Christ is the head of the church, his body, and is himself its Savior. . . . Husbands, love your wives, as Christ loved the church and gave himself up for her . . . husbands should love their wives as their own bodies. He who loves his wife loves himself. For no man ever hates his own flesh, but nourishes and cherishes it, as Christ does the church, because we are members of his body. "For this reason a man shall leave his father and mother and be joined to his wife, and the two shall become one." This is a great mystery, and I take it to mean Christ and the church.[9]

We must now allow certain philosophers and doctors of the church to ask these profound questions: Why is the Church a virgin? And what does her virginal character signify? These Catholic writers declare that "the mysterious glory which invests mystical love and its perfection as the crown of human relationships has no-

9. Ephesians 5:23, 25, 28-33 [8c].

where been depicted so vividly as in the Song of Songs." It will be remembered that in both Catholic and many Protestant Bibles, the bride calling passionately for her loved one is the Church and her bridegroom is Christ her Lord. (As everyone knows, there are several interpretations of the significance of the Song of Solomon. They vary from that of a romantic love song to a symbol of the relation of Christ and the soul, or Christ and the Church. The notations before each chapter in the King James Version, which for two hundred and fifty years influenced Christian thought, gave it the latter interpretation. More recent interpretations frequently do not. Catholic thought always emphasizes it. We will continue to examine the nuptial interpretation.)

The holy union of each soul with Christ is both a sister and a wedded relation. The Song of Solomon, the Canticle of Canticles, widely regarded as an authoritative and divinely inspired book, does provide a powerful foundation for the symbolic form and much of the emotional substance of the relation of the soul and Church as brides of Christ. Many other books of the Bible give evidence used by Catholics and often Protestants to substantiate this nuptial interpretation of the perfect relation between men and God. An introduction to the Song of Solomon in the family Bible of a Presbyterian home in Yankee City, for example, states an interpretation common to a number of Protestant churches. The notations at the beginning of each chapter of the book are similar to those found in the Bibles of many of the churches in Yankee City. The Song of Solomon, the introduction declares, is "a dialogue in which the speakers are Jesus Christ, the blessed bridegroom of souls; the church which is his body and bride . . . The scope of it is to represent Christ and his people's mutual esteem of, desire after, and delight in one another . . . the bride denotes either the church in general or a particular believer . . ." [8b]

In Chapter I in the Canticle of Canticles, according to the interpretative introductory notes of the King James Version, the "Church's love unto Christ" is passionately announced. [8d]

> Let him kiss me with the kisses of his mouth: for thy love is better than wine.
>
> Because of the savor of thy good ointments, thy name is as ointment poured forth, therefore do the virgins love thee.

"The mutual love of Christ and his Church," the cry of the loved and loving nuptial pair, is revealed in Chapter II:

> He brought me to the banqueting house, and his banner over me was love.
>
> His left hand is under my head and his right hand doth embrace me.

In this same chapter, "the profession of the Church, her faith and hope" about the bridegroom, is also stated:

> My beloved is mine, and I am his: he feedeth among the lilies. Until the day break, and the shadows flee away, turn, my beloved, and be thou like a roe or a young hart upon the mountains of Bether.

In Chapter IV, according to the interpretation, Christ "sheweth his love to her":

> Thou hast ravished my heart, my sister, my spouse,
> thou hast ravished my heart . . .

> How fair is thy love, my sister, my spouse! how
> much better is thy love than wine!

> A garden enclosed is my sister, my spouse; a spring
> shut up, a fountain sealed.

The Church is at once sister and bride to Christ in this seemingly contradictory role, a female symbol of the sister surrounded with moral rules and negative sanctions forbidding all sexual expression ["a garden enclosed"] and, on the other hand, the bride who like the hart longs to be united with her loved one. What can be the meaning of this sacred symbolic statement which seemingly contradicts some of the basic human values at the very foundations of human moral life? [10] To find our answer we must examine one other form of supernatural nuptial relations: the marriage of the consecrated virgin with Jesus Christ. Here we find this sacred theme and its values in their most extreme and detailed form and can examine them more easily. Moreover, since the sacred symbol of the consecrated virgin exists in substantial human form, the rules and regulations which order her life, the rituals which initiate her into the status, and those which continue to relate her to Christ are observable and recorded. It is therefore possible to obtain more explicit knowledge of the nature of this wedded relation of the sacred part of a human being to Christ and derive a better understanding of the meaning of the wedded relation of a brother and sister.

10. Ancient historical kinship factors having to do with the special use of sister also are involved.

Marriage of the Consecrated Virgin

"Among the ritual blessings having to do with the official worship of God," says Michel in the *Liturgy of the Church,* "the consecration of the church and the consecration of the chosen spouse of Christ are most imposing." The marriage of the virgin to Christ is presided over by the bishop who is the "highest liturgical dignitary" of the Church. The ceremony occurs in the Mass, "so that the obligation of the virgin's soul may be immediately united with that of the spotless Lamb on the altar." [11]

The candidates, escorted by previously dedicated virgins enter the church; a priest who is the assistant to the bishop sings, "Ye prudent virgins, prepare your lamps, behold the bridegroom approaches, go to meet him."

He presents the candidates to the bishop. The latter, as the representative of Christ, speaks to them: "God and our Savior Jesus Christ helping us, we choose these virgins, to present and consecrate them and to wed them to our Lord Jesus Christ, the Son of the highest God." The "brides" are then asked: "Do you will to be blessed and consecrated and betrothed to our Lord Jesus Christ the Son of the all highest God?"

They reply, "We will." In the ritual which follows each virgin is married to Christ: "Come, my chosen one," the song of the bishop calls to them, "thy King longs for thee. Hear and see, incline thy ear."

"I am a handmaid of Christ," the virgins reply, "therefore am I vested in servile habit."

11. Michel [74], pp. 258–63.

The bishop demands, "Will you persevere in the holy virginity that you have professed?"

"We will," they vow.

Each virgin is now a wedded spouse of Christ in eternal union with him. The perfect marriage on earth anticipates what will continue to be the perfect marriage after death in heaven.

Pure men and women in the marriage bed must control themselves and not yield to lust and abandon themselves to animal pleasures. Restraint and discipline are necessary if their wish to unite is to stay within the pre-established spiritual harmony and receive God's sanction. But no man or woman united sexually to another creature can ever completely escape from the lust of the senses and the vanities and snares of the world. Therefore, greater and further purification is necessary for any soul that yearns to achieve a more perfect state. Only ascetic practices can achieve this and allow such an individual to effect a perfect union with God. The vows of poverty, obedience, and chastity provide a way of life that by *self*-denial purify the individual. The symbolic flesh is reduced and some of it "removed" and the realm of the spirit expanded, thereby creating a larger opening and symbolic womb in which Divine love can enter and be contained. The ritual life of asceticism lays the foundation for a closer relation with God, but "the motive is no longer purification but undividedness in the strictest sense . . . The *inner emptiness,*—indispensable if we are to be filled with God—is complete inner freedom." Finally it is necessary for God to recognize the renunciation and make it acceptable to Him when "He and love for Him *fill the void* [italics mine] that has been left . . . He who invites the soul to the state of perfection will fill her with Himself if she obeys his invitation." Thus the marriage of the consecrated virgin, the bride of Christ, is spiritually recognized, emotionally experienced, and consummated.[12]

In this sacred marriage "there is delight and sacrifice for the beloved, and she leaves her worldly life just as the ordinary bride leaves her home to follow the man whom her love has chosen . . . Likewise, the soul that is inebriated with love of Jesus desires to forsake everything for his love, to stand before him naked, listen for his voice alone, draw his glance into her heart, and with loins girt and lamps burning await the bridegroom . . . The soul chooses suffering . . . that she may . . . celebrate with him the bridal of pain . . ." [13] This union is one of the highest and most spiritual of which human beings are capable. It is a living relation which completely surrounds and infuses the bodies of those involved in it so that such human beings are confined entirely within the limits of the sacred symbol, a sacred symbol of a sacred symbol, which in its turn is taken from moral man and his species life.

The marriage of the virgin to Christ reveals what the sacrament of marriage and the union of Christ and the Church signify. For the Church, the marriage sacrament in human marriage is an expression of the ecstatic nuptial union of the Church and her Lord. The marriage of the consecrated virgin indicates the emotional

12. Von Hildebrand [49], pp. 158, 185–6. See also pp. 150–6 ("The Ascetic Significance of Virginity") and in general pp. 183–91.
13. *Ibid.*, pp. 177–8.

depth and moral form of this relationship in more explicable, concrete form. Furthermore, this sacred symbolic union states these facts in their most extreme form. Such a person removes herself completely from the world, "dies to it," and devotes herself entirely to a life of consecrated purity within the loving arms of her Divine spouse. This human symbol of a symbol, set apart as the consecrated virgin, spouse of Christ, by her surrender to Christ as the symbol of the bride, emphasizes the extreme form of spiritual purity and expresses the emotional significance and the moral values of human marriage. The soul of the consecrated bride is wedded to Love Incarnate as a member of the Church, as a human soul, and as an entire person. She, made open and empty by ascetic practices and thus capable of containing more of incarnate love and closer union with God, can give and receive more of the love of the God-Man. Yet to most fully achieve this state of grace and earthly bliss she must be fully equipped with the sexual qualities of a human being. "The more fully a soul possesses the qualities of an earthly bride," says Von Hildebrand, "the better fitted is it to become a bride of Christ." [14]

Something of the emotional experience of the individual involved in such a mystical union is expressed by St. John of the Cross in a poem called "En Una Noche Oscura." The human lover's relations with the Divine Lover are deeply felt and explicitly stated.

> Once in the dark of night,
> My longings caught and raging in love's ray
> (O windfall of delight!)

14. For this entire section see *ibid.*, pp. 258–63.

I slipped unseen away
As all my hall in a deep slumber lay.

.   .   .   .

There in the lucky dark,
Leaving in secrecy, by none espied;
Nothing for eyes to mark,
No other torch, no guide
But in my heart: that fire would not subside.

.   .   .   .

O dark of night, my guide!
O sweeter than anything sunrise can discover!
O night, drawing side to side
The loved and Lover,
The loved one wholly ensouling in the Lover.
There in my festive breast
Walled for his pleasure-garden, his alone,
The Lover remained at rest
And I gave all I own,
Gave all, in air from the cedars softly blown.

.   .   .   .

Quite out of self suspended—
My forehead on the Lover's own reclined.
And that way the world ended,
With all my cares untwined
Among the lilies falling and out of mind. [55]

The problem becomes still more paradoxical when
we ask (at the sacred level) how it is possible to convert
the forms of social life into sacred symbols which express the values and beliefs of human society when these
symbols of purity place husband and wife in the incest
images of brother and sister? Any attempt to use rationality or the logic of evidence and propositional order

to explain this situation is certain to fail. Nor will justice be done to the meaning of these evocative and mythic symbols if we force them to submit to the rigid demands of logic and science. These mythic symbols are part of the *social logics* which may or may not be concerned about the requirements of evidence and rationality. They express real meanings and an inner constancy which communicate powerful and convincing truths to those who can accept and feel them. Their systems of mental life and moral order lie beyond the rational part of mental life and more often than not beyond the precepts and rules of official and formal morality. As religious collective representations they reflect and express, as Durkheim demonstrated, the moral and mental life of the group. Sometimes there is a mirrorlike reflection of its logic and even its most repressive morality, but more often than not such mental and moral symbols are part of the larger non-logical and non-moral context. Here there is something more than the social group ritually relating itself to the sacred representations of its own image; here life demands and gains full right to express what seems to be needed by men as members of this ongoing animal group we call the human species.

The several relations between the sacred symbolic life of Christians and the family structure are depicted in Chart 6. This chart and the discussion which follows are founded on the more general one (Chart 4) and the theoretical foundations previously discussed which it represents. The upward-pointing arrows on the left connect the species level of the human male animal and his sexual life with the status of male sexuality in the moral order of the family and, higher still, with Christ

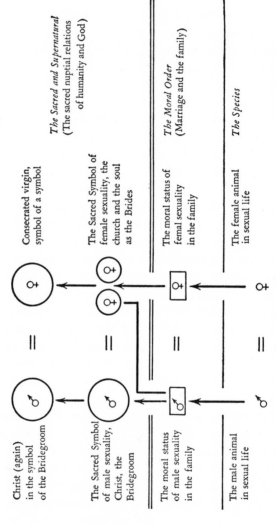

Chart 6. Man's Sexual Life and Family Structure in the Christian Symbol System

and the symbol of the Bridegroom, the sacred and supernatural symbol of male sexuality in the moral order.
The equal (marriage) signs show the male part of this
basic dichotomy related to the female (this chart should
also indicate that the male line of symbols, statuses, and
creatures is, in Christian values, superordinate to the
subordinate female line). It does indicate that the same
relations exist among the female parts of species, moral,
and sacred orders as on the male side. However, at the
sacred symbolic levels in the female line several developments take place that are significant. The symbol
of male sexuality, Christ the bridegroom, in the two
circles at the top of the chart, remains the same in his
marriages, but the female symbol changes: she is the
bride, the individual consecrated virgin, a ritual symbol of the Church as the bride; she is the soul of a man
or woman; and at the same time she is the Church in
holy nuptial relations with her Lord. This symbol of
a symbol in the "logic" of evocative, non-rational symbols provides, as it were, re-enforcement and symbolic
validation of the vaguer and less easily felt and understood symbols of the Church as the mystical body and
the soul.

The appearance of the two sacred symbols is an expression of the relation of the individual to the Church
and the community and of the social principle underlying the relation of the secular and sacred Christian
orders. The mystical body of the Church is composed of
all the souls who have been initiated into it through
the "rebirth" of baptism, which is also the "adoption"
of Christians into the family of God. Christ is the Head
of the mystical Body just as the husband is the head of
the wife. "The husband," says St. Paul, "is the head of

the wife, as Christ is Head of the Church." The mystery
here is great. The husband is recognized as spiritually
and morally superordinate to the wife at the moral level
and, at the sacred, the symbol of the bride is subordinate
to the superordinate male spouse, Christ. This sacred
symbol dominates and controls the moral and animal
worlds beneath it in the values of Christian thought.

The symbol, head, in this context has two important
references, logically impossible, but metaphorically and
evocatively sound and meaningful. The head of the
family is the husband status, and it is the "physical"
head, the directing and authoritative part of the mystical body. The congregation in its relations with Christ's
vicar, the pastor of a church, is in a subordinate role
to his leadership as is each of its members. The status
of the pastor in Christian thought is male in relation
to his flock. He is both father and husband; consciously
he is always father; unconsciously and sometimes with
difficulties resulting, husband to his congregation. At
the altar and in the Mass as priest he at times represents,
and is identified with, the female congregation—the
mystical body—and partly plays a female role. As an
individual soul he is always female. However, at other
times he is identified with Christ and is one of the
"other Christs" who compose the priesthood.

Thus the laity are female and the clergy are symbolically male; being so represented, they are made
emotionally meaningful for all times, all places, and in
all cultures. The significance of their male and female
relations can be felt and understood everywhere. The
Christ who enters the spiritual life of the community
and separately enters into the private world of each of
its members as the heavenly spouse can be felt and

accepted by all. The human being's subordinate yet blissful relation with Him is easily acceptable, for the soul can live in everlasting bliss and intimacy with her heavenly spouse. In the contemplations of the living, the pure soul at death, when separated from society, will not be alone or subject to the anxieties and desperate fears of the person who has lost his group, for as the bride of Christ such a being has special and altogether intimate relations with God himself. Moreover, the soul is always a part of the female body of the Mother Church into which she is first taken by the initiation rites of baptism and, through the rituals which separate the newly dead from the living, finally joined at death.

The ritually male priest as another Christ is the leader and authoritative father to his children who, as members of his congregation, are brothers and sisters to each other and children of God in the Christian world family. The higher clergy, bishops, cardinals, and the pope, are all fathers, each with an increasingly numerous and more widely extended family, until the world society of the Christian collectivity is joined with the one father as the head of the mystical body of one human community. He is the father of all fathers.

The images of what men are as sacred entities shift from family status to family status, but all of them are in the form of a family member. These spiritual identities are logically and scientifically impossible, but there is complete mythic congruence because the "logic" is structural and non-rational. Their diverse forms in a congruent symbol system are based on man's feelings and beliefs derived from his experiences within the family structure; they are expressions of his emergence as a person within the family's all-powerful matrix. In the human family, as we all know, an individual can be and usually is at one and the same time a child to his or her father, a spouse to his or her husband, and a father or mother to his or her sons and daughters. In the family, males and females share an infinite number of common formative experiences which not only differentiate them morally as sexual beings, but often encourage them to be, and mold them into, one likeness where sexuality is not recognized—this because as children of the same parents they belong to the same family. As siblings they are equivalent, which means that from the point of view of the larger society they are very much alike in status and in person. In the values of the sacred symbol system, functioning in part to integrate and hold the collectivity together within its reified system, which expresses common values and beliefs, the common qualities of kinship are stressed and differences often disregarded. The superordination of males to females may be expressed in a symbolic world of this kind in the dominance of the sacred spouse over the sacred female or of brother over sister, or it may be that authority will be given the form of the father as image for the enforcement of moral rules in the lives of his children.

One other major factor in the formation of these sacred marriage symbols which relate persons within the family such as brothers and sisters in spiritual sexuality must now be examined. The evidence from the psychoanalytic study of personality in family life is most important. The Church for Christians is also the Mother Church, yet she is sister and virginal as well as spouse; but she is mother to her children, the individual members of the congregation, and spouse and sister to her husband, Christ. The testimony of psychoanalysis and other evidence demonstrates that the strong negative rules which prohibit sexual relations between all family members who are not husband and wife are not "instinctive" nor a mere polite expression of man's "innate" goodness, but that these moral injunctions constantly function to forbid and prevent the powerful cravings of human beings to satisfy their species longings within the family. The emotional attachment of sons to their mother, daughters to their father, and brothers and sisters to each other, can only be recognized at the respectable level of precept and principle in socially acceptable sentiments. But at the deeper levels, in fantasy and in dream life where the evocative and emotional meanings are hidden from the scrutiny of the moral order, the non-moral and non-logical values of the species continue their existence and demand expression. The force of their existence can translate and transform the mental and moral system into fragments which are no more than parts of the non-logical and non-moral orders. Wish, desire, craving, emotionally remembered pain, and anxiety dominate here. Within them the moral and mental orders can be transfigured into symbols whose meanings on first inspection appear to be logical and moral but whose real significance belongs to the evocative world of species life.

The mythic, evocative symbols, related as they are to man's hopes and fears, to his wishes and anxieties about the risk of living and the certainties of death, to his desire for unfettered gratification of his longings as well as for immediate satisfaction of all his species appetites, allow man, under the highest and most revered auspices and sanctions, to express his species life and, at the same time and with the same symbols as moral representations, to project and act out his ordinary moral life at this sacred mythic level.

Thus the strict moral rules governing sexual life and marriage and the incest rules rigidly forbidding the relations of brothers and sisters at the mythic and sacred symbolic level can be congruently connected and given full honor and respect; yet the incest cravings in perfect non-rational congruence can also be expressed and used to help re-enforce the moral life of man. The whole man and the whole system of species and moral life are projected and expressed in the symbols of the sacred level. Logical and moral contradiction do not matter: the virgin is mother, incest is not incest, the incorporeal spirit implicates human flesh, yesterday is today, and today is yesterday or tomorrow, the one is the many and the many are one: these are the reality of mythic life.

The meanings of these logical contradictions are of vital consequence in the mental economy of man's existence. The evocative symbols at the sacred and mythic levels "talk" to man about *all* of himself, about *all* of his being; they speak from the profound depths of his species life and only secondarily from the superficial level of logic and thought. In the mythic symbol the species life of man in society and the values and beliefs of society in man are transformed and transfigured. They are made one in the sacred symbols of Christian society. When the several levels of the communicant's symbolic life are merged and joined with the sacred symbols of Christian society, an inward unity is achieved. To the believer this unity is felt as an integration of his own organic and moral life, but in each individual it is also an expression of the species and moral life of the human collectivity.

Mary, the Virgin Mother, Symbol of the Perfect Woman

The sacred symbol of Mary, the mother of Christ, is a collective representation in Yankee City and our society expressing in ideal form the culture's opposing and antithetical beliefs and values about women. For those who are Christians and believe, it embodies basic, nonlogical beliefs at two extremes of our values about women which state and define what women are and are not and what they should and should not be, to themselves, to men, and to God. The symbol carries within itself a series of implied negative and positive sanctions, a series of threats of punishment and promises of reward for approved or condemned sexual and moral conduct. It also expresses and gratifies the deep wishes found in each individual which are part of the species life of the human group. The threats and promises are addressed to men as well as women. To present, meaningfully and evocatively, the sexual and social definition of what a woman is and should be, not only is it necessary to define her to herself and all other women in extreme terms that are understandable, but it is also necessary to define her to the men who are in varying relation to the several basic statuses of women in this and other societies.

The figure of Mary, the Mother, is in many ways the most controversial one in the whole of Christian symbolism. The Catholic Church officially venerates her and many of its communicants worship her. Most Protestant churches recognize her position as the human mother of Christ who at the Annunciation conceived Jesus and gave him birth on Christmas Day. Yet for most Protestants and Catholics the amount of attention and significance given the Virgin Mary, the mother of Christ, is a crucial test of what it means to be a Catholic or a Protestant. In considering the father-son relation at the symbolic level, it is not difficult to speak generally about Protestants and Catholics. The role of the Virgin Mary is different. As the mother of Christ she is accepted officially by most Protestant communicants. At Christmas she receives their recognition, but it is largely secular in character, for she has lost her high official position and her rites no longer fill most Protestant church calendars. Meanwhile in the Catholic Church not only has she continued significant, but her place has increased in importance. Her rites have developed and the Church, by new dogmas, has strengthened the sacred quality of her symbol and its position in the Catholic pantheon, her immaculate conception without the defilement of original sin and her assumption into Heaven without the necessity of "death" being the most recent. They are co-relative, since the two combined change her into a symbol like Christ's, for she is— conceptually speaking—without beginning (birth without the human consequences of original sin) and without end (deathless). Her symbol, too, resolves the contradictions of eternity and of changing time, of immortality and mortality. She now is nearer the "being" of her Son. Her conception by a human father holds her to an earthly role bound by the limits of space and held within the changes of time.

The symbol of Mary is that of a woman who feels all the emotions of a woman, who yearns for her spouse and suffers the humiliations of her son and the pain of his and her death. However, the Immaculate Conception removes the feelings of guilt and shame associated with sexuality from the symbol. The sin of sex being removed from her creation, Godhead in the act which created Christ does not touch an impure thing. Mary becomes a pure object. The Immaculate Conception transforms her in very much the same way as the ritual of the Mass transforms the chalice in which Christ is recreated and born again. Ritually speaking, the forces of impurity and the forces of the profane are pushed beyond the immediate generation to a previous one. They are effectively walled off from the realm of the pure by the ritual force of the belief in the Immaculate Conception.

Mary was born without sin, to be the perfect receptacle of the semen of God (his essence, as the Holy Ghost) and the woman who would carry the foetus of Jesus and give birth to a supernatural being, a member of the Trinity and a Son to his godly Father. This immaculate collective representation strengthens the forces of ritual purity and the supernatural. God is further removed from the impure and the natural and ritually safeguarded from uncleanliness and pollution. The Annunciation purified the sexual act that produced a Son of God and removed male, but not female, sexuality from it.

When the mystery of the Immaculate Conception took place in the sexual act of Mary's father and mother, no male God intervened and implanted his impregnating energies within Anne. Her spouse was allowed to

be the father of his child, but the ritually unclean
forces present in the predetermined succession of sexually connected generations as conceived by Judaism and
Christianity and founded symbolically on the prototypical Eve and Adam, were removed by the intervention of Divine forces. The Holy Ghost did not enter
her womb as he did Mary; rather the effects of the
pollution were removed from the procreative act.

The great strength of such ritual symbols of pollution
and purification is that they mobilize the feelings and
values and beliefs we possess about sexuality, sexual
intercourse, and the institution of marriage and family
life, and relate them to the hopes and fears we possess
about our present condition and future prospects. The
feelings of guilt and moral inadequacy of everyone are
transfigured and reformed into the pure symbols related
to Divine sources. Thus each feels cleansed and reassured, his anxieties are reduced, and his hope for ultimate satisfactions and future reward maximized. He is
saved today, and by the happy consequences of the
efficacy of the sacred symbols' guaranteed victory over
his greatest fear: death and obliteration of the self.

The difficulties of bridging the great impossible divide of the sacred and the profane are accomplished,
yet the communicant retains the strength of the feelings
that flow unretarded from species behavior and, at the
same time, gains life-filling vigor from the increased
hope of immortality through the intervention of the
all-powerful forces of the Divine and the supernatural.

In the earlier pagan religions of the Mediterranean,
Osiris' mother, Isis, was also his much-beloved wife.
This same incestuous relation exists in many of the
great religions, where members of the immediate sacred

family who under secular circumstances would observe the rules of incest are conceived as perfect sexual mates. Christianity modified this. Although Christ is the Son of Mary and God, he is not conceived as the *spouse* of Mary. The idea of Christ being a second person in the Trinity and the Son of God the Father, whose Holy Spirit impregnated Mary, divides the Godhead into three separate roles and thus saves Christianity from worshiping what is in effect an incestuous god. But God is not the Son in sexual relations with the Mother nor is he the Father in direct intimate relations with Mary, the Mother. But it is his other spiritual self, the Holy Ghost, the symbol of his procreative strength and his intermediary with man, who becomes her sexual partner and is the male responsible for Christ's sacred conception.

Despite this Divine division, there is a very close parallel between the conception of the Virgin Mary as Christ's *mother* and the Church as the *bride* of Christ. Many of the same passages in the Bible, used to refer to both, indicate this incestuous conflict. "Christ is called the bridegroom of the Church," Mindszenty declares in his book, *The Face of the Heavenly Mother,* "That is why she is our mother. Her heart beats with the Holy Spirit. She conceives us in her womb. Joyfully, she brings us with our brothers forth to a new life. We are children of a sublime mother. New born in baptism, we may take the path to a new life." [15]

The Virgin Mother, for those who are conventional Christians and particularly for those who are Catholic, is a symbol of the ultimate and unattainable, yet always

15. Mindszenty [76], p. 131.

approachable, woman. As the Virgin she is the figure of sexual purity, taboo, highly desirable but as the Mother symbol always beyond any thought of sexual contact; yet at the very center of the incest feelings and beliefs, she is a woman who is necessarily—if not sexually, then procreatively—experienced.

> Two ineffable beauties [Mindszenty declares] are united in Mary: the charm of virginity and the dignity of motherhood. Mary is, therefore, the crown of nature, the wondrous flower of the new heavenly order. The charm of virginity does not disappear, the bright untouched snow of the distant virginal mountains does not melt away, but she becomes a mother. God is born into the world, the virgin proceeds in her blessedness—no man has intervened. She becomes a mother and remains a garden enclosed. She brings a child into the world not through desire of the flesh, but through obedience of the soul. . . . She stands alone in unspeakable dignity. Lovely virginity and sublime maternal fertility! [16]

Mary represents the two highest moral virtues that women can possess, symbolizing the basic contradictions implicit in the evaluations and symbols that we have of womankind in this culture. For men and youths, she is the queen of purity, the eternal idea of true chivalry. For if she is profanely touched, for those who are unwittingly involved there is a deep sense of guilt; better said, there is greater guilt for those who feel guilt in their basic emotions toward members of their family.

16. *Ibid.*, pp. 32-3.

The holy mother, for her earthbound sons, is perfect. She conceives and bears a child without sexual experience with her sexual mate. Her husband is not the feared sexual rival of her sons.

"Wholly of God," says Mindszenty, "is the fulfillment of this blessed wonder: mother and virgin at once. And virgin before, during, and after child-bearing! Virgin in body, virgin in soul, virgin for all time. . . . According to Hippolytus of Rome: 'The Pure One, in a pure manner, opened the womb of the virgin.' After her maternity, she remained untouched in soul and body, as though she had never been a mother." [17]

Mary also is always the yielding, soft, loving person. She forever acknowledges and accepts this superior masculine spirituality and power. She yields unresistantly to the male God.

Although as the Queen of Heaven, the spouse of god, and the mother of Christ she receives the veneration of those who love and believe in her, she does not receive the worship given the Son who was also flesh. Perhaps it is not without significance that he was male flesh.

As the good woman, Mary is obedient and yielding to masculine superiority, as the wife of Joseph, as the spouse of God, as the mother of the Divine Son, and as the dependent and bereaved mother of the dead Jesus, while under the sponsorship of John the Beloved. But as the sorrowful mother standing before the cross, suffering the final and ultimate pain as she watches her own son suffer and die to pay for man's sins, she becomes the ultimate appealing figure of the mother of all men. As her sons they can express their own love

17. *Ibid.*, p. 34.

and the guilt they feel in the presence of all mothers who unreservedly give them their love.[18]

> Stood the Mother, stood
>   though sighing,
> Tearful, 'neath the cross,
>   where dying
> Hung her only Son and Lord.

The virgin mother is provided with a husband, Joseph, who is her protector and moral representative in the larger world; God, the Father, acting through his agent, the Holy Spirit, impregnates her. The question arises as to what is involved symbolically that made it necessary for the male head of the family to be divided into two persons: Joseph and God. The immediate explanation that comes to mind is important but insufficient. Joseph, the human being, primarily in the role of the husband, and God in the role of the father and procreator—the one person being split into two—conveniently express this division in their persons. But why is this division necessary? It is not because God was too sacred and spiritual to be permitted symbolic human form, for Christ was one with him in the Christian Trinity and became human and suffered the degradation that all humans fear and never understand. It must be added that powerful gods of other religions have assumed human procreative roles and maintained their sacred authority. It could be said that the required symbol of the father is likely to be more reserved, withdrawn from his children and felt to be further removed from human approach and, consequently, less capable of assuming a human symbolic form. There can be little

18. *The Roman Missal* [96], pp. 847-9.

doubt that these values about the father do operate and keep him from too close contact with fearful and always distrustful man, but other societies have possessed family systems where the father was feared, yet they have worshiped father gods who were human procreators.

The principal factor is what might be called symbolic congruence. If sacred symbols express the idealized beliefs and practices of the social structure and are saturated with the idealized feelings and values human beings have for the statuses and relations which compose the various parts of the structure, then it would be expected that the several parts of the sacred belief system would eliminate conflict between the parts and harmonize them or provide satisfying explanations. Thus conflict at the human organizational level is less likely to be part of the ideal organization expressed in the sacred symbols.

For Joseph to be a human husband and a procreative god would make him far too substantial. His human sexuality would arouse the very conflicts which, intrinsically a part of the values and feelings of the human family, are most difficult to face and cause the greatest pain. To these ends, the present symbolic arrangement accomplishes several vital effects. It eliminates the husband, Joseph, as a father and sexual being and thereby removes the feelings of distress about the sex relation of the mother and father. It reduces the feared figure of the human father to a very secondary place. It increases the ease of accepting the mother of Christ as a virgin whose immaculate conception makes here the perfect expression of a moral purity which flees from the distress of the human sexual act. It elevates the role of the father as an authoritative figure to a spiritual place where, although greatly feared, he can be fully accepted.

This arrangement of Divine and human persons creates two highly approachable intermediaries, Jesus and Mary, who are far more able and much better situated to gain spiritual favors from a father who is always difficult to approach and who by his very nature arouses the very fears and anxieties that need to be assuaged. His very remoteness now contributes to his closeness. For the mother and her earthly son can intercede with this distant figure who no longer need to be the threat to man's basic sense of self-reproach. The structure of emotions within family life, particularly those which forbid and enjoin sexual expression, are thus idealized and the conflicts present in the ordinary world are by this symbolic phrasing eliminated in the sacred world.

The roles of the pure virgin and the saintly mother, combined in the figure of one woman, create a symbol of ideal simplicity to arouse and evoke the deep oedipus love of all males, particularly the love of those men who in fact retain their unloosened attachment for their mothers. The love for their own mothers is contained and bound by the worship of virginity. No other woman threatens the tranquility of this original love. The symbol of the virgin is strengthened and maintained by the deep attachment to the mother. It is quite possible that her worship by such men may release them from the guilt and terrors of the too deep attachment and the pain of a love of the mother that will not permit them a wholly satisfying attachment to someone else.

The Freudian conception of oedipus pain and the complex emotions underlying it being essentially psychological and *individually* oriented, loses sight of, and does not completely comprehend, their destructive power for those in the *group* in which such an individual operates. There can be no doubt that psychoanalysts have understood the grief and sorrow of those immediately attached to such a person, particularly the wife and children; but if it is a tragedy for Oedipus to suffer incest longings it is also a tragedy for Jocasta, his mother and wife, and for Laius, his slain father, and for Thebes, his community. All must suffer, since they are part of the society where such incompletely socialized men can never make satisfactory adjustments to those who are capable of living normal lives. It is possible that one of the principal functions of the sacred symbols of femininity is to help sublimate many of these asocial and antisocial longings and fears and drain them into areas that are approved and not dangerous.

It is probable that many in the celibate priesthood may feel a particular attachment to this wholly satisfactory sacred feminine symbol. They are officially urged to venerate her as first among the saints, second only to the Divine persons of the Trinity. "No created being can attain to so intimate a union with God as she. The saints live in the order of grace, but Mary shines in the order of the incarnation of Jesus." They are men capable of the same emotions as other males but under the strict ascetic discipline of celibacy. Yet scandal now rarely touches any member of the clergy. The love of the human mother can continue unmodified, and much of it without transformation can be passed over to the love of the Divine mother. Cardinal Mindszenty declares, "To the priest, a human being consigned to loneliness, the Lord gave Mary as mother when he gave her to His beloved disciple: 'Behold thy Mother!' The priest finds that warmth every heart needs in Mary. The priest, therefore, is obliged to love her with all the strength of an affectionate heart." [19] It will be recalled that it is officially stated that the perfectly pure man is not one without sex drive but he who learned how to control it and rise above it. The same statements, of course, hold for the attachment to the symbol of the female Church and, as we saw earlier, for some mystics in their relation with Christ.

The virgin part of the symbol of Mary reduces and largely eliminates the hostility to her. As such, she is not in the ambivalent position of human mothers. She is without immediate or original sin. She is innocent of sexual desire and accordingly the perfect mother of the perfect child. She is soft, warm, loving, merciful, and affectionate. She is the self-sacrificing, yielding mother who needs the love of her children. God, the father, fortunately remote, is harsh, unyielding, inhuman, largely without pity, the moral judge who punishes without mercy according to the harsh laws of a masculine universe. Their son, although masculine, is born in the image of his mother, yet he is also like his father. Christian doctrine has recognized him in both roles. As the gentle Lamb of God, he is the soft, innocent one who inherits the personality of his mother. As the fearful judge who will condemn the wicked to eternal torment, mentioned in the Gospels and the liturgies, who will preside on the Judgment Day at his second coming, he is created in the stern and fearful likeness of his father. Since he is both, different ages and different peoples have emphasized one side or the other of his personality. It is now fashionable to think of him only as

19. Mindszenty [76], p. 76.

the loving God, compassionate, and the source of loving kindness in human behavior.

God, the strong father, strikes terror in the hearts of men. Should they disobey his stern commands, he may condemn them to everlasting torment or personal obliteration. The mother continually appeals to the merciful side of her son, asking him to persuade his father to act in behalf of her weak human children who, as members of our species, forever misbehave morally and forever are sorry for their misdeeds. She can do this because, during the nine months she carried her Divine son in her womb—from the time of her impregnation by God at the Annunciation until his birth on Christmas Day —the blood and life forces of her human body nourished him, and her breasts comforted him and the milk drawn from her body fed him and became part of the infant—the same Jesus who, himself, grown into the mature male Christ, sought to save and redeem sinful man.

The harsh, not to say cruel and vengeful, qualities of the father image are transformed into the gentle, loving, peaceful son of the woman. The fighting, aggressive, male Jehovah becomes the gentle peaceful male Christ, capable of loving men as well as women, not in an erotic way but within the limits and bounds of the moral rules of a brother. In Christ as the brother, men and women are protected from sexual anxiety and fear because they share common incest bonds with him. He obeys the moral rules as they themselves hope they will act in any situation.

CHAPTER 8

Sacrifice: The Father and His Son

The Sacrificed God of Catholics and Protestants

For all Christians, Christ's death on the cross and his resurrection from the tomb after the brutal slaying are the climax and the wondrous denouement of the sacred drama of the gospel. [38] The public drama of the liturgies of Easter and Holy Week, the Mass, and the Lord's Supper are some of the present ritual expressions of the dreadful ending of his life on earth and of each Christian's involvement in the horrible deed. They tell, too, of the triumphal return of Christ to his spiritual home and of man's assurance of life after death.

In such rituals as the Mass (since the bread and wine are not symbols but Christ Incarnated) it is believed that each time the sacrifice is re-enacted the God-Man is brought back to life on the altar and slain again. Thus he is made to suffer the cruelty and pain of man's depravity not once but daily throughout human history. Why was one time not sufficient? More broadly, for both Protestants and Catholics, why commemorate this dreadful horror? And, one must ask, theoretically, what is present in the feelings of men as they are expressed in Christian belief which demands that this gentle God continue to be the ritual victim of their sadistic brutality? Why is it socially and psychologically necessary

314

now for men to re-enact this bloody and horrible event of two thousand years ago, when an innocent man was captured, humiliated, nailed to a cross, and killed because his human contemporaries collectively hated him?

Why do contemporary men, and the most devout, feel the need of continually remembering and re-enacting the great tragedy that their God was made to suffer when he was here on earth? Part of the answer, of course, is that he arose trimphant out of his suffering and thus, it is believed, reassured men that they could have eternal life. However important this reassurance is, at best it can be no more than one important part of the larger explanation. We must now further hypothecate that those of the faithful who are emotionally satisfied by this terror-filled drama—who unconsciously as well as consciously identify with the suffering God— not only receive vicarious satisfaction from his tragedy but, because they also unconsciously identify with the killers, can express their deep hatred of, and their desire to kill, their brothers and other members of the Christian and human collectivities. Moreover, their hatred is directed against themselves and what they are as moral beings.

We can also hypothecate that, by self-righteously loving their God and killing him, they can hate others and themselves and, through ritual usage, identify first with the hated human figures and later with the loved and valued God to forgive themselves for their hatreds and efficaciously release their feelings of guilt and self-condemnation. Such rituals as the Mass, later analysis will indicate, symbolically accomplish this transformation. The symbols of the myth of the Father and his Son supply the signs, buried deeply in the moral and species life of man, which evoke the human feelings that, when properly manipulated, accomplish this task. As long as this transformation can be done vicariously and unconsciously as a sacred act, the beneficial effects of such a mystical relation of God and man are incalculable, perhaps even beyond present human understanding, for to know what is meant is far beyond what we know now about the nature of life and about love and hatred.

The love of God for man and the effective form that it takes are expressed in such scripture as "God so loved the world that He gave His only begotten son that whosoever might believe would have eternal life." But there is a less recognized and unsanctioned set of feelings aroused, antithetical to the first, which are expressed in the sacrificial rites of the Church. In the drama man is put in the position of killing his God, his ritual older brother, and offering this slain kinsman to their father. The God, slain on his own altar by his human brothers, the human sons of Christ's own father, is offered to, and accepted with approval by, God himself. The whole of humanity's relation to Christ and all of its hopes and fears and all of its aspirations for itself are focused and contained in this relation of the adopted human brothers who, as members of the Christian family, are with Christ the sons of God. God not only accepts his Son as the slain Lamb but in varying rituals in the several churches becomes a member of the banquet table where all present dine upon the blood and flesh of the slain Son. The human members, refreshed, strengthened, and purified by this divine eating, receive grace and, by the efficacy of these most sacred rituals, are freed from a sense of guilt and the bonds of sin. How can this be so? How is it possible that such sacred beliefs and practices do free men from their feelings of guilt and do make them "whole again?" If this belief were newly invented and freshly presented to men and not sanctioned by sacred tradition and the churches, it is probable that contemporary men would draw back from it in horror and disgust. One must ask, What is this "myth's" deep appeal? Why should such beliefs become the very center of worship and the ultimate symbol of Christian belief? Why through it and its rituals do men feel cleansed and at one with themselves and with the members of their group?

In brief, what is the *meaning* of the myth and the several rituals of the Crucifixion and others having to do with Christ's death? How do they *function* in the beliefs and values of the collectivity and of each individual? Why are the beliefs and rituals efficacious? In sum, what is their validity in the non-rational mental life of the society?

To begin our analysis, we will briefly examine some of the variations of belief about the rituals of Christ's death and resurrection. When the wine and bread of our Lord by the ritual action of transubstantiation become the Blood and Body, they have their own particular significance to Catholics and some Episcopalians. As the sacrament of the Lord's Supper for many Evangelicals they "convey the Gospel in dramatic form" and "portray forgiveness and life which Christ imparts in response to personal faith. The sermon is in the Supper. In accepting the Sacrament we remember His death. It brings to mind the redemptive death of Christ; it is an expression of Communion with God, as we have access to the Father through Jesus Christ, the one mediator between God and man; it is an expression of fellowship among the disciples of Christ, emphasizing their oneness in Him. In the word 'Eucharist' we express gratitude to God for redemption and dedicate our lives [to Him] and lastly 'The Sacrament brings assurance to us of the ultimate completion of our redemption when the Christ comes again.' "

For the authority of the Holy Word such passages as 1 Peter 2:24 are often quoted: "Who his own self bore our sins in his own body on the tree that we, being dead to sins, should live unto righteousness; . . ." Even better known are those from John 6:54–57:

> He that eateth my flesh and drinketh my blood hath everlasting life, and I will raise him up on the last day.
>
> For my flesh is food indeed, and my blood is drink indeed.
>
> He that eateth my flesh and drinketh my blood abideth in me, and I in him.

Whatever may be the variation among Protestants about the meaning and ceremonial form of the sacraments, most churches of Protestant faith officially recognize only two—the Lord's Supper and baptism. Their retention by Protestants during the Reformation and after Puritan destruction of liturgical signs demonstrates their deep significance to all Christians. We have previously examined some of the meanings of baptism as they are expressed in the yearly liturgy on Holy Saturday before Easter Sunday. Here we will analyze those of the Lord's Supper and the Mass. Although different in form and symbolic intent, the sacrament of the Last Supper and the Mass are symbolically related to two significant forms of human experience, the sharing of food at a common meal of intimates and the fear and fact of human death. The symbol system of Calvary and that of the last meal of Jesus with his disciples in the upper room are treated as separate and yet as one in Christian ritual. The "meat and drink" of the Last Supper, the bread and wine, become one with the live Christ who died and lived again.

To further our understanding of the myth of the voluntary sacrifice of the Son to his own Father, and the Father's acceptance of the voluntary death through which all humankind were "redeemed" and given the gift of immortality, we must analyze the symbolic communication involved in the rituals of sacrifice. What supernatural meanings do the signs of sacrifice convey in the symbolic dialogue between God and man? What functions do they perform? [1]

The Mass—an Analysis of the Constituent Parts of an Act of Ritual Meaning

To arrive at a better understanding of the meaning and functions of the myths and rituals of the Lord's Supper and the Mass we shall first ask ourselves, What are the assumptions and methods followed in the act of ritual communication? How are the various elements in the communication—the signs, the communicators, and the objects—evoked and referred to and related to each other? How do its signs function? Why is the rite efficacious as a system of communication?

To accomplish our ends we shall analyze the whole interaction of the basic parts of the Mass and compare

---

1. Those who are theoretically inclined might read Chapters 14 and 15, on symbolic theory in *The Living and the Dead*. [114f]

the component parts of the ritual with the ordinary forms of sign usage and acts of meaning.

As all Catholics and many others know, the Mass is divided into two basic parts, the opening half, or Mass of the Catechumens (the initiates of an earlier period who were not yet baptized), and the Mass of the Faithful (those who had been previously baptized). [38] Each is redivided into two parts. In the first part of the Mass of the Catechumens, the faithful (through the priest) give prayers to God and in the second part he, in return, gives instructions to them. The present ritual maintains the symbols of the ancient rite of initiation of adults into the mysteries of Christianity.

The first half of the Mass of the Faithful is the offertory of gifts and consecration to God. The latter part, Communion, is "the true enactment of the liturgical mystery of Christ's sacrifice." In the second part the "sacrifice-banquet" is God's return gift. (In official belief this rite is made effective by "our intimate union with Christ who is both God and man.") Formerly and prototypically, "the people went up to the altar of Christ, they placed themselves in their gifts on the very altar of the sacrifice as living oblations to God, and in the consecration they were most truly merged in the very passion and death of Christ, sharing fully in the redemptive action of Christ made really present in the liturgical mystery."

Thus there is a gift exchange, an exchange of signs and meanings in the two Masses; the reception by God of the gifts from men obligates each by the "intimate nature" of man's and God's relation to the Divine victim to exchange gifts. [69] Thus Michel writes,

The Mass is an interchange of gifts; we give to God and God gives to us. This double motive is the basis of the entire Mass-structure. It determines the division into two parts of both the Mass of the Catechumens and the Mass of the Faithful. In the Mass of the Catechumens we first give to God, in the prayer-part, and then God gives to us, in the instruction-part. Likewise in the Mass of the Faithful, the sacrifice-oblation is our gift to God, while the sacrifice-banquet is God's gift to us. In both cases the interchange is effected through our intimate union with Christ who is both God and man, according to the ever-recurring phrase: *per Christum Dominum nostrum:* through Christ our Lord.[2]

The obligations of the gift and gift exchange in the two parts of the Mass are illustrated in Chart 7. This symbolic interaction is the fundamental mold in which the ritual signs of the Mass are given meaning and efficacy for those who believe as well as for scientific analysis as we see in the Missal.

The priest offers the bread with the prayer: "Accept, O holy Father, almighty and eternal God, this host for the all-holy sacrifice, which I, thy unworthy servant, offer unto thee, my living and true God, to atone for my numberless sins of sinfulness and neglect; on behalf of all here present, and likewise for all faithful Christians, living and dead, that it may profit me and them, as a means of salvation unto life everlasting, Amen."

The exchange takes place at the altar which stands for God the Father, and for the cross of Calvary. It is

2. Michel [74], pp. 162-3.

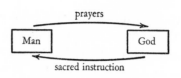

Chart 7. The Obligations of Sacred Gift Exchange

1. Sacred Sign Exchange in the Mass of the Catechumens
2. Sacred Sign Exchange in the Mass of the Faithful

here in the holy of holies that the consecration can and usually does occur. In brief, here while the Mass proceeds: (1) the signs of the bread and wine become Christ himself, (2) the priest becomes (a) Christ, the victim offered, and (b) the Christ who offers himself as the Son to his Father, and (3), through the efficacy of the rites and the original perfect act of love by the Son for his Father and for mankind, the audience of the faithful become one with the priest and with the Son, the entirety in the symbol of the Son being accepted by the Father. Lastly, in the sacrifice banquet the return gifts of immortality and fellowship with God are given by God to man. "In the sacrifice-banquet we receive back from God the gift we gave to him in the sacrifice-oblation but in the meantime it has been consecrated into the living Christ. Our acceptance of it is in the form of the Bread of Life. We thus assimilate ourselves most intimately with God, by uniting ourselves with the sacrificial victim." [3]

3. Ellard [38], p. 160. See also chart in *The Roman Missal* [96], p. xxv.

The ceremony, although concentrated on the literal death and rebirth of God, "is also a celebration of Christ's entire life work—" including the mysteries of the human conception of Jesus, the virgin birth, his suffering, crucifixion, and resurrection and ascension. The audience vicariously lives through it all and is initiated into God's family; a collectivity of kindred made one in the holy birth and death partakes of the banquet at the family table.

Not only are the priest and the immediate *individuals* in the audience involved in this symbolic transformation, but the entire collectivity as a corporate body is assimilated into the signs of the bread and wine which as Christ are slain and offered to God. St. Augustine in *The City of God* states the official interpretation: "The whole ransomed city, that is, *the Church and the communion of saints, forms the universal sacrifice* offered to God by the High Priest, who in His passion gave up His life that we might become the Body of so great a Head . . . This is the Christian's Sacrifice: we being many are one Body with Christ, as the Church in the Sacrament of the Altar, so well known to the faithful, wherein is shown that in that oblation *the Church is offered* [italics mine]." [4]

The bread, product of the many broken grains of wheat, and the wine from the bruised countless grapes, symbolize the unity of all in the signs of the Body and Blood of Christ. St. Augustine in an Easter sermon uses these symbols to express the supernatural significance of these earthly unities and to evoke the feelings of spiritual unity in the faithful.

4. Quoted in Ellard [38], pp. 124-5.

When you were enrolled as catechumens [says the
saint], you were stored in the Christian granaries.
Later, when you handed in your names as candidates for Baptism, you began to be ground by the
millstones of fasting and exorcisms [in the Lenten
exercises of the catechumenate]. Then ye came to
the font, and were moistened and made one paste;
and then the fire of the Holy Spirit coming upon
you [in Confirmation], ye were baked and became
the Lord's Bread. See what you have received. See
how this unity has been brought about, and be of
one accord, cherishing one another, holding to one
faith, one hope, one love . . . Thus, too, the wine
was once in many grapes, but now is one . . . Ye
now dine at the Lord's Table, and ye there share
in His Cup. We are there with you; *together* we
eat, *together* we drink, for we live *together* [italics
mine].[5]

The symbolic gift exchange of sacred signs between
man and God, depicted in Chart 7, is not just an exchange of signs which refer to separate objects, as it is
at the secular level of communication. In the language
of symbolic analysis, the signs (bread and wine) become
the object (Christ), and the communicators (priest and
congregation), through the efficacy of the changing signs,
also become the object (Christ), and all are received and
accepted by the other communicator (God, the first person of the Trinity; the Son being the second is one with
Him).

To summarize, the supernatural communication involves two actions and results: (1) The signs and those

5. *Ibid.*, p. 199.

who use them become one with the object and are so received by the (symbolic) receiver, God. (2) Their meanings, signs, and communications *transport* and *lift* them from the natural and profane level to the superior supernatural where they possess qualities in kind of the Trinity and Divinity.

> When a man is "in Christ," forthwith He and Christ are vitally united, and Christ offers Himself and His Christian in Himself, and the man offers Christ and himself in vital unity, and God, looking upon Mass, sees both His Son and those who are "in one" with Him. Hence you cannot but perceive the incredible cogency of Mass. It is a gift that God cannot resist: the priest, and the layman too, since there is solidarity between them, have omnipotence in their hands. Mass is an act—not a prayer recited, not a ceremony contemplated, but the supreme act of history unequaled in the world.[6]

These products of supernatural communication, sign into object, communicator into communicated, and all into the One, are a supernatural aspect of the technical facts of communication. They are portrayed below in Chart 8. It will be noticed that everything engaged in the visible human process of communication moves from beneath the broken line and the realm of the profane and is transported, through the sacred efficacy of the ritual, to the supernatural realm, these including priest, communicants, and the signs of bread and wine. This is accomplished by "magically" identifying sign with object (arrow *a* in the present chart) and sender (priest) and human congregation with the transformed

6. Martindale [68], p. 115.

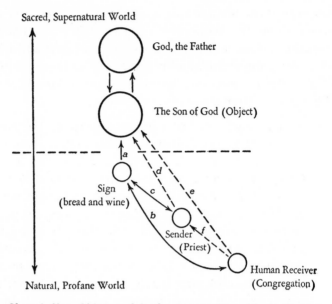

Chart 8. Sign, Object, and Sender Become One with the Receiver

signs (see arrows *b* and *c*). Broken lines *d, e,* and *f* indicate the ritual identifications made possible: the congregation with the priest and both with Christ in direct
relation with God the Father. In the rituals of "consubstantiation" (Luther) and the symbols of the Lord's
Supper representing the history of Christ's life and
death and man's redemption and immortality, the object does not become the sign, nor the sign the object.
In the theology of consubstantiation, however, Christ,
the object, moves through the actions of the sign's
manipulation and is present, never becoming one in the
substance with the bread and wine.

By the acts of meaning in the sacred dialogue of the
Mass, the words and gestures are not only verbal signs

but actions whose effects in the meanings of God who receives them *cause* change to occur in man's state. Ritual pollution is removed from sinful man and, in a state of grace and in the symbol of Christ, man moves from the natural to the supernatural, from mortality "up to" immortality. The purification is accomplished in the images of the slaying of a son as the Lamb of God and the communal eating of him by the family of God.

Wherein lies the great validity of these symbolic themes? To repeat a question asked earlier in this chapter, What in us, expressed in Christian belief, demands that the God-man be the victim of attack? Why must men re-enact these horrible details of a man being nailed to the cross? And, adding disgust to horror, eat the innocent victim?

The Father and His Son

Let us first repeat what is traditional knowledge; the rite of sacrifice is a very old and widely spread ceremony inherited in part by the Christians from the Jewish rite of the Passover. [54b] This said, we can ask why the meal and the slain victim are now used as the central myths which provide the non-rational mental forms in which the collectivity has contained their meanings of the rite's significance and its public display of signs. The writings of Frazer, Durkheim [35a], Hubert and Mauss, Freud, Robertson Smith, and others have been drawn upon to help us progress to the interpretations offered here. We will begin with Smith.

In his classic *Lectures on the Religion of the Semites* W. R. Smith establishes two types of sacrificial rituals. "Sacrifices slain to provide a religious feast, and vegetable oblations presented at the altar, make up the sum

of ordinary religious practices of the older Hebrews."
"The animal victim was presented at the altar . . . but
the greater part of the flesh was returned to the worshiper, to be eaten by him under special rules."

"Everywhere," he continues, ". . . a sacrifice ordinarily involves a feast and a feast cannot be provided
without a sacrifice." [7] Smith develops his analysis by his
commensal interpretation that "those who eat and drink
together are by this very act tied to one another by a
band of friendship and mutual obligation." The sacrificial meal in which the community of men share their
victim with the host, their God, is a "solemn expression
of the fact that all who share are brethren . . . and the
duties of brotherhood are implicitly acknowledged . . .
By admitting man to his table the God admits him to
his friendship . . . The very act of eating and drinking
together was a symbol and a confirmation of fellowship
and mutual social obligations." The circle of those obli-
gated was "the circle of kinship" where . . . "the whole
kin is answerable for the life of each of its members."
Finally, the ritual action of the ceremony purged those
who participated of their sins, bringing them into actual
union with their god. According to Smith's account,
when the small *kin* group grew into *national* aggregates
there was greater need for reconciliation with God.
Mystic religions then developed and man fled from divine hostility "by incorporating himself in a new religious community." [8] In such religions man atones for
his sins through a holy victim, pure and sacrosanct; the
ceremony commemorates a divine tragedy for which,

7. Smith [105], Lecture VI, p. 239.
8. *Ibid.*, Lecture X, p. 359.

like that of Tammuz or Adonis, there was annual mourning:

These early rituals of atonement contributed their share to the myths and images of Christianity. Despite their historic significance, Smith's emphasis on the obligations of the kinship community is of most use to us. The divine father and his mystic family, in heaven and on earth, recognize mutual obligations and give mutual aid and brotherly care and affection to each other. The efficacy is in the signs of a shared meal where each incorporates the food of a holy victim into himself and thereby is so constituted that part of him is also incorporated into the others whose entirety make up the spiritual group of kindred. The symbol of the family meal that becomes a sacred ritual image and a sign of mutual aid and the obligation of God and his human kinsmen to each other is part of a basic myth all built on the family structure and the sharing of food at the family meal. The emotional efficacy of such symbols for understanding the meaning of the ritual relations to God and the feelings attached are clear. Their non-rational validity in the feelings of men is also satisfied by this analysis. But what isn't clear is how at the deep non-rational level of human mentality these images of kinship relations and the horrible killing of the holy victim are interrelated in such a way that they satisfy the celebrants and contribute to the felt validity that such rituals evoke in the minds of the faithful. We will first examine this problem by returning to the whole question of the sacred family, this time examining the relations of the father god and his son and that other principal father-son image connected with the supernatural: Adam, first son of God and father of all living.

The father-son relation with its many complexities and contradictions, with all the importance and the depth of its significance for society, is at the core of Christian life. It pervades all faiths, its mysteries involve some of the most important rational problems that beset metaphysicians and scientists, yet it successfully deals with the practical problems that constantly face men. "I believe in God the Father Almighty," the faithful repeat, "Maker of Heaven and earth; and in Jesus Christ His only Son our Lord who was conceived by the Holy Ghost, [and] born of the Virgin Mary, suffered under Pontius Pilate, was crucified, dead and buried . . ."

In Christ as the human Son of God, the hopes, fears, and dilemmas of creation and all existence are resolved in Christian thought. Through him the Eternal One becomes Father to that which is opposite to eternity, the human Son, who as a *person* of God in another image, is transformed into ephemeral man to live, die, and become a part of changing time and finite space. The unlimited and abiding Eternal is meaningfully articulated to, and expressed by, its opposite where there are a human here-and-now and beginnings and endings. Mortality and immortality are no longer antithetical and opposite, but one, yet still opposite and different.

These profound logical contradictions of existence are easily solved by the Eternal One becoming the Father to his other person, the Son, through the action of the third, the Holy Spirit, in the womb of the human mother, the Virgin Mother. Problems founded on rationality which are thus insoluble and their terms contradictory, when translated into the non-rational symbols of the family circle of relations, can be and are easily resolved. The great mysteries of life, often no more than contradictions based on external logic, which frustrate and frighten men, when translated into non-rational terms (social logics) are easily understood and accepted, for now they are founded on the known experiences of family life. Under these conditions, logical contradiction and the rules of rationality lose control and men's convictions are allowed to rest on empirical evidence and use the deep feelings which attach to beliefs founded on the persons of the family. Such symbols place human faith in a human family mold that is "feelingly" understandable to all human beings.

The Father and the Son are then meaningful and symbolically acceptable to men in all their most peculiar yet profound manifestations. A loving father who sends his son out in the world to be horribly crucified and a son who goes out from the father into a sadistic world and offers himself to be slain to return *obediently* to his father, although monstrous at the secular level, are easily accepted by the faithful at the sacred level. The moral, animal, and sacred orders are fused, and each within this undivided whole has another and fuller meaning. The loves and hatreds of men, the problems of discipline and authority, of social order and individual autonomy, the dependence of men on society and of sons on their fathers and families find expression in this magnificent drama of the Father and his Son. The earthly son's need to be with his father yet escape him and the right of access and help from him are portrayed. The oneness of the two in the family "blood" and in shared experience and *their unity and oneness in the spiritual semen of the Holy Ghost* are fully stated, yet their difference is made clear. The dependence of the

Son on his Father, his need for his help, his freedom
from the Father to make his own choices, even to being
tempted by the Father's greatest enemy, are all acted out
in the sacred drama of the Father and Son. Yet the discipline and authority of the Father are supported; the
Son, after paying a terrible price, returns willingly to
his Father. Thus God, "who so loved the world that he
gave his only begotten Son that whosoever might believe
would have eternal life," once more repossesses his Son.
With him, when he takes him back, he accepts rebellious mankind. In the Son who loves perfectly, a hostile
mankind, hating its fathers and its brothers, can momentarily find peace and a belief that transcends much
of its daily experience and rises above the deeply buried
hostilities of those who love.

Adam, as the first son of God and father of all human sons, in sacred symbolism is the image that expresses what man is that Christ is not. Whether he is
believed to be true in the literal or metaphorical sense,
the son and father symbols express some of the deeper
meanings in the cluster which surround the human
father. Adam is not only father to all mankind and husband to Eve, but he is the first son of God just as Christ
was his only "begotten Son." Through Adam's hus-
bandly relations with his wife, Eve, original sin, the
curse of mankind, was passed on to all succeeding generations of his children; thus a father-god's curse on
(his and) Adam's children becomes part of man's eternal
inheritance.

Adam, the son, autonomous and free and by free will
capable of knowing and choosing between good and
evil, chose Eve and evil and thereby rejected the father.
It was then that he was banished and cut off from his

father. Christ, the other son, refused to reject his father and, when tempted, resisted the tempter, returning to sadistic mankind to suffer and be slain that he might save his cruel human "brothers" and return to his father. The hostility of a father to his son and of the son to him is movingly portrayed by the image of Adam; but he, too, is a son lost in a world his father made, yet which he, the son, feels responsible for. He is the guilty man who lost perfection for himself and for his children because (he feels) his father cannot forgive him. When he clung more closely to his wife (and by implication to their own family) than to the paternal family of his father, he thus chose earthly evil as against heavenly good. But, in fact, Adam is also the father who in the attitudes of his "sons" is blamed for the pollution of all his progeny because of his relations with his wife, their mother. When he is forced out of the Garden of Eden he is thrust out of the household of God. He is the unforgiven son with a father with whom man has not made peace. Adam, the father, although blamed "by all mankind" for their human ills and their destinies, is more important as the rejected son who loses his first birthright and is cut off from the father. In him the faithful can punish themselves and express opposition to all fathers.

This image of Adam may be seen as a perfect fantasy of what a spiritually rejected man should be, and wishes to be—the model of thwarted physical, moral, and spiritual perfection. Adam before his defeat was the perfect man; in the present interpretation he represents for those who believe a projected dream of human perfection. In the beginning he was ritually clean, not in need of prayers, sacrifice, or any Christian rites which now symbolically relate men to God, the present inadequate substitutes for the wholly satisfying direct face-to-face relations believed once to have existed between Adam and God. When he ate the fruit, Adam—symbol of man's innocent self—became ritually unclean and therefore out of relation with the sacred world and his God. The pollution of all mankind and the inception of original sin occurred when Adam, by an oral and alimentary act, swallowed sacred, ritually forbidden fruit. Adam, the human father of all, becoming ritually unclean, pollutes all men generated from him. When Adam, image of all men, fell, man (the referent) fell too. Thus man's vision of his pure self is symbolically always accompanied by guilt and the moral accusation that he is inadequate because he cannot live up to his ideal of moral and spiritual perfection. For those who believe in these symbols, the biological generations listed in the Sacred Book, supposedly tracing their beginnings from Adam, validate their feelings about mystical contagion and transmission of spiritual pollution. "After Adam's fall, Adam's progeny is like a race of wingless birds still destined only for God's spiritual sky yet only able to crawl along the earth."

Sacrifice, Suicide, and Tragedy

The Christ symbol, "the New Adam," is the image of man's moral self and the moral life of the collectivity stated in the form of family life and expressing much of it. In him men can give perfect moral love to their fathers and, through their kinship to him and the father, as brother to all others. Hostilities are suppressed. The images of the rebellious Adam and his attractive wife (mother of all men) functioning to express human

faults and to evoke the deeper and forbidden fantasies
of the non-rational levels are pushed aside and in the
drama superseded. Each man and the entire collectivity
are "saved" from themselves and their sense of guilt.
The sons kill themselves and in the image of Christ as
a "perfect act of love" voluntarily and vicariously offer
themselves to their father. In this perfect act there can
be no hatred. In him fathers and sons are one and
brothers are united in heavenly grace.

> Even as in the first Adam [Michel declares], the en-
> tire human was virtually *persona ingrata et
> maledicta* (displeasing and accursed) before God,
> so in the second Adam, Christ, all mankind be-
> comes virtually before God a *persona grata et bene-
> dicta* (acceptable and blessed of God). Christ, re-
> plete with sanctifying grace and with charity not
> merely as an individual but rather as head of the
> Church, as universal man in whom the entire race
> is as it were condensed, achieved an act of perfect
> love of his Father. As a result of this act he is ever
> the man universal in whom all mankind is con-
> centrated, the object of the infinite pleasure of his
> Father.[9]

The "family" meal provides a perfect set of images
for the evocation of the deep feelings involved. Food
and drink as facts are in the very center of man's feeling.
[27] In the family meal and sharing with brothers, sisters, and parents the food assumes moral significance.
Around it the meanings of family life can be expressed
and the moral authority of society made significant.
Here, too, the deep positive feelings of love that men

9. Michel [74], pp. 40–2.

feel for each other can be expressed and those motions belonging to the deeper levels of the species which Kropotkin categorically dealt with as "Mutual Aid" can be symbolized. [62]

And by them and with them their opposite, hostility and hatred, can also flow and be purged in the symbols of the brutalities of the killing on the cross. The elder brother is killed and offered to a father, who, they implicitly believe, is sufficiently in the fantasied image of their own families to approve and demand such sadistic collective actions. The myth of the Mass and the Crucifixion purges men of the pollution of their own self and collective disapproval. Their guilty selves can be free from the distress of each life and from the collective accumulation of generations. The competitive hostilities of organized life can be submerged or transformed into the spiritual identification with the sacrificed son. Purgation of hatred and guilt in his slaying and the assumption of grace at the "banquet table" of kindred —perfect sons before a benign father—are symbolized in the giving and the taking of the two parts of the Mass of the Faithful. This is the dialogue, the exchange of signs between God and man. The sacred image of the family provides its powerful symbols to arouse the totality of men's feelings and mobilize them for moral action.

Durkheim's conception of the altruistic form of suicide often found in the actions of human beings [35b], Kropotkin's theory of mutual aid among the members of different species, including men [62], and Freud's theory of totemism [41c] help us to understand the positive factors contributing to the efficacy of the sacrifice and its emotional validity among those who believe. The altruist may give up his life for the good of the moral life of the collectivity or for the maintenance of a moral principle. Many species, including the other primates, "sacrifice" their own egoistic satisfaction to help or benefit others in the group. All is not competition and individual struggle for existence. This form of "love," a feeling for the good and benefit of others, in its extreme form is expressed by the sacred concept of Agape. Nygren declares: "Agape is spontaneous and unmotivated . . . a free gift" that is "indifferent to value" in evil or good men. It "freely spends itself." [10]

Complete unselfish love is the epitome of self-sacrifice and mutual aid carried to the point where the self may be destroyed for the collective moral order. In the Mass each son dies for the father, and in so doing subordinates self to the authority of the moral order. Since the rites surrounding the sacrifice are partly death rituals expressing the wish for immortality and the fear of death and the destruction of the self, they also allow men, by anticipating their own deaths and by voluntarily and vicariously living through His sufferings and death, to train themselves and thus prepare for death. This long preparation for death in the constant re-enactment of Christ's death helps to release their anxieties and control their panic. The myth of human triumph over the human tragedy of death, in the gift of the entire self to God through the image of the sacrificed Christ, allows each voluntarily to sacrifice himself and in so doing save himself.

When viewed as a drama, the Christian myth's basic theme is seen to be the fearful struggle between life and death for each man's destiny, and its climax: the ultimate triumph of life. The life of a Divine being—his

10. Nygren [84], pp. 75–6.

birth, suffering, death, and resurrection—provides the plot. The efficacy of the sacred play lies in the dominant identification of the audience with the sacred hero and secondary identification with his adversaries. Just as the human members of an audience identify with the human hero who triumphs, so the worshiper and the audience of Christ also triumph over death.

But this sacred drama represents the collective history of ten thousand years of authoritative fathers and submissive and rebellious sons and a multitude of cults and cultures. Its symbols contain the non-rational meanings of the species and collective life of men in societies. The truths it contains, the significant non-rational beliefs, feelings, and actions it expresses and evokes, cover the entirety of what man is and wishes to be. This kind of understanding is beyond the simple logic of rational men; too often, in this scientific age, men, proud of their disciplined intellects and rational inheritance, have dismissed it as unworthy equipment for those who seek to know the nature of reality.

The rational pursuit of knowledge of course must continue; its value is self-evident. Ways must be devised, however, by which men can enter the non-rational domain of human understanding and there find the secrets and strengths of individual and collective life. Through the ages our species has lived in the harsh realities of the world and collectively accumulated a store of understanding on which it successfully operates. This is a product of its organic evolution, its non-rational world of meaning and the thin crust of rationality. All of this knowledge is part of men's adaptation as a highly successful animal species. For the last few centuries we have partly succeeded in developing a scientific understanding of ourselves and the world around us. For further aid we need to turn to our non-rational collective and individual mentalities, for the tools of rationality are not enough. With equal ingenuity and skill, we must learn how to develop those deeper understandings of human beings. Perhaps when we do so we shall achieve even more spectacular results in our understanding of this subliminal world of belief and feeling than we have gained from rationality and logic. Myth and non-rational belief may need their own rules of inquiry. In them we may make new discoveries about the older meanings of man and develop new and better ways of solving his problems and determining his fate.

Part V

Transition and Eternity

Introduction

Rituals, whether they be formal and explicit or informal and implicit in human behavior, symbolically state the meanings and social values of some part of the world in which the group is involved. What is concerned may be an object in the natural environment, such as water or food; some part of the social order, such as the family; a status, such as that of a ruler; or at the supernatural level the meanings and values attributed to a god. Sacred rituals may combine all three at once; for example, a sacred ceremony of totemism expresses the meanings and values of the animals of the natural environment, the significance of the family and clan, as well as the values and meanings attributed to the totemic deities. *Rites de passage* are transition rituals, which are given particular attention in Part III. They mark the critical moments in the life career of the individual, particularly those of birth, puberty, marriage, and death. Those of birth, puberty, and marriage are likely to give more emphasis to the here and now, those of death to the spiritual significance of eternity.

The problem of sacred time as organized and symbolized in the liturgies and public worship of the Protestant and Catholic churches is studied, and evidence about collective and individual time is examined in the first chapter of Part V. The secular time of objective physical reality and science and the non-rational time of the species and the moral order, realized in the several systems of thought, are investigated and their significance for human existence discussed in the next chapter.

The last chapter deals broadly and directly with the structure of non-rational thought as an important way of knowing on which man depends.

CHAPTER 9

Sacred Time

The Problem: Time Symbols and the Sacred Year

Since in the rational and non-rational thought of Yankee City notions of time are basic and penetrate all mental life, and since faith in Christian symbols, founded on the family and the species, permeates most of the collectivity, it would seem that an inquiry into the possible interrelations of the two systems of signs and the worlds of meaning they represent should give us increased understanding and possibly be rewarding, too, with a view of some part of the master plan which holds the several systems of belief and value within one mental universe. The worship of the Christian Trinity brings forth the deepest and most persistent primitive emotions of the animal world of the species and relates them to those from the moral and spiritual orders which are the highest and most recent achievements of man's collective life. The notions of social time, largely founded on the cultural adaptations that men make to each other, and the constructs of objective time, [46] products mostly of technological adjustments to the outside world and the universe, are united in Christian symbolism, [17] as in all systems of religious thought. The youngest school child in Yankee City knows that "Christmas comes but once a year" and that Easter Sun-

day is different from all other Sundays of the year. [3]
Still others in many of the present Protestant congregations of the city know about and are fostering the "liturgical revival" and the institution of sacred seasons and
holy days and an ordered public worship in their
churches. Meanwhile, the Catholic Church continues to
maintain the yearly liturgical cycle of seasons, with
Advent leading to Christmas, Lent to Easter, and the
other holy seasons with their own days of significance.
In them the symbols of time and those of the Christian
supernatural join and are one, and in so doing become
something more than what they are separately. [74]

To examine this problem, direct our inquiry, and
determine our theory and choice of method and relevant evidence, we will begin by asking a series of questions: How are the several notions and symbols of time
related to the Christian symbolic structure and the non-
logical mental world it expresses? What is the scientific
and social significance of this relationship? Given these
answers, what can we learn that will provide explanations about the mental life of the society? The several
answers will be derived from, and refer to, several levels
of thought and behavior. To begin our inquiry we must
briefly review the relevant facts about the signs, seasons,
feasts, and fasts and their relations to each other in the
sacred calendar. The visible sacred calendar, a sign system which refers to the Christian signs of public worship, will be a major part of our evidence. The variations among the evangelical, non-liturgical and liturgical churches, including Episcopalians and Catholics,
will be considered and the variations and uniformities
noted. [32, 106]

We will ask about the meanings of these signs as rep-

resentations of the rhythms of collective life and how
their meanings are related to those of social and objective chronological time. Since the holy days and sacred
seasons advance not as cold arithmetical numbers, as
they appear on a secular calendar, but in dramatic
rhythms of emotional intensity and modes of emotions,
we must learn what the emotional rhythms are and
inquire about the significance of the recurrent periods
of affective intensity and relaxation, even perhaps
apathy. What are the periods of sacred joy, sorrow, love,
and other human emotions? And what are the meanings
of their rhythmic evocations to the functioning of the
collectivity?

We will begin by examining the present state of
yearly public worship in the several church calendars of
Yankee City. [102a, 102b] The evidence runs from the
great liturgical structure of Catholicism, which has held
firmly to the holy days and seasons of the past and has
added to and strengthened them, through the liturgical
Protestant churches such as the Episcopalian, with its
prayer book and outward signs of sacred worship, to
local and national variations of the evangelical churches
and the Unitarians. Furthermore, these differences and
similarities cover a history from the time when the Congregationalists and others in Puritan times destroyed all
liturgical worship to the present and what we are here
calling the Protestant Counter Reformation and liturgical revival in Yankee City and America.

Stafford in his *Christian Symbols in the Evangelical
Churches,* discussing the "restriction of the forms and
symbols" of Christian tradition, says,

> The various Catholic, Episcopal and Lutheran
> churches are professedly liturgical and make exten-

sive use of the traditional forms and symbolism inherited from the early Christian Church, or developed in the period of magnificent flowering of
medieval religious art which preceded the Reformation. During the early stages of the Calvinistic
Reformation, much of this heritage was thrown
into the discard by wrathful reformers, who
wrought havoc on priceless treasures of religious
art in Scotland, England and other parts of Europe.
Of three hundred sixty Celtic crosses, said to exist
in Scotland prior to the Reformation, only two
exist today. John Calvin permitted gratification of
the ear through poetry and music, but denied gratification of the eye. Genesis 1:31 was overlooked.
In attempting to uproot "superstitious" and "idola-
trous" usages, the Calvinists committed many destructive excesses and, for the sake of stark contrast
to Roman Catholic custom, kept their churches almost completely bare of everything that might
appeal to the imagination and the esthetic sense of
the worshipers. Every candid student of history will
admit that they had much provocation. Nevertheless, it now appears that the catharsis was too severe.

The present liturgical renaissance, after a passage of
time, he says,

> . . . has brought the inevitable backward swing of
> the pendulum from the extreme Calvinistic posi-
> tion regarding forms and symbols, and today we
> find a considerable number of Presbyterian, Con-
> gregationalist, Baptist and Methodist churches in-
> troducing enriched forms of worship, altars, crosses,
> candles, vestments and other ecclesiastical equip-

ment that would have been darkly frowned upon,
even as late as the beginning of the century. Apparently a concomitant of all this is a deepening of
reverence for the sanctuary as such. . . .[1]

The liturgical renaissance in the evangelical churches
such as the Congregational and others in Yankee City,
once the icon-breakers of Puritan times, makes it less
easy to draw sharp distinctions among churches about
the use of the liturgy in public worship. The present
*Guide for Members of Congregational and Christian
Churches,* used in Yankee City and cited to our research
to describe what Congregationalists do, declares, "The
observation of the Christian Year goes back to the
very earliest days of the Church . . . when the Christian religion became established . . . the celebration
of memorial days significant to the Christian religion
grew in importance . . . Within a few hundred years
the Christians had developed the observance of two
great seasons—Lent, the period preceding Easter, and
Advent, the period preceding Christmas." The Puritan
Reformers, in their efforts to free themselves from the
control of tradition "retained only the Bible, some of
the hymns, and the observance of Sunday. . . . They
rejected," the *Guide* continues, "the beautiful and
symbolic ideas which have helped to make the older
churches places for reverent worship . . . In New England this attitude went to the extreme of preventing
by law the observance of Christmas."

The Protestant liturgical revival has reached the point
where the Congregational *Guide* in Yankee City provides a full calendar for the Christian year with a

1. Stafford [106], pp. 21–2, 24.

liturgy of over sixty pages presented for the sacred
season (see Chart 9). "The Congregational and other
non-liturgical bodies," it declares, "have been making a
study of the values in historical Christian culture . . .
Christian symbolism is [now] being used, the cross appears in many churches. The revival of interest in the
observance of the great days of the Christian year is of
special significance to the worship program of the
Church."

Despite the surge of new interest and liturgical manifestations in the "non-liturgical" churches and the present elaboration of full liturgical seasons, including
many of the great festivals (the Annunciation of the
Virgin Mary on March 25th, for example), the evangelical churches have yet to develop the elaborate rituals
and accompanying myths with detailed biblical and
traditional references that are common in the Catholic
and liturgical Protestant churches. The forces of rationalism and revolt are still strong. However, this new
Counter Reformation in the Protestant Church, emphasizing the visible signs of sacred thought to communicate the non-rational mysteries of the spiritual world
more effectively than words, continues to gain strength.

The Protestants, once fearful of the distortions and
"earthly impurities" believed to come from the generations of churchly men and women who, in the thousand-
odd years after the "books" of the Bible were written,
added their own signs to the liturgy, are now filling the
old liturgical seasons with their own feast days and
their liturgies with words and sentiments and interpretations of sacred life now considered appropriate for a
given season. Meanwhile they are reincorporating the
older liturgical symbols and seasons into their calendars

Catholic [a]	Episcopal [b]	Congregational [c]	Presbyterian [d]	Methodist [e]
Advent	Advent	Advent Season	Advent Season of Expectancy	Advent Season of Expectancy
Christmastide	Christmastide	Christmastide	Christmastide Season of the Nativity	Christmastide Season of the Nativity
Time after Epiphany Septuagesima Remote Preparation	Time after Epiphany	[Sundays] After Epiphany Three Sundays next before Lent	Epiphany, Season of the Evangel	Epiphany, Season of the Evangel
Lent	Lent	Lent	Lent Season of Renewal	Lent, Season of Penitence and Renewal
(Holy Week)	(Holy Week)	(Holy Week)		
Paschal Time Eastertide	Paschal Time Time after Easter	The Sundays from Easter Day to Whitsunday	Eastertide Season of Resurrection	Eastertide Season of Resurrection
Time after Pentecost	Time after Pentecost	Whitsuntide the week following Whitsunday	Whitsuntide Season of Holy Spirit, Expansion of Church	Whitsuntide Season of Expansion of Church
		The second half of the Christian Year from Trinity Sunday to the Advent Season	Kingdomtide Season of the Kingdom of God on Earth	Kingdomtide Season of the Kingdom of God on Earth

a. Dom F. Cabrol, O.S.B., "The Liturgical Year and Prayer of the Time," *The Roman Missal*, in Latin and English (P. J. Kenedy and Sons, 1922), pp. xiv–xxi. Rt. Rev. Fernand Cabrol, O.S.B., *The Year's Liturgy* (New York, Benziger Brothers, 1938).

b. Calendar for 1952, *The Living Church Annual*, Yearbook of the Episcopal Church, 1951 (New York and Chicago, Morehouse-Gorham Co.). *The Book of Common Prayer* (New York, Oxford Univ. Press).

c. Calendar, the Congregational *Guide* (Pilgrim Press, 1952).

d. Calendar of the Christian Year, 1952–53, *Presbyterian Plan Book*.

e. "A Calendar and Lectionary for the Christian Year," *The Book of Worship* (The Methodist Publishing House, 1945), pp. 209–12.

Chart 9. The Seasons of the Sacred Year

(see the earlier discussion of Mother's Day). These include days of significance to the Church and those taken from the larger collectivity's holidays. For example, in the Christian year of the Congregationalists are "Race Relations Sunday" to be celebrated on the Sunday

nearest February 12, Lincoln's Birthday; Independence
Day, "the Sunday next before July 4th"; Labor Sunday,
Thanksgiving Sunday, as well as Forefathers' Day "in
honor and memory of the Pilgrim Fathers." Reforma-
tion Sunday is placed on or near October 26th by the
Presbyterians.

The testimony of some of the local ministers brings
out the Protestant situation in Yankee City and provides evidence about the liturgical movement and the
surviving sense of local independence and concern
about visible sacred signs. "There is a strong liturgical
revival in the Protestant churches here in Yankee City.
We wish to bring in more beauty," the minister of the
largest Congregational Church said (1952). "There is
a general feeling that it is a good thing to bring the old
symbols back into the church. For the last ten years
we have been following the Congregational Calendar
[see Chart 9]. Both we and the First Church follow it
entirely. If you get the church calendar it will tell you
exactly what we do. We also place more emphasis on
the ordinances. The two [he used the word sacraments
later] we observe are Baptism and Communion. Marriage can either be an ordinance or a sacrament according to the decisions of the minister."

The minister of the liturgical Episcopal Church
(1952) said with considerable satisfaction that "all the
churches in Yankee City are beginning to reinterest
themselves in the liturgy. A number of the liturgical
seasons are being recognized again, particularly Advent
and Lent, by such churches as the Congregational. The
Episcopal Church here has always followed the seasonal
cycles of the prayer book and observed all of the

ordinances and sacraments that the Episcopal Church has always observed."

The Presbyterian minister stated that "we follow local judgments about what will be done and not done to celebrate the seasons. Although we don't place much emphasis ourselves on the liturgical seasons, I myself follow the *Presbyterian Plan Book* (see Chart 9) of the General Assembly of the Presbyterian Church. We pay attention to such days as Christmas, Easter, Thanksgiving, and sometimes Pentecost [Whitsuntide]."

It was clear from the general tone of the interview that he took pride in the local independence and freedom from what he thought might be domination from outside sources. However, it was also apparent that he used the information sent out by the central authorities to guide his selection of topics appropriate for the several seasons of the liturgical year.

Catholic authorities testify that the liturgical year "is one united whole"; the most cursory examination shows that it traces "the different phases of Our Lord's life from Advent to Pentecost," and thereafter the development of the Church and its relation to the Holy Ghost.

The several seasons usually recognized in the various churches are: Advent, Christmastide, Time after Epiphany, Septuagesima (Period of Early Preparation), Lent, Eastertide, and Time after Pentecost or Whitsuntide (see Chart 9 for each church). The several periods (the Catholic Missal says) "are regulated by the three chief feasts of the year, Christmas, Easter, and Pentecost"; the first appearing on a fixed date, December 25; the second, a movable one, on the first Sunday after the first full moon of the vernal equinox; and the last appearing fifty days after Easter, also a movable feast, dependent on Easter. Advent, with four Sundays, is a period of three to four weeks from Advent Sunday to Christmas Eve. The length of Christmastide is dependent on the time of Septuagesima Sunday, which may fall on any day from January 16 to February 22. It includes all Sundays after Christmas "to the number of six."[2] (See Chart 10).

2. *The Roman Missal* [96], pp. xiv–xx.

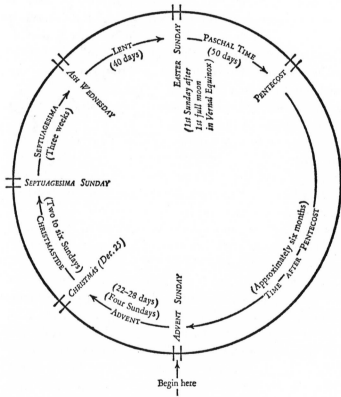

Chart 10. The Sacred Cycle of Time

The extent of Septuagesima is only three weeks; "the duration of the season is invariable," but its beginning is dependent on the position of Easter. Lent is always a period of forty days, extending from Easter Sunday (March 22 to April 25) back to Ash Wednesday (see Chart 10). Eastertide extends forward from Easter Sunday for fifty days to the Feast of Pentecost or Whitsunday. At present it is the practice in some churches to extend it "to the Saturday before Trinity Sunday." Time after Pentecost, the longest liturgical period—approximately six months—varies in length depending on the date of Advent Sunday and the end of Paschal Time (certain churches divide it into two seasons). This season, of secondary importance, expands or contracts according to the demands of the more important ones directly related to the great feast days celebrating the two crises in the life of Christ: his birth and death.

Starting with Advent, it is immediately evident that the liturgy follows very closely a series of irreversible events directly related to the life cycle of Jesus. Beginning with the preparation for his birth and continuing thereafter with his childhood, his presentation in the Temple, later fasting and similar events, and ending with the last few weeks of his life, the liturgical drama exactly parallels the biblical accounts. The last periods portray his passion, crucifixion, the events of his resurrection, his ascension into Heaven, and finally, at Pentecost, the descent of the Holy Spirit from Heaven to the apostles and the birth of the Christian Church. This whole period, from the beginning of Advent to Pentecost, can be viewed as one sacred cycle. The feast days and other liturgical events after Pentecost are not chronologically arranged. They may or may not follow an objective time order.

As symbols the central and minor characters of the Christian calendar are infused with the ultimate values and beliefs of the moral order and the emotional needs of the species. Each year they act out a story which narrates and expresses in material form the symbolic significance of man's existence and the meanings of the social and natural world which invade and surround his species. The human attribution of meaning to them is not merely individual projection but the group using common symbols which it has produced. In them the psychic needs of men are fulfilled.

The sacred characters and their actions, the Father, the Son, the Holy Ghost, and the Mother of the Son, being signs of man's long experience as a social species —a species whose physical acts are never free of social and spiritual infusions, whose spiritual life is filled with his physical and species nature—are collective expressions which are multi-determined. To take a parallel from another culture, the meanings of Bapa Indi, the great python god of Australia, are at once a deity, a snake, the weather, one of the seasons, the male half of the age-status structure, several clans, as well as one of the moral and spiritual forces of the whole society. [114a] Jesus Christ, the Son of God and the second Person in the Trinity, is not only a male with a human body born of a woman, the friend and leader of man, but the abstract Word and the summation of modern man's spirituality and supernatural beliefs. The Holy Spirit, the Ghost of God, the least corporeal of the three Persons of the Trinity, is a moral being who is the Comforter, Paraclete, and Christ's substitute in man's present life; yet even so he is infused with physiological and species significance, for in his most important act he is the symbolic energy and spiritual power which impregnated the Virgin. The differences, great as they are, between the Holy Ghost and Christ, the God-Man, as well as between God, the Father, are of degree, not of kind. All three Persons of the Trinity in the liturgy in varying degrees refer to and evoke feelings and beliefs which express all levels of man's existence.

The efforts of the logicians and some theologians to explain God's significance in a set of propositions are as futile as they would be dangerous should they be effective. The yearly story of the life of Christ expresses and evokes some of the deepest and most significant emotions men feel about themselves and the world in which they live. The great drama necessarily releases them from quandaries and dilemmas for which rational and moral values have no answers. Social and technical sources, in the ultimate sense, have no adequate solutions for man's will to live and his need to die. Furthermore, since the world of man is fundamentally a species world, to be significant the basic symbols which organize his private world must be images whose meanings remain close to the meanings of his individual membership in the species life of his group. This statement becomes dramatically true at crucial moments such as birth, marriage, and death, when the behavior of the species interconnects, or fails to interconnect, him and other (separate) individuals as ongoing beings in the flow of species behavior. At these moments there is the greatest concern, anxiety, and fear among those involved. The symbols of the death rituals, for example, express the sorrow and guilt of those who have lost someone they love and the anxiety of the survivors for their own anticipated death, as well as the disquiet and disorder felt by those involved. Rationally, morals and technical knowledge should suffice, but the brutal ultimate facts of death, felt and experienced at the animal level of species life, can be expressed only by the physical and oral acts of sacred ritual. A dead Christ brutally slain and his human body nailed to a cross, in fact once and in liturgical observance beyond count, can tell all that must be said; the identification of his passion and men's pain at their deaths allows each human animal to feel and know what it means to die. But since individual transience, in Christian drama, is merged in the myth of the collective Christ with the eternal myth of the eternal species, the pain of death is assuaged by the healing assurances of this symbolic transformation.

The liturgical calendar as a comprehensive system of signs relates the several non-rational time orders to each other and to the rational chronology of objective, solar time (see Chart 10). The sacred calendar is a sign system ordering certain events of the sacred myth into the form of a cycle beginning and ending at the same place. The sacred signs are meaningful directives to order the public worship of the collectivity. The sacred symbols, given linear time dimensions "bent" to the form of a circle, as Chart 10 depicts, are transformed into the *space* of a circle which is non-rationally given a beginning and an end. The beginning and end occur at the same liturgical point. The liturgical year covers the same length of time as the secular; like the secular year it, too, has its seasons; but whereas the natural year has four seasons, in fact or by ascription more or less equal

in length, that correspond with the course of the sun
and the changes in external nature *felt* and conceived
to be of significance to man's adjustment, the seasons of
the sacred calendar are more numerous, vary greatly in
length, may or may not have close correspondence with
the solar cycle, and are variable according to the usages
of church denomination. All of them, however, have to
do with the life crises of Christ.

The sacred calendar as a yearly structure of sacred
symbolic events is represented in the circular representation of Chart 10. In it objective time with its
beginning and ending, with duration in a linear series
of unending days, is transformed into a sacred circle
where duration is contained and forced to repeat itself
in the pre-established eternal forms of sacred time. At
the bottom, with Advent Sunday, the liturgical calendar
starts and ends. The breaks in the outer circle (||)
indicate the principal holy days when the seasons are
said to start and end. The arrows running clockwise
show the course of the seasons and their approximate
periods of time. Some of the principal holidays of some
of the churches are marked on the outer circle.

The liturgical year transforms the feelings of the
species as well as technological and social time, conceptually and emotionally, into the powerful symbols
of the life span of a god-man. Social and technological
time is thereby securely bound to, and confined within,
the significant emotional crises of human individual
experience. The cold, desireless technological time of
recurring nights and days, of equinoxes and solstices,
extending from infinitesimal divisions of a second
through a mathematical order into eternal duration,
yields to the fantasies and wishes, the hopes and fears,

that are intrinsic parts of the crises of birth, life, and death. The rhythms of our social order, expressed in the social calendar's weeks and months and other secular conceptions, are transformed into symbolic birthdays, deaths, and other important days of Christ and those who surrounded him. Thus social time is transfigured and "raised" to the sacred level through the individual time of incarnate God; accordingly it has become emotionally meaningful to everyone who believes, since everyone from his own experiences with his own life crises can project his private and public values and beliefs onto the action of this sacred drama. What is projected is not the idiosyncratic differences of individuals and the social world that they and others have experienced during their lives in the group, but the life cycle of Christ, God become human, who was born, lived, suffered, and died as a man, symbol of all men, although individually conceived, symbolically structured into a sequence of individual events that mirror the essentials of the life of the collectivity.

The sacred seasons, directly related to the symbolic structure of Christianity, and through it to the human social system and the species order, consequently evoke and express the non-rational meanings of life through its sacred symbols by the rational arrangement of objective time. Spiritually stated, the liturgy is said (by Pius Parsch, Augustinian canon) to have "a twofold function: to lead men to a worship of God pleasing to Him, and to conduct His grace to men."

For those who believe, the dull, discordant realities of ordinary existence are transfigured by the symbolic power of the liturgy. For them the fearful, separate beginnings and endings of human life are lifted from dark obscurity into circular, timeless tranquility. At this sacred level the brutal facts of secular mortality lose their harsh significance. They merge with and lose their meanings in the peace and quiet of the sacred symbols of immortality. The sequence of past events and their projection into the changing future disappear within the liturgical stillness of an eternal present. The self-contained sacred conceptual system expressed in the outward forms of the liturgy symbolically transforms yesterday and tomorrow into an eternal today. The recurring yearly feasts and festivals, forever in a self-contained, circular continuity without beginning and without end, express and refer to the eternal quality of the group and the human species. The liturgical circle of holy days and holidays celebrating the human life span and godly existence of Jesus Christ allows those who believe to escape some of the pain of life and their feeling of doom within this symbolic sanctuary. Here each mortal's fate is transformed by identification with the immortal fate of his God. Through the symbols of the liturgy one can say, borrowing from the theater, that "death takes a holiday," not for a brief interlude but forever and in all ways.

The system of sacred belief and ritual is not only an organized expression of the social and species life of the human individual and his group, but one of the effective controls exercised on the animal life of man. By use of it the ongoing species, with its interconnected members, maintains and controls part of the life of the group. The several types of ritual usage directly or indirectly constrain and control the physiological processes of the separate human organisms and the outward actions which interrelate them in time and space as members of the species. The biological crises, including those of birth, maturation, procreation, and death, and the feelings of the individual about them, the sensations of hunger, thirst, sex, and the satisfactions felt in eating, drinking, and copulation, as well as the feelings of cold and heat and other emotional reactions to the natural environment, in the liturgy are given recognition. The ritual usages employed are the several *rites de passage,* those of fasting and feasting, commensalism, and other forms of ritual eating, sexual prohibition, license, and the ritual usages of sexual contact.

The Sacred and Secular Rites of Passage—
Reified Signs of Age and Ritual Status

Since the whole liturgy is a drama, or several connected dramas, it can be examined by a methodology similar to that used for historical dramas. As research materials the two are quite similar, the several elements being: (1) the principal sacred characters, Christ, the other personages of the Trinity, the Mother, and the human and divine, positive and negative, characters; (2) their actions and the involvements of the hero, those of his birth, life, and death; (3) the actions as plot (story line) in his, and our, tragedy and triumph; (4) the several scenes—for example, Bethlehem and Calvary; and (5) the emotional involvements, identifications, and evocations officially assigned to the audience and to the actors who present the drama. For the liturgical and some of the evangelical churches there are a series of directions for moral conduct and the control of physical activities. To learn something more of the significance of this little understood and vastly unappreciated mode of human understanding, the empha-

sis in the discussion will be upon deriving a clearer
delineation of the non-rational clusters of sacred meanings.

The feast days of Jesus are the marks of his own
rites of passage, conforming in broad outline to Van
Gennep's classical conception of what they are in all
societies. [44] They include birth, naming, circumcision, the miraculous events that mark his maturity,
the Crucifixion, Resurrection, Ascension—and, in his
other Persons, his conception at the Annunciation and
the coming of the Holy Spirit at Pentecost. In Catholic
myth the rites of passage of the Virgin, beginning with
her immaculate conception and her nativity, through
the birth of her son until her death and assumption into
heaven, paralleled those of her Son. They provide a
spiritual age structure for women similar to the one
of Jesus for men. The worship given to God by the
faithful is paralleled by the veneration (hyperdulia),
not to say worship, given the Mother. Through the two
in Catholic worship, and the one in Protestant, the
(felt) meanings of species events that flow through the
family structure and their crucial moments are significantly marked and made symbolically meaningful. The
sacred ceremonies of baptism, confirmation, marriage,
and the death rituals symbolize the significance of these
events in the life of the devout.

The sacred symbols of the family—the Father, the
Son, the spiritual semen, and the Mother—exist outside the dimensions of time. They have their being in
eternal simultaneity. As such they symbolically express
the ever-present finality of the family system. As such
their meanings are circular in conformance with being
parts of a larger unity. It is only when the events in

the life of one of them (Christ) are viewed in sequence, or when the sacred family is related to the reckonings of human collective time, that the linear time of past, present, and future enters. It seems likely that the logical and very abstract concept of simultaneity, a comparatively recent acquisition of logical thought, is little more than what was once only felt by the individual as the oneness of the sensations coming from his separate bodily parts and—collectively—as the primitive nonrational sense of those elsewhere existing now as do those who are (spatially) present. Passing events change all this, and for the individual age becomes the dominant mental organization of experience.

The several sacraments and ordinances, various in number according to denomination, reorganize the sacred symbols of the family into a linear order of the changing events of individual age and rechannel the notions and feelings they express about the life cycle for those who believe and are involved with them. [65] The unchanging yearly cycle of spiritual eternity is given human meaning by the projection of the significance of the meanings of the individual life span and human rites of passage onto those of Christ as a symbol of the general collectivity. The family structures, those of birth and orientation and of procreation, are represented in new symbolic forms. The factual events which establish parent-child relations are first transformed into the symbols of individual time and a linear time extension. Thereafter the symbols of the human life cycle are reified into those of the Christ cycle and as such they meaningfully interpenetrate. In Christian thought, as we stated earlier, the family and its extended kinship structures, along with the Church, stand for the total collectivity. The age crises of the individual, made sacredly significant in the several sacraments, and the Christ symbols of the collectivity as an age aggregate blend and merge in the liturgy.

The symbolic events in the life of the Virgin, for example, carrying the unborn child in her womb for nine months from March 25 to December 25—in the liturgy from the Annunciation to Christmas—her accouchement and period of recovery from the birth of Jesus, her flight with him into Egypt, all accent the age and species relations of Jesus and his mother. In one period he is physically connected with her, his human life dependent on her human life, a foetal member of the species and a participant in the ongoing, continuing behavior which commits him to the physical and social generations of men. The given facts of his foetal life and his mother's life during that time correspond with the natural age order of the species and of all men and their mothers. As a sacred drama, it is a series of interconnected acts involving human beings and their gods, the natural and the supernatural. The center of the whole drama is in the transitional rites of the family and the life cycle of each human being.

The flow of species events and the related structural changes in the family's moral order and their liturgical recognition are depicted by Chart 11. It shows how the changing feelings and sensations of the growing individual and the moral and symbolic structures are ordered in an age-time arrangement. On the left the interlocking families are translated into a time order, running from the generation of ego's parents, through his birth, marriage, and the birth of the new generation. Immediately to the right are the critical events, species

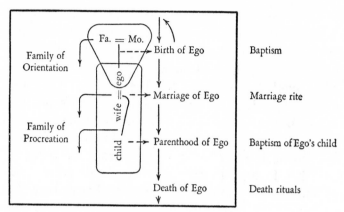

Chart 11. The Symbolic Recognition of the Flow of Species and Moral
Events in an Age Status System

and moral, and to the extreme right the symbolic age
rites that mark the passage of individual time. Out of
this intimate and, for those involved, easily comprehended system, a symbolic structure, world-wide in its
distribution and existing ages before Christianity, takes
form and attains non-rational validity. Species events
miraculously defined, but humanly felt as portrayed in
the collective symbols that comprise the life of Christ—
birth at Christmas and Easter, death in the events of
Good Friday and Holy Saturday—give human meanings in the collective worship of the liturgy.

The symbol system of the liturgy, responding to the
significant cultural and species meanings of human
facts, marks the objects and relations among them with
ritual expressions, the sacred meanings of which are
mysteries. At the points where the age and family facts
of the ordinary world of natural reality are connected
with the truths of religion, the church and religious

tradition erect a symbolic marker pointing to the critical changes of age and interpreting their meanings with
supernatural meanings. The liturgy provides an interrelated system of age symbols which refer to the facts
and provide their supernatural meanings. When the
logic of reason can apply, it is used freely; when it fails
to correspond with the order of natural facts and provide a "reasonable" and "believable" relation between
the sacred and natural orders, sacred symbolism is employed and the supernatural becomes the cause (the
"pre-established" form) which explains the natural.
Those who can avail themselves of faith readily move
from the starting point and progress from ascertained
fact to symbolic reified truth.

Chart 12, of the emotional rhythms of the sacred
season, depicts the rise and fall of intensity of feeling
as it is officially defined by the liturgy and by the human
and family nature of the events symbolized; the symbolic seasons (moving from left to right) are listed and
numbered. The degree of emotional intensity is shown
by the height or depth of the seasonal curve. Below the
list of liturgical seasons are the principal sacred characters and crucial actions occurring during the great divisions of the year. It will be noted that the principal
holy days and the occasion for their celebration are
given.

In general the emotions rise from Advent to Christmas and the birth of Christ and fall slightly thereafter;
the curve for the Period of Remote Preparation (Septuagesima) that leads up to Ash Wednesday rises rapidly
and reaches its highest peak at the death and resurrection of Christ at Easter, then lessens towards Pente-

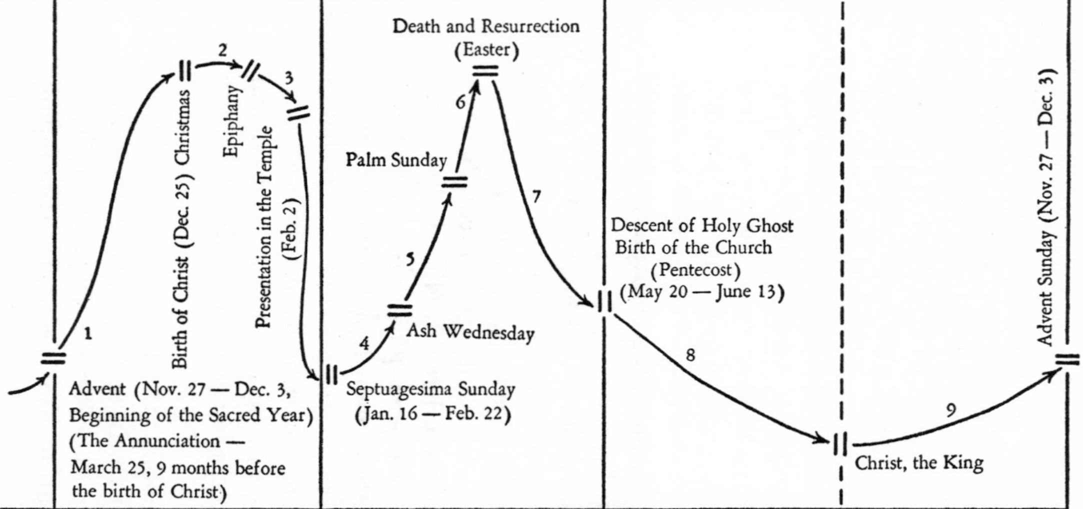

Seasons	1. Advent, 2. Christmastide, 3. Time after Epiphany.	4. Septuagesima, 5. Lent, 6. Holy Week, 7. Eastertide (Paschal Time).	8. Birth of Christian Church, 8–9. Time after Pentecost.	9. Kingdom of God on Earth.
Characters and their actions	God the Father, Holy Ghost and Christ and Mary (and Joseph). Impregnation of Mary, birth and baptism of Jesus.	Christ, the Apostles, the Passion, Lord's Supper, Crucifixion, Resurrection, Ascension.	The Holy Ghost, the Apostles (Peter and Paul and John). Forming of the Church and conversion of Gentiles.	St. Paul and the Apostles. Expansion of the Church.

Chart 12. The Emotional Rhythms of the Sacred Seasons

cost and falls into the period of least interest, Time After Pentecost.

Dom Cabrol, one of the great authorities on the Sacred Year, in his commentary on Holy Week makes abundantly clear the emotional rhythm and the liturgy's increasing intensity from the Period of Remote Preparation to Easter. He says, "We might compare the time from Septuagesima to Palm Sunday to a long road, which has brought us by a gradual but continuous ascent to the summit whereon we now stand. The three Sundays before Lent and the five which follow them are all really a preparation for Holy Week." [3]

The significance of the family structure, and the species and non-logical significances given to the Easter period, most clearly marked in the rites of Holy Saturday are secondarily accented on "Low Sunday" after Easter and the rebirth of Christ. Remembering that the symbols of this period were of direct significance to the initiates who were to be baptized in the womb of the font, previously impregnated by the Holy Spirit (see next section), we see the joyous theme of the celebration following Lent expressed and interpreted by the joyful melody of that Sunday's Gregorian setting. "The newly baptized," Cabrol says, "are as new born infants, who already instinctively long for the natural milk, a symbol of the first element of the Christian doctrine."

Paschal Time following Easter is a time of joy. It is the Holy Fifty Days, "a long continuous feast," once so in fact, now only by sign and emotion. This period is believed to be the oldest of the liturgical seasons. On Ascension Day, fixed by the Gospel text as forty days

3. Cabrol [17], p. 164.

after Easter, Christ ascends into Heaven. The Catholic Mass for the day makes its symbolic function clear: "Christ Our Lord, after His resurrection, appeared to all His assembled disciples, and, while they gazed at Him, ascended to heaven, in order to make us participants in His divinity . . . it is on this most holy day that Our Lord, the Only Son of the Father, placed the substance of our fragile nature, united to His own, at the right hand of the glory of God the Father." The scriptural reference in the Congregational *Guide*, "The Ascension" (Mark 16), also provides the biblical significance of the day.

Whitsunday, fifty days after Easter, a date exactly set by scripture, "celebrates the Day of Pentecost, the gathering of the first church, when the disciples were met in the upper room in Jerusalem, and Jesus' spirit was manifested to them, making them realize again that he lived. This sending of the Spirit," continues the Congregational *Guide*, "marked for the disciples the great new day of Jesus' continuing leadership of men."

"With the Feast of Pentecost," Cabrol explains, "the Holy Ghost has taken possession of the Church." [4] The ritual is the same as for Holy Saturday on the night before Easter.

During Time after Pentecost the Catholic liturgy uses once more St. Paul's Epistle to the Ephesians on the Nuptial Mass which relates the belief about the feminine nature of the Church with the masculinity of Christ in wedded union with the love of human males and females in marriage.

Michel, in speaking of the liturgy of the Trinity, presents the non-logical cluster of meanings and their

4. In general see *ibid.,* pp. 197–204.

theological significance. "It is he [Holy Ghost] who is
sent down to complete the fullness of Christ's mission,
sent down by both the Father and the Son after the
Son's return to the Father." He quotes Dom Grea to
interrelate the scriptural metaphors about the relation
of the Third Person to Christ as the Head of the
feminine body of the Church: "The Holy Spirit could
not be absent, and in the mystery of the Church united
to her Head, he is given to the Church; he lives in the
Church, breathes and speaks in her. And his presence
in her is a mysterious necessity of the hierarchy,
founded on the eternal necessities of the divine life and
of the society that is in God. And as he unites the
Son to the Father, so he unites the Church to her
Head . . ." [5]

The Holy Ghost has an important role in several
acts of the drama, particularly at the time of the Annunciation in the impregnation of Mary, where he
represents God and, for this particular event, symbolically is sacred semen, and at Pentecost when he returns
as one of the persons of the Trinity to the Church
and once again, in effect, plays a similar symbolic role.
This time, as with Mary at the Annunciation, he enters
the Church and fills her with his spiritual power. The
primary role of the Holy Ghost is essentially that of
being a substitute for the other two major figures of
the Trinity. In the Trinity, the unity and diversity of
men in society are represented, the three separate autonomous personae made one in the collective image
expressing the unity of the group—the Father, the
Son, and their connecting principle, the Holy Ghost,
separate yet one, the collectivity made in the image of

5. Michel [74], p. 36.

the family. He provides an abstract and formless spiritual image for the more material forms of the other two when the presence of either in the sacred acts involved might be awkward or embarrassing to the sentiments of Christians. A too close and realistic representation of the impregnation of Mary by God at the Annunciation would be embarrassing and difficult for the faithful to accept. The appearance of the Holy Ghost on earth after Christ's departure makes it possible thereafter for the resurrected Christ to be felt as an ever-present reality, permitting the faithful to reduce their sense of loss and deprivation by his disappearance to the sacred world. The return of the Holy Spirit at Pentecost and his entrance into the female body of the new church and into the spiritual life of each Christian as the Holy Spirit provide an intimate, enduring relation of the sacred with the ordinary world of men.

Whereas the Roman rite repeats the coital symbolism of the early initiation of the Catechumens as new Christians at the celebration of Whitsunday (see next section), the Presbyterians list Whitsuntide as the "Season of the Holy Spirit and the Birth and Expansion of the Christian Church," thereby clearly recognizing not only the biblical account of the "fiery tongues" of the Holy Spirit descending into the assemblage of the Apostles but the *birth* of the Church from this mythical union. In keeping with this masculine-feminine symbolism they also place the Annunciation and the impregnation of the Virgin Mary by the Holy Spirit, which resulted in the birth of the other holy symbol, Christ, on March 25th, nine months before his birthday.

The liturgical drama acts out the Christian myth as it is told in the Bible; it is also clear that what it expresses are the deeper emotions of the species, particularly those of the family and the age-grade system.

Holy Coitus and Sacred Procreation

The present Catholic rite and many Protestant rites of baptism, originally sanctioned by Christ himself and by the appearance of the Holy Spirit when he was baptized by John the Baptist, are greatly dependent on the early Christian rites of initiation used for *adult* pagans who went through a long period of training to be crowned and completed by the Easter rites of rebirth. During the rites of the catechumens on Holy Saturday night the initiates died with Christ and rose with him from the dead. The Catholic liturgy for Easter preserves and makes symbolically explicit what the shortened and more oblique Protestant and Catholic baptismal rites express in condensed form.

The principal ceremonies of the night before Easter are the blessing of the new fire, the rites of the paschal candle, the reading of the twelve prophecies, and the blessing of the baptismal font.[6] All of these overt rituals and oral rites, some of them with an extreme degree of literalness, symbolize (among other things) the power and significance of man's sexual life as a member of his species. Let us examine and analyze the symbols of this most important ceremony.

The candle, a principal emblem in these Holy Saturday rites, with its light and fire is officially a "symbol of Christ," to "enlighten the minds of the faithful" where "grace enkindles their hearts." When at this very solemn moment of bleakness and stark darkness which symbolize death and the end of things, when all lights

6. See *The Roman Missal* [96], "Holy Saturday," pp. 399–446.

are out in the church, fire is struck from a flint, the priest blesses the new fire (as the symbol of beginning and renewal) and appeals to God for his aid as "the author of all light." Then the triple candle is lighted and blessed and the deacon sings, "Light of Christ." Once more every year a new world begins, an old one ends, and new life triumphs over the deaths of all men.

"The darkness of sin" is overcome by the light and spiritual splendor of Christ. The feared symbol of death and feelings of ritual pollution and darkness are defeated by the triumph of light, symbol of life and spiritual purity. This is the symbolic "night which broke the chains of death," and man, with Christ, "ascended, conqueror, from hell." It is "the time and hour when Christ rose again from hell and man and the world were sanctified." "It is the time when Jesus Christ," says the Roman Missal, "paid for us to his eternal Father the debt of Adam and by his sacred blood cancelled the guilt contributed by original sin. The sanctification of this night blots out crimes, washes away sins, restores innocence to sinners and joy to the sorrowful. It banishes enmities and produces concord . . ." [7] After the reading of the twelve prophecies of the Old Testament, including those having to do with ritual pollution when the sin and wickedness of the earth are washed away by the flood and the earth purified, and the destruction of the evil Egyptians by the waters of the Red Sea, the priest begins the solemn rite of the blessing of the font. Water, sanctified and transformed into a sacred symbol, washes away pollution and cleanses the sinful earth.

Some of the more significant passages from this aes-

7. *Ibid.*, pp. 399–406.

thetically beautiful and symbolically significant rite of purification need further analysis. (The material used is taken from the Roman Missal.) In the rite, after the twelfth prophecy, Psalm 41 is quoted. "As the hart panteth after the fountains of water so my soul panteth after thee, O God. My soul has thirsteth for the living God." In the collect it is implored, "Almighty and eternal God, look mercifully on the devotion of the people desiring a New Birth who, like the hart panteth after the fountains of thy waters; so mercifully grant that the thirst of their faith made so by the sacrament of baptism sanctify their souls and bodies through our Lord." In the same collect, the priest invokes, "Almighty and eternal God, be present at these mysteries, be present at these sacraments of thy great goodness and send forth the spirit of *adoption* to regenerate the *new* people whom the font of baptism brings forth . . ." [8]

The priest continues saying, "O God whose spirit moved over the waters of the beginning of the world that even the waters might receive the virtues of satisfaction." He also says, "God, by water, washed away the crimes of the guilty world and of the deluge which gave the figure of regeneration."

The symbolic "fountains of water" which refresh the soul, the primal waters over which the Spirit of God moved at the beginning of the world, and the purifying water of the deluge which regenerated sinful man, are all symbolically invoked and with God related to the waters of the font of adoption where the "new people" are to be brought forth and "adopted" into

8. *Ibid.,* pp. 434–5. See the Missal for passages cited from the continuing ceremony.

God's spiritual family. The holy font is being formed into the image of the other spiritual water symbols and prepared to become the efficient symbol for the rebirth of the initiates. The female symbol, water, is being acted on by the male representative of a male god.

The priest divides the water in the font into the form of a cross and refers to God "who by a secret mixture of his divine fruit may render this water *fruitful* for the regeneration of man to the end that those who have been sanctified in the immaculate womb of this divine font, being born again a new creature, may come forth a heavenly offspring, and that all that are distinguished either by sex and body or by age and time may be brought forth to the same *infancy* by Grace, their spiritual Mother."

The officiant then touches the water with his hand. He says, "May this holy and innocent creature be freed from all of the assaults of the enemy" and "purified . . . by the operation of the Holy Ghost, the Grace of a perfection purification." The priest then makes the sign of the cross three times over the font. He says, "Therefore, I bless thee, O creature of water by the living God—by the Holy God—by the God who in the beginning separated thee by his word from the dry land, whose spirit moved over thee."

During this ritual the water in the font and the font itself take on a spiritually female significance, the priest being the male representative of the male God. Meanwhile, the transformation of the water continues. The priest declares, "I bless thee also by our Lord, Jesus Christ, his only Son who in Canaan of Galilee changed thee into wine by a wonderful miracle of his power— walked on thee dry foot—was baptized *in* thee by John

in the Jordan—and made thee flow out of his side—
and commanded his disciples to baptize and to be
baptized." The priest adds that the water's "natural
virtues of cleansing the body are also effectual for the
purifying of the self."

At this point the water and the font have not only
become spiritually transfigured into feminine sacred
symbols but have also been transformed into effective
ritual instruments for the purifying of the soul when
it is reborn and becomes Christian. For the first time
the priest sinks the paschal candle in the water. While
so doing he sings, "May the virtue of the Holy Ghost
descend into all of the water of this font and make
the whole substance of this water fruitful and capable
of regenerating." The waters of the Jordan into which
the Holy Spirit descended when Christ was baptized
are likened to a symbolic womb, the water made fruitful and the font capable of regenerating sinners.

When the priest divides the water, he declares, "May
he (i.e., the Holy Ghost) fertilize this water prepared
for the regeneration of man by the secretive mixture of
his light that by a holy conception a heavenly offspring
may come forth from the spotless womb of the divine
font as a new creature and may all who differ in sex or
age be *begotten* by parent grace into one and the same
infancy."

The sexual act is thus dramatized. The paschal candle
inserted in the font overtly states it. The oral rite in-
voking the intervention of the Holy Ghost cries for
a holy conception "in the spotless womb of the divine
font." The rite of baptism is formed in, and validated
by, the equated female symbols of the Annunciation
and the waters of the River Jordan.

The priest withdraws the paschal candle from the water. He intones, "Here may the stains of all sins be washed away. Here may human nature created to thy image and reformed to the honor of its altar be cleansed from all the filth of the Old Man; that all who receive this sacrament of regeneration be born again *new* children of true innocence."

The people are sprinkled and the priest pours oil of the catechumens in the water in the form of a cross. He says, "May this font be sanctified and made fruitful by the oil of salvation, for such as are regenerated therein unto life everlasting." He pours chrism (consecrated oil and spices) into the font. "May this infusion of the chrism of our Lord, Jesus Christ, on the Holy Ghost, the Comforter, be made in the name of the Trinity." The officiant then mixes oil and water and baptizes the candidates in the usual manner.

The candle as the symbol of the holy male God, Christ, is inserted in the fruitful waters of the "immaculate womb." The pure wax symbol of Christ (a product of the social labor of a community of bees), the spiritually potent chrism, and oil are dropped into the waters, and the spiritual womb of the ritual is thus made fruitful and capable of regenerating all men who come from it. They enter it sinful adults and come out innocent infants. But, symbolically, they do not come out of it for, by intent and ideally, they remain forever in the secure containment of the Mother's spiritual body. It need not be said that this rite and the beliefs which it expresses are a non-logical analogue of the Christian belief in the spiritual conception of Christ, the New Adam. Mary, the immaculately conceived, is impregnated by the Holy Spirit, the third person of the One God, and at this time she hears the words, "Hail Mary, full of Grace, the Lord is with thee. Blessed art thou among women and blessed is the fruit of thy womb [the Lord Jesus]."

The candidates, spiritual progeny of the baptismal symbolic sexual act, are "babes crying for the milk of salvation." The rite of baptism, an initiation of rebirth, is a symbolic statement of the marriage act, the resulting conception, and the birth of a new generation. More abstractly, it symbolizes the species relations necessary for biological continuity and the persistence of the social group. This rite dramatically acts out the spiritual union of Christ, the Bridegroom of the Church, with his holy spouse, and the spiritual birth and regeneration of the candidates. At baptism, Christ and the Church procreate a new Christian, recognize and mark this new creature as a member of their eternal family by "christening" him. The newborn in name, substance, and form, is in the likeness of the Father.

To go back to the ritual: meanwhile, the time being Holy Saturday, Christ lies dead in his tomb waiting for his return to life. The neophytes, too, are spiritually dead awaiting a rebirth to eternal life. On Easter morning they with Christ will come to life from death. The immaculate womb of the font of baptism "receives" the body which has "died unto sin," the initiate being immersed by the waters of salvation. The grave also receives the corruption of the body that has died and is to be reborn and, for many believers, restored as the same organism and the same person on Judgment Day. Thus birth and death are joined in the one transition rite. Moreover, both are related to the conjugal connection of Christ, the risen God, and the Church, his spouse.

Michel, in *The Liturgy of the Church*, makes this vividly clear: "The mystical union of the Church with Christ in his risen splendor puts her in a transport of joy that continues to vibrate through the liturgy of the whole Eastertide till the very consecration of this union on Pentecost Sunday. The newly baptized, who for this week will wear the white garment of their new bliss, rejoice at their rising with Christ to the new glory." [9]

There are several symbolic consequences of the symbolic transfiguration of death into birth. The open tomb of Christ and each human earthen grave out of which resurrected and reborn individuals come forth are implicitly feminine. The Christian symbols thus parallel, and are identified with, the idea of the earth as female and fruitful. In the rites of dedication for one of the principal cemeteries of Yankee City, which transformed secular ground into sacred soil, it was said to be the Mother and the grave, like Christ's tomb. The dead body like the sinful initiate polluted by the experiences in the world, following Christ's prototypical experience, and by use of the final rites and sacraments, would arise once more, born again from the womb of the earth. Symbolically death is but the beginning; it is the "conception" which becomes the final birth into the heavenly family of God.

9. Michel [74], pp. 138-9.

CHAPTER 10

Secular and Sacred Time: A Collective Product

The Calendar, the Clock, and Reality

Within the exact time-forms of the calendar, Yankee City's social and individual life rhythms ebb and flow, expand and contract; new experiences or old ones repeat themselves as the community's activities endlessly pour through its numbered days, its cycles of weeks, months, and years. Looking at the symbols of the calendar, Yankee City faces signs of reality; eternity flows through their ordered confines and finite existence is fixed and made meaningful. Their words and numbers are the visible signs of a system of concepts and values, a moral and mental order of social control, which organizes and gives meaning to much of the life of Yankee City and contemporary society. Its meanings reach beyond reason and the precise logical order of reference, stretch through the intangible, uneasy guesses of science and theology, and finally touch the edges of an unformed meaningless void which is nothingness. "Science is inevitably tied to dealing with time, but is ultimately driven to aesthetic or imaginative rather than logical grounds for selecting the way to formulate time relationships." [56]

Without the calendar, the contemporary life of

Yankee City as it is now lived would be impossible; with it, the events of today and yesterday are invested with form and significance. People's fears for tomorrow become more bearable, their hopes and wishes for the future more believable, because their emotions about what might happen are subjected to the control and meaning of the calendar's precise and invariable sequence of well-known and securely connected words and numbers.

Objective time is forced on each individual by his culture, but its meanings are never given more than the right to remain in the vestibule of each man's inner life. Objective time must recognize and adjust to the non-rational levels of personality and of the collective mentality—to the time of the self and to subjective, social time. Within each of us, far below what are said to be the "realities" of logic and culture, lies that "obscure inaccessible part of our personality" which Freud called the id, where "there is nothing corresponding to the idea of time, no recognition of the passage of time and . . . no alteration of mental processes by the passage of time." [1]

The calendar (and the clock) divides duration into a manageable series of interconnected representative compartments and thereby transforms its vague meaningless expanse into a time that men can conceive and understand. "A calendar," says Durkheim, "expresses the rhythm of the collective activities, while at the same time its function is to assure their regularity. . . . Try to represent what the notion of time would be," he exclaims, "without the processes by which we divide it, measure it or express it with objective signs, a time

1. Freud [41a], pp. 103-4.

which is not a succession of years, months, days and hours!" "Time," he says further on, "is an abstract and impersonal frame which surrounds, not only our individual existence, but that of all humanity. It is like an endless chart, where all duration is spread out before the mind." [2] Time thus conceived is a yearly cycle which tidily begins, contains, and completes a unit of duration. Each yearly cycle is related at its two ends with connecting ones that form a chain conceived to extend in a line from the present back into the past and on into the future. Often a festival marks the point where one link ends and a new one begins, thus ritualizing the separation of past from future time.

The conception of the earth's yearly movement around the sun, used by Western man (as well as others) to give precise form and human significance to the bleak, unyielding, and unmeaningful extension of duration, provides fixed points that give accurate, safe places on which to put marks saying that a bit of meaningless duration ends and another begins. The marks of the repetitive movements give Yankee City and Western man a feeling of security, of being on familiar ground where they know, feel, and can be sure about what is likely to happen. Enclosed within this system, collective memories of yesterday become a reliable and dependable map for knowing what will happen tomorrow, thus reducing anxiety about the future's uncertainties. If the facts of reality are obdurate and will not yield to technical efforts for the fulfillment of all man's wishes, then they must be dealt with in some other manner to allow him to survive as a species and permit normal affective and physical feelings to ex-

2. Durkheim [35a], pp. 9, 10.

press themselves. If man cannot control his fate, mold harsh reality to fit his creature wishes, and destroy the validities which feed his fears, he can do the next best thing by fitting the outer realities to the strict rational, conventional symbolic forms which he himself provides and controls. Many can go further and subject the rationalities of objective time to the evocative claims of the sacred year and non-logical demands of the past.

The Non-logical Structure of Time

The meanings of life were thus represented in the non-rational symbols of the Procession as events of ordered time which, moving out of the unknown toward, and into, a timeless region of earth and water, became the living time and space of Yankee City. There resting briefly, the significance of time developed into enduring importance in the recorded activities of the community. Then, at an ever-accelerated speed, we see the significant present move out beyond the city to the vast western distances, to the great metropolises, to the more important economic and social life of a powerful nation. The importance of time in Yankee City is not in the here and now but as it once was, in an enduring yesterday that has remained while present time has gone elsewhere. Since the end of the nineteenth century events are felt to be "too recent" and, while important, lack significance. They are not invested with the full social power of the mental life of the group. Yankee City is now enmeshed in the huge, dull world beyond it. Recent time in the meanings of the Procession lies sprawled and mired in the ordinary rounds of unimportant events. The splendor is gone; the power and the glory are elsewhere. Yankee City must go to them; they no longer come to Yankee City.

Within the non-rational feelings of today, time has run down. [7a] The spiritual and absolute certainty of the Protestant faith of the early fathers has been drained from the people, the great period has gone and only a diminished secular prestige remains. Yet as the nation grows into world greatness we, the people of Yankee City (the symbols of the Procession seem to say), who started and established things as they are, possess a unique kind of prestige shared only with those who were present when the Great Society came into being. Our present power is relatively weak, our contemporary prestige not conspicuous, but properly viewed in the context of the past we are identified with the most powerful symbols of the Great Society. To establish their claims as legitimate heirs and present holders of the great tradition, they who live elsewhere—the hundred-odd million—must come to us. In us the great tradition lives and our symbols legitimately express it.

Analysis of the forty-two scenes of the several time periods demonstrates that, although the whole Procession is a representation of the passage of time, and time as movement and change, in these same symbols there is also present a non-rational eternal finality. This static, unchanging, eternal quality has to do with the ultimate nature of man; it is in the fixed-forever of the species group. The eternal verities of the drama were in the unconscious assumptions that created it. By their sequential movement before the stationary reviewing stand, the scenes of the great Procession, precisely following each other chronologically, stressed the rational

and linear qualities of time. But the symbolic conventions of such dramatic processions demand that the
reviewing stand, those in it, and the public they represent, be still and rest in one place.

For that moment the lives of those who viewed the
spectacle were suspended and timeless. In them the
meanings of the Eternal City of St. Augustine were
present. Coming from the past, time moved by them.
The time-ordered events of the parade moved from the
starting place in Yankee City through the streets of the
city as *one* thing. The Procession itself, while trying to
emphasize the rationality of time, played havoc with it.
The meanings of objective time were non-rationally
contradicted. Although first things came symbolically
and logically first and the beginnings of history were
spatially and logically at the beginning of the Procession, while last things appeared at the end, to those in
the stationary reviewing stand their own time stood still.
All the scenes were parts of one timeless thing.

In the feelings of the people, past and present life
were one. Governor Winthrop and his Charter were of
a piece with Greely, the ancient living hero, for they
were of one substance. [123a] In this symbolic unity
the simultaneity of 1630 and 1930 was non-rationally
stressed. The great past of the ancestors was evoked and
symbolically lived in the present. Many sensed this. On
the first day of the celebration the minister of the oldest
church, which traced its being to the beginnings, said
to his congregation, "The Great Book of Life lies open
before our generation; today, in the scenes we produce [its] notable characters seem again to walk our
streets . . ." Those in the reviewing stand saw the
forty-two scenes move as the "one Book of Life" across

their vision, and pass on through the spaces of the city. In their diversity there was logical empirical time; within the non-rational meanings of their unity was the static, fixed quality of being. The timeless sense of species existence, felt as eternity, was present. The rationality of Durkheim's "Chart" depicting the points of time, and the deeply felt unconscious sense of total existence where, in Freud's findings, there is no time, were both present.

Despite the prevailing and perhaps necessary belief in the unitary character of time held by members of our culture, there are nevertheless many kinds of time. For our purposes we can divide them into what some philosophers have called objective and subjective time, forgetting their quarrels about one or the other being true, or all time being one or the other.

Objective time, as we said earlier, supposedly has to do with the world beyond man, particularly the movements of the earth, stars, and planets. Objective time is numbered and measured. [46] We think we take account of it by the clock, calendar, and the instruments of the physicists and astronomers. We relate objective time to our social life and regulate much of our existence by clock and calendar. Events are accordingly timed and regulated. The individual, being part of this action context, learns and internalizes it and makes it part of himself. Such "objective" time concepts are then applied to social age status, to biological change, and to the transitional activities of the individual through the age statuses and the events of his life history. Days, weeks, months, and years, anchored to a birthday, produce a person forever measured by "objective" time, but by a time to which he and others also attribute human values. By this means the time of the individual and the society can be named and numbered.

The time symbols of the Procession were multiple and diverse. There was the objective time of chronology and verifiable historical references. Events of men and the chronology of the planets were synchronized. Such references can be validated by many people and the self-correcting devices and criteria of science. Then there were the subjective levels in which the individuals involved possessed non-rational beliefs and feelings about time. Rational concepts were rearranged in a non-logical manner. These were systems of feeling non-rationally organized. Ideas were syncretistically arranged.

The symbols of non-logical or subjective time, on the other hand, are laden with affect. These non-logical feeling systems are not necessarily individual; more often they are social. The vast world of feelings and the images which express them are passed on from generation to generation and change as experience affects them. The subjective, non-logical (social) time of Yankee City can compress the objective time of half-centuries into nothingness and extend a mere ten years into what, measured by objective time, would be a century.

The symbols of time (and of space and all other meanings) are not only signs of constructs and logical thinking, but are available and used by the non-logical feeling systems of a people and their culture. Moreover, they are subject to the needs and demands of a still deeper level of being and understanding. The non-logical meanings of our mental life are products of the species group in interaction with its environments; meanings accumulate in, and are reordered by, the organisms that compose the species. The limitations of the species, and the actual extension of its capabilities into experience and environment (accepting or not accepting available stimuli), provide the limits of knowing. For time, and indeed all knowing, cannot go beyond the nature of species being. The turtle, the chimpanzee, the firefly, and the angleworm, as species, by their own nature and being have their inherent limitations and extensions of understanding. So it is with man. That which makes the human species different from all others makes its knowledge different.

The logical objective categories of time and space, the non-logical affective systems, and the species sensations constitute three levels of understanding. Each refers to worlds of reality. They refer to the physical objective world beyond man, to the ongoing organismic world of the species, and to what the individual experiences when he experiences himself. In terms of time, physical time is the sequence of events (which may or may not have the form it is believed to have) that occurs in the world beyond man. Social time is beyond the self; it is a sequence of happenings, with or without form, which take place in the world of social relations. Self time is a sequence of events, with or without form, having to do with what it is I am and do.

We thus have three broad categories referring to the several realities: objective time and space references to physical, social, and self phenomena; non-logical systems of feeling, which refer to the same three; and species sensations, which order experience about the objective world, beyond other organisms as they are socially related to each other, and the self as a being apart.

Tradition and the Emergent Society

We must return to our consideration of the *delayed, indirect,* and unintentional use of signs. In the literature the economic, political, and religious aspects of autonomous men have been stressed. [89*a,* 89*b*] This is not enough. Above everything else this shift in the Western world's culture was related to the release of secular and sacred words from oral control and from the face-to-face control of their meaning and overwhelming power to influence action and behavior. When they were freed from the bodies of the users and were no longer bound by the necessities of direct action, in which mouths and ears create and consume perishable sounds and signs, a whole set of new possibilities developed. If men can symbolize saying-what-they-mean so that it is no longer a momentary act of attribution but something that persists in time, the possibilities are limitless for extending the number and kind of people to whom signs can be "sent" and who may be influenced *indirectly* by the sender.

In the simpler stages of man's life, for words and other objective signs to continue circulating in the limited environment of those who create and maintain them, it is of course necessary that individuals of each generation relearn and refashion them as signs of communal agreement as to what they mean and are signs of. It is said that words are exchanged in communication between the sender and receiver. More correctly, sender and receiver, when conversing, stimulate themselves with *socially selected sounds and silences.* As long as this verbal stimulation is labial and auditory and strengthened with the auxiliary gestures of an interpersonal and imme-

diate context, those who know what the words are meant
to convey and who choose to speak, or choose not to,
are in positions of great strength. They have control
over these vehicles of collective knowledge, which can
be, and often are, of incalculable power. When they
speak, those who cannot understand what is told them
may be placed fortuitously in positions of helplessness.
They do not have some of the tools necessary to control
their environment; the others do. The control of the
use of words demands that their meanings be known by
the user, and he can choose to speak or not speak, hear
or refuse to hear.

When words are written, being no longer dependent
on the *immediate* organic environment where sounds
and silences stimulate meaning in live organisms, several powerful new factors enter. Freed from immediacy, words can now go elsewhere, beyond the interpersonal context. The secret intimate written words of
two people—for example, a love letter—freed from
sound, may leave their first context and move into a
space limited only by human environment and into a
time limited only by mankind's survival. Those who
use words in the present or future by the use of the
written form of delayed communication may "converse"
with the past. Delayed communication, which at times
may be more accurately called continuing communication, between individuals of generations widely separated in time and space, is one of the important ways in
which words are freed from their immediate controls
and, thus circulating, become autonomous—move beyond the bounds of mortality (where to live they must
be consumed) toward immortality.

Being still dependent as signs on human beings, they

must be protected to attain full autonomy. The autonomy of each individual person is dependent on a social
structure with values and beliefs which do not fix his
position but allow him freedom to move from one social place to another, from one social context to others.
So it is with words. When the morality which controls
their proper use defines them autonomously, they can
move more easily from context to context, from B.C. to
A.D. In oral tradition, their meanings can move through
time in a chain of live interaction from mouth to ear,
from ear to mouth, within the continuing flow of human tissue, but unbroken generational continuity must
be present.

The written word, an object whose form is an agreed-
upon sign, is by nature so constituted that the objective
part of the sign—the material object—does not need to
be refashioned or recreated each time a new individual
or a new generation uses it. If used, however, the meaning must be under the influence of intervening generations. The archaeologist may unearth unused inscribed
tablets whose signs belong to a culture long forgotten
and never before known to this civilization. Although
the signs remain the same and the meanings intended
have not passed through any transformation of changing
belief and value, the receivers of this delayed communication have been influenced by the flux of cultural
transition of perhaps a hundred generations. What they
know and feel cannot be what those who invented the
delayed message could have meant, even though the
message comes directly from the forgotten source. In
this sense the sign is autonomous—dependent, like the
autonomous individual, on the values and beliefs of society for its freedom of movement. So long as its exist-

ence in the human mind is important, involving the value of wanting to find out what it meant to those who sent it, then within the human limits of such a term it has sign autonomy. And as such it is both free and bound—free to move within the limits of human mentality; bound to serve the meanings attributed by those who use it.

As such it also acts both as a conservative force, strengthening the hold of the past on the changing present, and as a liberalizing one, freeing the present generation from dependence upon oral transmission of the immediate older generation's interpretations of the sacred tradition. Not one, but a hundred generations are now sending their own delayed interpretations of what both they and we are. If a written sign like the Massachusetts Bay Charter or the Constitution of the United States has passed through continuing generations of interlocked interpreters, then not only is the original sign present as a whole, but the inscribed meanings are also directly sent to help distant ancestors communicate with their present "contemporaries." This is in fact the purpose of such a document as the Constitution, with its effort at "wise provision" for the future. The written sign loosens the control of time and modifies its effect upon us, for as we can now send words to the present and future, those in the past have been able to send directly these same signs of meaning to those born long after them. The signs of delayed communication have a quality of simultaneity about them—they "speak," we "listen," in the same moment of interpretation, as it were. Like receiving a telegram sent across the distances of a continent, to be read a brief moment later, reading these signs of distant meaning changes the significance of space and time. Through the unity of meaning between sender and receiver, the realities of time and space are transformed into *social* realities of meaningful nearness. "The" meaning that was "instantaneously" "put into" the signs which is the Charter, three centuries ago and a continent away, by the sign-maker, in the receiver's act of interpretation today in Yankee City can be "instantly" and "immediately" shared.

Thus the autonomous word, for instance, within the guarantees of freedom of speech and press to tell the truth, has a variety of meanings in Yankee City which have clashed. All played vital roles in the symbols of the Procession and in the historical events symbolized in the signs of this collective rite. The Word of the first settlers was in two forms: the Sacred Book which put them in direct communication with God through the literal signs of his Truth, and the secular Charter which Winthrop and the proprietors of the Massachusetts Bay Colony brought with them. Those early ancestors thus had the absolute power of the Word of God and the great but less powerful word of the secular covenant in their hands. As such, the Bible, the Holy Word, was the ultimate source of all authority; its truth was absolute. Those who controlled the interpretation of the scripture could be—and some were—theocratic tyrants, but since the truth was believed to be in the Word, directly communicated by God to those who were the instruments of his communication, this infallible Book, freed from the controls of an ecclesiastical hierarchy, potentially gave to each man who could read absolute autonomy and power. For there he could find the truth and, thus informed, be not only free to know it but duty bound to tell it to others. Each man might become his own private sect, at peace or war with all others.

Since it was believed that it was each man's duty to learn the truth and read the Scriptures, it was necessary that he learn to read and have immediate access to the Holy Word. From the very beginning, Massachusetts and Yankee City taught their young to read. Public schools were believed necessary, and they were publicly supported. Private academies were endowed and Harvard College founded, all primarily because of implicit faith in the written word, particularly the Sacred Word. The second float after Winthrop and his Charter was "The First Class at Harvard. Benjamin Woodbridge of Yankee City ranked highest in this class of nine . . ."

The social and symbolic processes which, through time, formed the symbols in the minds and hands of the modern symbol-makers to create the signs of the Procession representing things past and evoking and expressing contemporary beliefs and values about them, emerged from the most diverse sources. As such these signs of the past were given *delayed attribution of meaning*. The action of meaning took place over hundreds of years rather than in the immediacy of a moment. Meanings deriving from three hundred years, tens of thousands of hours, and millions upon millions of past words and events were condensed into a few brief hours and forty-two passing symbols. The condensation of the meanings of experience stored in the unconscious of one individual is slight compared to the condensation of social significance in the symbolic equipment of each generation and the special signs of historical works or rites used by collectivities to speak to themselves about their past.

Necessarily in such signs there is *displacement* of significance; necessarily many of the older meanings are no longer allowed explicit expression. Unconscious meanings, never permitted open expression even during the occurrence of an event, still seek and find covert acknowledgment. The older meanings of signs, implicit or explicit, rational or non-rational, also change their accent. Some retreat into somber obscurity, not being publicly acknowledged and celebrated; others once not publicly admitted come from their closets and parade before an approving multitude. Through time, as everyone knows, signs and symbols stand for something more —something less—something quite different—or cease to exist. New signs stand for old meanings, old ones for new—sometimes the opposite of what they once meant.

The flow of signs, events, and their meanings takes place, of course, in the interconnected organisms and species events which have composed the collectivity during the span involved. The flow of events through the social and status structures influences the content of each symbolic form. The continuing interpretation and reinterpretation of the events and the society in which they occur contribute an important share to the significance of symbols of the past wherever they are being used by the collectivity. The conceptualizations of what man is, what the world is, and what the supernatural is, flow through the social and status structure, influencing and being influenced by its changing values and stream of events. All of these—status and social structure, values and beliefs, and the events of time—persist and change and add to and subtract from the meanings of the past as they are caught and momentarily held in today's symbols. Logical or non-logical, rational or irrational, conscious or buried far below in the organic life of the species, adequately or not, they find expression in man's collective symbols. [35*b*]

Time, Space, and the Species

The non-rational ritual year, systematically related to the mathematically rational, objective time of the solar and lunar years, incorporates all levels of man's experience and mental life into a symbolic unity. As a sign system conforming outwardly to a time cycle founded on the movement of the earth and the planetary system, it gives "visible form" to what is believed to be reality. It embodies all forms of man's ordering of time and relates them to all levels of his mental life. Sacred time relates in one system the rational and verifiable references of objective time—of calendar, clock, and construct—to the feelings, moods, and significances of the emotional and non-rational orderings of social time and those of the species level. By reification it reconstitutes them and translates them into a divine and sacred order. The symbols of Christ's life become syncretistically interrelated with the physical changes of the earth, with the universe and the species, and with the non-rational world of the collectivity. The facts of species life, the earth, and the universe are transfigured into *signs* of meaningful sacred significance. Their meanings refer to the supernatural; it assimilates their multiple meanings into clusters whose cores have commonalities. The commonalities are modes of feeling, of pleasure and joy, of pain and sorrow, or of love and hate, security and anxiety, good and evil. The cores of

significance and their feeling systems spread out to the
several worlds of reality: the non-rational world of men
and the rational one of referential objects.
Liturgical time is but another expression of the sense
of time in men. In our culture, as we said earlier, are
present the objective references that can be validated.
These are to physical, social, and self phenomena. The
non-rational expressive and evocative signs and meanings of time also have their physical, social, and self
objects of reference. There is time felt and reacted to
at the species level which is syncretistically related to
the objects of the physical, social, and self environments.
The species level, being limited by the nature of the
species itself, determines what can be experienced,
what can or cannot be accepted. Responses to cold and
heat, to the opposite sex, to what is food, what is light
and darkness, to hunger and thirst, are so determined,
and their rhythms lend themselves to notions of time
and thus contribute to their non-rational ordering in
the self and in the mental products of collective life.

The nature of these non-rational clusters in the sign
system of the liturgy needs to be further analyzed and
broken down into objective and rational terms. But in
doing so we must constantly keep in mind that, for purposes of translating them into the foreign universe of
rational thought, the meaningful life and truth of such
mental systems is being damaged. The system of non-
rational thought holds man's entire universe together
in a valid whole, where the species can live a full life
and the rational worlds of both constructs and objects
can be made useful in the sacred system of thought. For
those who can believe and practice its beliefs and rit-

uals, the liturgical year helps admirably to perform this function. We will begin our analysis of the several components by first examining authoritative statements issued by theologians.

> There is a rhythmic ebb and flow running through the liturgical year as through all else in the world [Michel declares in *The Liturgy of the Church*.] The universe of the heavens has its changing cycles and periods; the solar system gives us our four seasons and the earth gives us the regular recurrence of night and day, the rhythms of which are copied by the various forms of life here on earth. In life itself there have been the vast cycles of species coming into existence in geological time and again disappearing; the stages of youth, maturity, old age in the individual; the seasonal changes in many forms of life; the daily periods of wakefulness and sleep . . .[3]

The figure of Christ is identified with the sun. "The liturgical year," says Cabrol, "is the revolution of the year around Christ." Dom Michel makes the myth's objective reference even more clear.

> In nature the most resplendent, most beautiful object is light, and for us it is the natural light of the sun, which is also the source of the power of growth in life. Hence in the liturgy the sun is the symbol of Christ and of his light-giving mission, just as darkness represents the powers of evil and of sin. Christ appeared on earth as man in the midst of the

3. Michel [74], pp. 75–6.

darkness of night, both literally and figuratively, and around him as around the sun revolves the true life.

On Holy Saturday the triple candle, lighted from the newly blessed fire, is saluted as the "Light of Christ." [13]

Colors related to light and darkness and to the solar year and change of night and day have their own sacred significance. White, the color of unrefracted light, "is the symbol of God, the father of Light, and of Christ, the Light of the World." White accordingly is the sign of purity, angels, virgins, and joy, and is used at the nuptial Mass. Black is the color of mourning and is used on Good Friday and in services for the dead.

Finally the end of the solar year arrives, the time of harvest and the death of seasonal life, entering the liturgy at the end of Time after Pentecost. Says Michel,

> The Ember days of the September harvest time occur after the seventeenth Sunday [after Pentecost]. While the spring Ember days had to do with asking God's blessing for an abundant harvest, the September days are those of the gathering of the fruits, and they point to the final consummation of things. The harvest in time directs the Christian mind to the eternal one . . . It is within these last Sundays that the feasts of All Saints and All Souls occur, which are distinctly feasts of the next life . . . [and of death].[4]

In joyous anticipation of the birth of Christ, Advent, the opening season of the Christian year, once again

4. *Ibid.*, pp. 77–8.

starts the new cycle: death and its sad reveries are now forgotten. Since Christ's actual birth date is not known, any day might have been chosen. [38] The feast seems to have originated in Alexandria. January 6 was first chosen, but by the third century December 25 was being celebrated. [25] The latter date was connected with the popular festival of sun worship. By imperial order, the return of the sun after the passing of the winter solstice was the occasion for a great pagan feast. Christmas took its place. [3, 115]

It is necessary perhaps only to mention *The Golden Bough* of Sir James Frazer to bring the numerous pantheons of nature and vegetative gods to mind and see our problem in its larger historical and comparative setting. In his chapter on "The Myth of Adonis," Frazer summarily states that

> under the names of Osiris, Tammaz, Adonis, and Attis, the peoples of Egypt and Western Asia represented the yearly decay and revival of life, especially of vegetable life, which they personified as a god who annually died and rose again from the dead. In name and detail the rites varied from place to place: in substance they were the same. The supposed death and resurrection of this oriental deity, a god of many names but of essentially one nature, is now to be examined . . . In the religious literature of Babylonia Tammuz appears as the youthful spouse or lover of the Ishtar, the great mother goddess, the embodiment of the reproductive energies of nature . . .[5]

5. Frazer [40], p. 325.

The several statements of the theologians about the sacred time of the liturgy interweave solar and objective time with those of the vegetative seasons, day and night with winter and summer. Heat and light alternate with cold and darkness, and these are given connotations of good and evil. Growth and development in nature and man alternate with decay, sterility, and death; and all of them with Christ, "the Light of the World" and Savior whose life and death atoned for man's sins and purchased Paradise for all men.

These syncretisms—which include all man's experiences as a species with all his non-logical relations and interpretation—can only be expressed by visual representations supplemented by textual descriptions and explanations. Two charts will display them. Chart 13 shows the clusters of species experience which have accumulated through time and taken on symbolic significance. The cluster of primitive, not to say species, feelings and notions at dawn, noon, sunset, and midnight are partly noted. They are notions, feelings, and sensations that the simplest societies experience and are possible in the communities of most primates. The syncretistic clusters, partially differentiated or not at all, are the beginnings of light, of brightness, at times of heat, the rise of the sun, the beginnings of day, and the end of darkness. In species-centric thought and feeling they involve the beginning of body and social activity, more effective use of the senses, particularly seeing things and seeing what it is one does as an active being. There is increased social participation and with it greater maximation of the self in the physical and social world about one. The group increases the amount and kind of its interaction; there is greater interstimulation and exchange of collective symbols. The quiet privacy of sleep yields to public life.

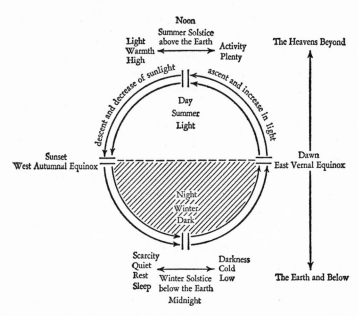

Noon
Summer Solstice above the Earth

Light Warmth High

Activity Plenty

The Heavens Beyond

descent and decrease of sunlight

ascent and increase in light

Day Summer Light

Sunset West Autumnal Equinox

Dawn East Vernal Equinox

Night Winter Dark

Scarcity Quiet Rest Sleep

Darkness Cold Low

Winter Solstice below the Earth

The Earth and Below

Midnight

Chart 13. The Synchronized Meanings of the Sun Cycles

The sun moves and rises to its height at noon. The primitive undifferentiated feelings and notions of increased heat and brightness, of the apex and end of the rise of the sun, cluster together deep within the animal and non-logical life of the group and the individual. Non-logically it is the felt moment when things are least private and secret and most public.

The sun moves downward to sunset, leaves the world and is gone. In non-logical thought there cluster the notions: end of day, of light, the waning period and the beginnings of darkness, possibly loss of heat, usually individual withdrawal from public activity to purely private and family life. It is the beginning of the reduction of the full use of the senses and public use of symbols.

Midnight and night—generally when light is gone with the sun and there is the greatest darkness, conditions are most private and least public and, during sleep, there is least use of the senses and intellect. The symbolism used then is private, unconscious, and nonrational. There is regression to more infantile stages when words are not used; the images are dramatic, mythic, not propositional and rational. In general there is a lack of form, of order and clear definition of things.

The notions of the yearly cycle (Chart 13) can begin with the vernal equinox when night and day, darkness and light, shadow and sunlight are equal. The sun is beginning to be nearer and more evident and the dark nights are shorter and less cold. Spring is starting and winter ending. There is the promise and expectation of more pleasant bodily sensations (and less of the unpleasant)—of warmer and more pleasant days. Seeds are to be planted, vines and trees bud and bloom, and new creatures are born. There is more food, the promise of abundance, and a reduction of the fear of scarcity—in general, an increased sense of individual and collective hopefulness and well-being. At the middle of summer (summer solstice) the sun is warmest, the days are long, growth is abundant, the plants and animals are ready to be food for man. At the autumn equinox the sun descends and leaves, it is colder, vegetation stops growing, crops are gathered, and plants wither and die. At the winter solstice, the sun is at its remotest angle, the days short, the nights long, and the weather cold. Annual vegetation is gone and men are less free and active. The feelings and notions of the yearly and daily cycle interpenetrate each other and form syncretistic clusters of meaning. These symbols accordingly are multidetermined. Space, time, feeling, sensation cluster tightly together. In the meanings the species gives to each there is something of all the others.

In Chart 14 the headings to the vertical columns list these external and internal influences felt by the species, perceived and evaluated by men, and syncretistically projected into the symbols and activities of the social world and on the self. Along the left side the horizontal columns are listed. They include the cycles of day and night, the seasons, light and heat, plant rhythms, annual life cycles, and that of the human species. A horizontal reading of day and night, for example, shows dawn, noon, sunset, and midnight. Of the human life cycle: conception, sexual intercourse, birth, infancy, and marriage, followed by later periods ending with old age, senility, death, and burial.

A glance down the left column shows dawn, spring, solar vitality, early growth of plants, the mating of animals, and the birth of the young equated with human copulation, conception, and infancy; and on the right, winter, night, low solar energy, the decay and death of plants, harvesting, and slaughter of animals, the old age and death of other species equated with senility and death for man. [115]

None of these equations is as exact as denoted here, but the clusters of meaning syncretistically expressed in the non-rational thought and symbolic expressions of men are vital and driving parts of the collective life and man's sense of what he is. These are the inchoate notions, the emotions felt, and the sensations which sig-

	The Beginning	Transition	Transition	The End
Day and Night	Dawn Morning ↓	→Noon Middle of the Day	Sunset Evening	Midnight (→ to *dawn*) Night
Seasons	Vernal Equinox Spring	Summer Solstice Summertime	Autumn Equinox Fall: after summer and before winter	Winter Solstice Winter └→ to Spring
Light and Heat	Beginning of increase in light and heat and solar vitality	Maximum of light and heat and solar vitality	Lessening of light, heat, and vitality	Least amount or no light, least amount of heat and natural vitality └→ to return of light, etc.
Plant Species	First vernal signs of activities, early growth	Fruition, ripening of fruit and grain, full growth of plants	Changes in leaves, plants, drying of grasses. Beginning of decay	Decay and death, quiescence, disappearance of vernal life └→ to the beginning
Technology	Planting and sowing, animal breeding	Protection and care, cultivation, etc.	Harvest, slaughter	Harvest of plants Slaughter of animals for food
Life Cycle Animal Activities	Mating, animal herding and birth of the young	Full maturity, strength and power, greatest sexual and productive power	Decrease of power and lessening of sexuality	Old age, senility, and death
Life Cycle Species	Marriage, sex intercourse, birth, infancy and early growth, conception, children in the family of orientation	Growth to full man- and womanhood Height of sexual and productive power Parents in family of procreation	Decreasing strength and energies, lessening of sexual and productive power Grandparent generation	Old age, senility, and death Cemetery

Chart 14. Transitions and Syncretisms: the Species, the Seasons and Solar Time

nificantly motivate men and, by use of non-rational symbols such as those of the sacred year, find ordered expression.

The Church writers on the liturgy, with different objectives and interpretations in mind, clearly recognize these modes of thought. Professors and doctors of the

Catholic Church through the two millennia have ordered and rationalized them. Thus Ellard says,

> . . . man has his complex corporeal structure so closely linked to his spiritual powers, that when he thinks, his imagination, his bodily emotions, and his nervous system, all to some extent come into play. The more intense his mental operations, the more necessary also it becomes for him to give corporeal expression to them in some way . . . man does not hesitate to employ any word or tone, any gesture or posture, fire or water, light or darkness, oil or incense, or any object about him as an aid in expressing his religious sentiment . . . The symbolism of the liturgy is fundamentally natural . . . being the expression of the relation of the Author to nature itself.[6]

6. Ellard [38], pp. 60–1.

CHAPTER 11

The Structure of Non-rational Thought

The Significance of the Species Group for Understanding Non-rational Symbols

Human beings cannot be understood when studied as separate units for, although separate in space, each is a dependent and interconnected part of the species. In their physical entirety they compose a biological ongoing system of interaction at the subcultural level. The actions of all individuals, from the time of conception, are dependent, integral parts of the continuing actions of the species. During their lives they closely interact with other human animals within the limited framework of species life. The observable actions and cries of the bodies involved in the interplay of species life are only the manifest parts of the whole action system, the rest taking place as it were subcutaneously in the internal physiological processes of the bodies involved.

The infinitesimal, momentary, individual speck in the infinite species expresses and reflects what the nature of his species permits him to do and learn to do. The private world of each individual is largely the product of the efforts of our society's moral order to control and constrain the non-moral and non-symbolic continuity of species behavior and to channel some of these somatic energies into technological, moral, and supernatural contexts.

Since men are cultural animals, the influence of species behavior and its contexts on symbolic life can be studied only by analytical and indirect methods which conceptually separate the species way of life from culture. Since symbol systems by their very nature are social, they can be understood only as integral parts of the larger social systems which they express, interpret, record, refer to, and help to maintain for members of the group. But symbol systems must also be recognized as belonging to the varying kinds of species action groups which are given affective expression by the several forms of symbol system.

The principal species action groups are the family of procreation, the sexual pair, the parents and offspring; the food-gathering and using groups; and the physically and sexually mature and immature. Since man is physically most like certain other primates which do not possess symbols of language or culture—for example, the chimpanzee—the contexts of species behavior which infra-human primates exhibit are useful indicators of what man's species groupings may be. Many studies of groups of monkeys and apes demonstrate that they possess and "recognize" in their behavior the simple family group consisting of such relations as the procreative pair, parents and offspring, the relations of siblings, and the external relations of this kind of group to other members of the band and other subgroups within the larger one. In addition, other groupings can be recognized in primate behavior, including sex and age groupings as well as feeding and defense groups. [124]

The social groups discernible in the behavior of members of such simple and loosely organized human territorial cultures as the Andamanese, Paviotso, Negrito, and many other primitive tribes approximate the simple biological grouping of the other species of the primate order. Our own society, despite its great complexity, has a common core of basic groupings which seems to correspond with those mentioned for the simple and primate societies. Certainly our system of social interaction is still strongly founded on the elementary families of orientation and procreation and the closely interrelated age and sex divisions. For the purposes of our present analysis, no more evidence of species contexts is needed than those just mentioned. [33]

Each individual of the infra-human primates (and presumably man) by nature grows into, and learns by experience to be, an ordered and functioning member of an orderly persistent group. The non-symbolic, non-moral ordered life is maintained through time. The animal energies of each species are expressed and discharged in an animal organization. There is very little that is amorphous or a "cauldron" of seething emotions about the life of an ape. His sexual life is ordered, his child-rearing conforms to a development pattern, and his feeding and eating conform to the status usages of his animal group. The uncontrolled violence hypothecated for the uncontrolled id when free of the constraint of the cultural ego and super ego is not observable. The adaptations in behavior necessary for animal interaction for survival have been made. It seems probable that man during his transition from a non-cultural to a cultural and symbolic animal brought these adaptations with him and that they continue important and crucial factors in the social and biological life of man. The resulting order reduces individual variability, decreases immediate satisfactions of unfulfilled desire, and restrains the immediate satisfaction of pleasurable "wishes."

It is reasonable to assume that our species, since it is closely similar to many other primates, possesses a core of non-verbal and non-symbolic meanings and gestures closely related to our animal nature, which express many of the needs and demands, the fears, satisfactions, and deprivations, the frustrations and gratifications found in these other primate species. It seems equally reasonable to infer that our cultural symbols and the non-verbal animal symbols are integrally interrelated and that some of the former are more fully suffused with the meaning of our animal signs and meanings than others. The meanings derived from our experiences with what a mother is, for example, must be in large part a product of the early animal behavior with her in which her gestures, sounds, and action systems became cues interpreted and responded to at the non-verbal level. The taboos, restraints, and limitations which later became a part of her meaning and the meaning of "mother" as a sign are part of the moral order of our culture.

If the cries and actions of the animal group directly express the meanings of the species and these become integral parts of the accumulation of such symbol systems as language and moral rules governing the relations of the sexes, of parents and children, and of the dominant and the dominated, it must be supposed that much of the meaning of some of the more basic parts of man's symbolic life must be sought beyond the signs and meanings of the conventions of culture. It must be looked for within the signs and meanings of species behavior and within the physical world of the human animals who embody its biological composition.

Furthermore, the non-logical expressive symbols which make up most of our symbols used in daily action —particularly those of religion—will be valid for those who use them, not because they can be proved to be true or false or logically congruent, but because they make emotional sense and are emotionally valid for those who *feel* them.

Moreover, if this is true, rational and scientific truth can be no more than one form of "knowing" reality and —this being assumed—reality as now defined can be no more than one form of what is real. The non-symbolic species behavior is the result of millions of years of accumulated adaptation. [41e] What the species inherits biologically and each individual member learns socially at the non-symbolic level, and is felt and experienced by the individual organism and by the organized responses of the group—being outside the realm of reason and its logical and scientific operations—contains orders of significance and truth far removed from even the suppositions of rational thought. The accumulated, condensed experience transferred and integrated into the species and its behavior and felt intensely by its members, individually and collectively, has meanings and validities and forms of truth for men beyond the capacity of rational thought to conceive and to order into sense-making symbols. Man's sense of what he is cannot ever depend solely on rational thought; too much is left out of what we know.

Non-rational Symbols: Their Development and Function in Species and Social Life

The meanings of non-rational and rational symbols, conscious as well as unconscious, emerge in the internal world of the individual during his development. They become part of his self and his relationship with those around him, being fitted inwardly into the structure of the personality and outwardly into his relations with his species, his society, and the physical world.

For the natural environment, the signs and contexts reflect previous and past learning situations of what is present beyond the organism. "Outward" experiences with the natural world are somewhat different from those within the world of the species. Outwardly there are no immediately shared contexts of direct experience. The gestures of others, and one's own, do not here become intermeshed and blended in common, simultaneous interpretations which in themselves re-influence the situation and become part of the stimuli helping to redefine it. The inanimate world can be experienced as something to adjust to purely on the technological level—as something to manipulate and handle or not handle. Of course, members of a society can and do "share" these relations with the outside world, but here the relations can be direct, denotative, and in terms of what the object is and what I do and do not do with it. This may be done through the tools and the skills of the technology. The inanimate environment may also be defined indirectly by the symbols of the social order and conceived of as something alive, either like other non-human living things or in the image of human beings, living beings which are not human, or beings which possess human attributes. Or the biological world may be divided into those who share some but not all of man's social nature. Usually such conceptions of other species are redefined and re-expressed at the supernatural level.

In the species environment the individual's experiences take place with other members of the species; interaction among them is primary; the only reality is the peculiar nature of the species itself. Each individual is directly involved in the learned and learning contexts of the others. Each member of the species is implicated, as George Mead indicated, in the other's meaning by being involved in his own. What is learned by each is how to act towards the other, and in so doing how to act towards himself when acting in relation to the other. The species cues and acts are interchanged in a continuing series of adjustments interpreted and organized by the participants. The action is composed of continuing, adapting acts of each as integral parts of the continuing acts of the other. The learned context of each includes much of the learned contexts of the other.

For men, therefore, the sign situation for one is similar to, and part of, the sign situation of the other. The significant cries and other significant gestures which refer to what is going on inside and outside both organisms can later refer to what has taken place and express and evoke for each what was felt at the time. When similar cries and actions are heard or seen and become symbols and symbolic gestures whose meanings are found in previous contexts of social and species interaction, each individual will have shared in a core of similar yet different meanings. The accumulation of such shared meanings among all members of a society, past and present, constitutes its living heritage. The continuing investment of these mutual meanings in objects, signs, and their relations transforms the world and men into a significant whole.

From the very beginning of each individual's life, what he feels, sees, hears, smells, expresses, and does, and his intensity of feeling are directly related to what other humans experience and do in the situations in which he finds himself.

The mother's initial meaning, for example, is not only the taste of warm, satisfying milk, the hard feel and tactual pressure of the nipple on the soft lips, the soft feel of a breast against the baby's face and fingers, the filling belly, and the satisfaction and support of her arms and lap, and the sound of her voice. She is also the soft voice saying something to herself. She is (to herself and others) the woman who holds the child in her lap and bares her breast to feed her child as a nutritive and loving gesture to a being sexually constituted but one with whom overt sexual experience is forever taboo. The reciprocal sounds and gestures and other overt acts compose the socio-species interaction of the mother and the child. Each has shared meanings and the significant actions, gestures, and sounds of the other. Each internalizes part of the other in the context of a common experience. The two share a species relation defined in the social context of a family. Although the relations and experiences are different with others in and out of the family, the infant learns from them by a similar process.

The child learns what the mother (and others in his immediate environment) is as an object to feel and know. The mother learns what her child is to feel and know, while at the same time the woman who is mother learns what she is as a mother, and more generally what a mother is while the child is experiencing her as a mother, in the same context of experience and defined social situation. The interdependent actions implicate the other in this mutually defined context of social and species experience. The shared experiences of each internalize part of the other in each. [12]

When these basic and continuing experiences take place within a previously defined cultural context—in which a mother, father, or sibling is defined as someone who, according to the rules and feelings and beliefs, is a person who must do this and not do that, and where a child must learn to to do this and not that—symbolic usages are internalized into the behavior of the child and the mother. The meaning of child becomes son or daughter to a mother and father, with a specific name to designate this person with whom they share certain experiences, responsibilities, rights, and privileges. For example, the actions of the mother in which the child's behavior is implicated are learned in time, and implicitly and explicitly the meaning of mother for him becomes one with whom he has shared certain kinds of experiences, felt certain obligations, certain privileges, and whom he has recognized with a set of symbols. The symbol for mother must forever reflect the mutual experiences of the two with each other, experiences which are different, yet the same, but always experiences molded in a context of "permanent" meaning socially defined. Through the family the vast, infinitely powerful, and largely unknown, forces of species life flow into the moral forms of the society and human personality.

When a baby makes a sound or a gesture it expresses one or more emotional states. These sounds, as Malinowski pointed out, are signs which have meaning to adults —to people who have learned the culture. The emotion of the child has to do with his situation as it is related to the internal workings of his organism, his outer environment, or a combination of the internal and outer environments. Sound behavior which expresses emotion breaks up into units of sound. The actions of the child in time also break up into parts which are significant gestures. As this differentiation proceeds in time, the growing individual is acting by sound as well as by muscular, overt behavior. Sound-making and certain gestures get sign-attention from adults and cause action to take place in the immediate interpersonal environment. Most of this behavior occurs in the family context. Adults, particularly family figures, give aid and comfort to the needs of the child. Gradually sound-making and action gestures are roughly adapted as signs to the surrounding adults and to the emotional and mental states of the child. These adaptations have pragmatic validity, since they work to relieve the child's tensions and irritations. Thus an anatomically helpless infant is socially adapted and becomes a more effective part of the action system of the species and the social group. The child acts through the parents and instigates acts through them by sound and other appeals which later become verbal and symbolic. From the time the child uses words, they not only express feelings but are a form of action. [67b]

A biological arrangement of sound-making and overt acts permits words and gestures to produce the effect that they mean. Words, as one form of sign, are active forces and instruments to relate the individual to social and species life. Words and symbols relate the child to the realities of life, not just because the child has learned to use them but because social tradition has given them common meanings as ways of interacting and as objects which refer to the rest of the world around them. Such symbols when used with the child not only attract but also repel. They act as controls over the interpersonal relations of an individual, and they give others control over him.

While the growing individual learns the various systems of symbols, he does this for the most part unconsciously—which is to say, he is not aware of what he is doing and rarely separates feeling from concept. The child uses the name of the object to express an emotional bond. The expressive jargon for a toy does not depend so much on its properties as on the feelings the child has because of his experiences with it. The meaning of a thing and its signs are the total set of experiences a child has had in using them. Such meaning is part of the meaning that other people attribute to the symbol and the object for which it stands. It is probable that in most cases the meaning of an object or symbol for each person will be similar to its meaning for most other persons who live and have been trained in similar contexts.

Although conscious symbols vary greatly in meaning among the members of the community who interpret them, they do have a common core of agreed upon and customary meaning. Even though the unconscious ones are always important parts of each individual's social interaction, and usually possess significance which is generally felt and implicitly understood, they rarely become explicitly meaningful. [19b] There may be a little conscious agreement about their ideational meanings in the community, but the degree of emotional agreement among those who respond to their stimulus is high, despite the fact that they may be unaware of the significance of their responses. The testimony from the psychoanalytical couch as to the meanings of various dreams shows strong resemblances among the meanings attributed to various kinds of private symbols and the unconscious responses elicited by them. The typology of implicit meanings found in the unconscious symbols produced in the responses to the various projective tests, including the TAT, the Rorschach, and similar tests, clearly shows that there is a whole submerged world of general implicit meanings where collective agreements are not referential so much as emotional and evocative. The processes of socialization have reduced them to a submerged life fitted below rationality, embedded in the feelings related to species behavior. The increasing demands of the technology in our society have decreased the social area where such evocative and expressive symbols can be explicitly used. Consequently, they live a hidden life in the demi-world of human thought and can only be understood by translation into rational thought by a scientific interpreter.

The testimony of research in the mental and moral life of children demonstrates a pattern of non-logical thinking and behavior. Piaget's research led him to the conclusion that the child was *egocentric* in his thinking and that the logical thinking of the society only appeared after the child was socialized. The egocentric thinking and moral behavior of the child, he said, must be stripped of what he called *personal schemas* of anal-

ogy and supplemented by the thinking of the group.
The "motivated" individual thinking must give way to
the "arbitrary," obligatory, abstract thought of the
society. The problem he poses is one of the *individual*
child becoming socialized and a thinking member of
the group. [89a]

A re-examination of his concept of egocentrism leads
to a re-formulation of the problem. The egocentrism
of the child, according to Piaget, occurs when he does
not distinguish himself from the world around him.
He interacts as an organism with other organisms about
him without distinguishing *himself* from the *others*.
He treats cultural things and organizes them "syncretistically" into his own affective way of life.

And what is this way of life? The infant and young
child act largely according to the action systems of the
species. They interact in the group more as members
of a species than as self-directed socialized beings. The
action system of the biological family still operates as
a powerful influence on what the child thinks and does.
The insistent needs and wants, pleasures and pains, of
the body related to other bodies dominate the feeling
system of the child. The meanings of things are organized in the pattern of the feelings of species action
systems, always under the continued and increasing influence of the cultural system.

The social symbols are present and used, but they
are used according to the feeling order of the organism
behaving within species action systems. Their significance and ordering are largely determined by the species
context and only secondarily by social contexts. They
are not irrational but non-logical. Their validity lies
not in testing but in feeling and conviction.

Freud's and others' evidence about the nature of dream symbols and the mental life of much of the unconscious, where logic and rationality do not organize the mental life, adds further demonstration of the relation of non-logical order and species life. The mental world of the child—a feeling system which in early life dominates each person—continues to exist in the life of the adult individual and the group. The feeling system operating in the interaction of human animals as part of the action system of the species lies below the reality system of the ego and the society. Although Freud conceptualized mental life in individual terms, he treated it within the context of the family. The family is a biological and species system for the child, but for the mature it is dominated by the moral order and incest taboos of the society. Freud's "id," touching and being charged with energies from the organism, the source of our strongest feelings, indicates how the non-logical feeling system operates as part of the social life of man. [41b]

Such symbols as dreams, reveries, hallucinations, many of the ordinary symbols of everyday life, those of many of the arts, and supernatural symbols such as myths—Durkheim notwithstanding—can be understood only when referred to the context of species relations and events. They are never free from cultural influence, for the symbols have a cultural *form,* but the feelings they express are largely those of the ongoing species life.

There are at least two classes of unconscious symbols: those which operate covertly in the inner world of everyone, evoking emotionally charged similar meanings among sizeable proportions of the population of the community; and a second class, still unconscious, or largely so, which functions quite differently in the life of some individuals and the society. The latter type, instead of being powerful forces integrating the society and relating the individual in a deep, meaningful way to those around him, separate the individual from his fellows, distort prevailing relations, and create problems wherever they exist. These private symbols and the irrational emotional meanings they attach to the flow of private and public events are usually born in experiences which tear painful lesions in the inner world of the persons who have them. Although they are evocative and charged with the powerful energies of species life, belong to the type of expressive covert symbols first referred to, and emerge from the same milieu where the species life and the moral order merge and normally interpenetrate each other, they prevent the individual and others around him from discharging their emotions as "adjusted" animals. They force their emotionally powerful but distorted interpretation on what takes place, so that the maimed individual cannot adapt easily to the present or the future. They are irrational and usually result in non-adaptive behavior, whereas the non-rational type supports, strengthens, and provides the foundation of our social life. [114c]

The deep, unconscious, latent meanings connected with manifest signs during sleeping and waking must be considered as more than the unique and hidden symbols of an individual. They, too, are part of the total action context in which other individuals are involved as animals and persons. Their full meaning can only be learned after similar knowledge about conscious and unconscious signs from *all* individuals in an action context are interrelated as integral parts of the meaningful whole. Their full meaning can only be found by studying the rest of the system of unconscious understandings out of which the individual ones have been taken, and in which they were learned and have been maintained.

Much of the collective life of man is carried on by an exchange of signs part of whose meaning is unconscious, and whose function allows the animal life of man to be expressed. The expression may be entirely hidden, or it may find a vehicle in collective signs, whose conscious conventional meanings are so related to unconscious meanings that they are accessible for their expression. Psychoanalytical techniques allow us to learn how to study them as part of the action system of a society. Research must learn how to relate them to the conscious collective signs of the community as a system and—at the other extreme of the mental life of man—to the sociological behavior of the ongoing species. The findings of Freud and other depth psychologists must be reconceptualized. The deep, unconscious id of each individual must be conceptualized, not so much as a component of individual mental life, but as an integral and significant part of the action life of the species—as a segment of our mental life, much of whose meaning must be sought within the context of the action groups. What are called the ego and super ego are not only individual phenomena but integral parts of the society; of the moral and sacred relations of group life. The interconnections among the three should be viewed in the total context of the life of the species as it exists in the groups which compose the observable eventful life of men.

The underlying themes of non-logical symbol systems, to be learned by research through an examination of the special parts, are basic arrangements of dominant meanings expressed in varying designs at the sign level. The motifs (themes and their designs) are patterned in traditional or newly invented forms. The proportionate amount of thought or emotion involved in the construction of an art product, liturgy, or whatever the symbol system may be, varies greatly. The form may be professionally sophisticated or naive and simple. The response of the interpreter also may be simple and folk-like or highly sophisticated. There is no necessary relation of similarity between the forms of response and the degree of artistic professionalism. The simple folk-like creation of an early blues song or cowboy ballad may receive a sophisticated or folk-like response, depending on the interpreter and on the context in which he is acting when the response takes place. Part of the satisfaction in slumming, by both white and Negro sophisticates, in a "hangout" where popular jazz is played is not only to feel superior but to give the direct, immediate, naive response that the unsophisticated give, and "do it like gone guys" among others who can only respond in the naive, direct way.

All popular arts are capable of being translated into the rhetoric of the sophisticate. The oral action rites of the emotional religions of the crowd in time may develop a style expressing greater use of thought and professional competence. When this change occurs in a religion it usually means that the leader, and later the congregation, has moved up in class position, that the concepts of God expressed by the leader and felt by the congregation have changed and acquired a new set of meanings; as a consequence, many lower-class members, to receive the symbols they need, must once again go to another church.

When "rhetoric" is said to be present in a symbol system, professionals have usually entered either as creators who give thought to the evocative signs and their relations and to their meanings, or as critics of folk and other unsophisticated products, attributing a rhetoric which may or may not be present in the way they assert. [16b] Essentially such a process usually indicates that the art forms of the masses are being translated into "fine" arts acceptable to the superior classes, to those aspiring to such levels, and to a few of lower station who have learned to appreciate them. [16a]

The popular arts that satisfy and engage the attention of the masses are the rallying points where the people arrive at the common points of meaning and feel again the deep memories of past experience. Here diverse adults can find, re-live, and re-feel the central areas of what they themselves are and the emotional core of their culture. The fine arts allow many in the superior classes generally, and a selected few among ordinary men, to withdraw from the meanings of the common world to an aloof and protected one where they enjoy what they experience and at the same time are rewarded by a feeling of exclusiveness and superiority.

The creators of all types of symbol systems in effect first define the meanings of the meaningful forms they have produced. The interpreters in the audience in varying degrees accept or reject these meanings. The signs, objects, and their environments to which the "producers" refer may or may not be the same as those assigned by their interpreters. Ordinarily the audience and producer, in the immediate context of interpretation, are not identical (in dreams they may be). The problem of how much the meanings of the product for its creator and those who interpret it coincide is a special one and need not presently concern us. What we must consider are: (1) the meanings signs have for an audience as judged by an analysis of their conventional meanings and the relations of signs, meanings, and audience to each other as part of a whole symbolic assemblage; and (2) the meanings the signs have for the varying kinds of individuals composing the audience. Consequently, to adequately cover and collect evidence, the skills and instruments of the field investigator must include those from the social and psychological disciplines.

Non-rational symbols are basic parts of the animal organization of man. They express and evoke the feelings and sensuous observations of animals in an interactive group. The signs and gestures used are not private but part of the basic sociality of man. They relate to his deepest emotions. Within them flow the vital energies and emotional significance of species behavior. When individuals grow up these symbols are not "stripped" of their egocentric meanings, but undergo modification and become part of the symbolic equipment of mature men and women, remaining deep within their mental and moral selves. Such symbols are not unadaptive because they are non-rational; on the contrary, these evocative symbols, directly related to the species organization of man, allow this part of man's essential nature to be expressed and justified without the restrictions of cultural and moral life interfering. With their aid, man remains a *full* participant in the life of his species. Without their help he encounters painful difficulties. A logical mind is not a good one to reinforce the pleasures of sexual communication. It will not increase and maximize the exchange of sign and gesture which enhances the physical and moral worth of the sexual act to the participant pair. The language of love is non-rational; its symbols are evocative. They arouse and evoke some of the deepest and most profoundly significant feelings and "understandings" of what man is to himself and others, but they do not need the denotative symbols of logical speech.

These symbols are part of, and refer to, the species organization of man, culturally reformed but still lived and expressed in the social organization and in the person. The constant pressure of the natural environment, beginning long before man was a symbol-using animal and up to this moment, modifies his full expression of his species urges. Obviously, as an animal acting in direct relation with other animals, he does not directly attend to any reality beyond that of his species.

The way of life identified as egocentric does exist as a phase of individual development, and it continues to exist and is an important and vital part of all human existence. But it is not so much egocentric as species-centric; it serves as a vital part of species interaction. Species-centric symbols in human beings are largely family ones. They find their freest and easiest expression in the arts and religion. Here, sometimes hidden but often in very transparent disguises, they are available for the full charge of animal emotions released from the moral restrictions and logical controls of secular life. Men can murder their brother gods—the father can be accused of knowingly permitting this, incest can be indulged in, and the father can become the son and the son the father, each with one woman as mother and wife.

The suppressed species life partly excluded from expression in the moral life of the community takes refuge in the sacred symbols of religion and art. Unfettered by the conventions and inhibitions of social and cultural isolation, the family unites the understandings of men—sometimes thousands of years apart—by creating persons who share a common core of human experience. Great literature, great drama, many of the other arts and much of religion rely on the shared meanings of family life to permit communication and understanding across the barriers of cultural diversity and long passage of time.

The faith of the group in supernatural symbols, the sense of "integration," of "oneness," and the sacrifice of self for the survival of these sacred symbols now become meaningful. Whenever an individual can identify sacred symbols in which he believes with the integrated socio-species symbols of his ordinary life he can have enough faith to believe in their supernatural efficacy and power. The source of their power is in and beyond him; these symbols unquestionably express for him a feeling of belonging to a vital eternal world which is all-powerful and—although beyond human understanding—knowable and true because of what he feels the symbols have "within them" and express for him.

The knowledge of science is necessarily limited and incomplete. Part of the great authority we presently grant it is given because it, too, reduces anxiety and maximizes our sense of control over nature. Until now, when the symbols and skills of science have marched into a new area of man's adjustment, the sacred symbols of religion have retreated. The rapid advance of science and the confused retreat of religion in recent history have given to some the impression that science will ultimately conquer the whole world of religious life. This may be a false impression. Science, a recent superstructure built on the solid foundations of empirical knowledge supplied by earlier technologies—a product of realism—cannot be directly related to, and fused with, the evocative symbols of species life. The two systems can only be bound indirectly and mediated through the moral structure of the society in each individual. For example: the science of psychoanalysis cannot be a total way of life, although some of its adherents attempt to use it as such. At best it can only heal an injury to the human psyche resulting from the dislocation of species life from the moral and technical life of the group. The individual who has lost his faith can no longer express his hopes and fears, his sense of belonging and togetherness and thereby his feeling of "wholeness," for the sacred symbols which combine the emotional world of the species and the moral world of the society are the only ones now available that can function in this manner.

Those who have faith may be on more solid ground in their understanding of reality than those who cannot find a way to believe. What they *feel* in their thinking may refer to a larger reality—mystical and supernatural or not—which speaks of truths beyond the present power of scientific thought. That this may be so should do no more than make the scientist truly humble and deeply respectful of other kinds of knowing; it should in no way influence him to abandon or reduce his efforts to know and understand.

References

1. ADAMS, JAMES LUTHER. "Ethics," *Handbook of Christian Theology.* New York, Meridian Books, Inc., 1958.
2. ARISTOTLE. *Aristoteles,* ed. and trans. S. H. Butcher. London, Macmillan, 1911.
3. BARNETT, JAMES H. "Christmas in American Culture," *Psychiatry, 9,* No. 1 (February 1946), 51–65.
4. BEARD, CHARLES A. and MARY R. *The Rise of American Civilization.* New York, Macmillan, 1949.
5. BECKER, CARL C. *The Heavenly City of the Eighteenth-Century Philosophers.* New Haven, Yale University Press, 1932.
6. BOGORAZ, V. G. *The Chuckchee.* New York, Stechert, 1904–9.
7a. BERGSON, HENRI L. *Time and Free Will. An Essay on the Immediate Data of Consciousness,* trans. R. L. Pogson. New York, Macmillan, 1913.
7b. ———— *Creative Evolution,* trans. Arthur Mitchell. New York, Macmillan, Modern Library, 1944.
8. Bible, editions of
8a. American Revised Version, New York, Thomas Nelson & Sons, 1901.
8b. Brown's Self-interpreting Family Bible, Edinburgh, Daniel Chadwick, 1778.
8c. Revised Standard Version, New York, Thomas Nelson & Sons, 1952.
8d. Riverside Parallel Bible, Boston, Houghton Mifflin and Company, 1885.
8e. Westminster Version of the Sacred Scriptures, London, Longmans, Green and Company, 1913–

9. BIRKHOFF, GEORGE D. *Aesthetic Measure.* Cambridge, Harvard University Press, 1933.

10. *Book of Common Prayer.* With the additions and deviations proposed in 1928. New York, Oxford University Press, 1951.

11. *Book of Common Worship,* rev. of Hugh Thomson Kerr and Others. Philadelphia, Presbyterian Board of Christian Education, 1946.

12. BOSSARD, JAMES H. S. *Parent and Child. Studies in Family Behavior.* Philadelphia, University of Pennsylvania Press, 1953.

13. BRIFFAULT, ROBERT. "Festivals," *Encyclopaedia of the Social Sciences, 6,* 198–201. New York, Macmillan, 1930–34.

14. BRYSON, LYMAN and Others, eds. *Symbols and Society.* (Fourteenth Symposium of the Conference on Science, Philosophy, and Religion.) New York, Harper, 1955.

15. BULTMAN, RUDOLF. *Primitive Christianity.* New York, Meridian Books, Inc., 1956.

16a. BURKE, KENNETH. *Philosophy of Literary Form. Studies in Symbolic Action.* Baton Rouge, La., Louisiana State University Press, 1941.

16b. ———— *A Rhetoric of Motives.* New York, Prentice-Hall Inc., 1950.

17. CABROL, FERNAND, O.S.B. *The Year's Liturgy. The Sundays, Feriae and Feasts of the Liturgical Year.* Vol. *1* of 2 vols.: *The Seasons.* New York, Benziger Brothers, 1938.

18. CARPENTER, C. R. *A Field Study of the Behavior and Social Relations of Howling Monkeys.* (Comparative Psychology Monographs, *10,* No. 2) Baltimore, Williams and Wilkie, 1934, 1–168.

19a. CASSIRER, ERNST. *An Essay on Man. An Introduction to a Philosophy of Human Culture.* New Haven, Yale University Press, 1944.

19b. —— *Language and Myth*, trans. Susanne Langer. New York, Harper, 1946.

20. *The Catholic Encyclopedia*, ed. Edward A. Pace and Others. 16 vols. New York, Gilmary Society, 1936– .

21. CIRLOT, FELIX L. *The Early Eucharist*. London, Society for the Promoting of Christian Knowledge, 1939.

22. CLARK, ELMER T. *The Small Sects in America*. Nashville, Tenn., Cokesbury Press, 1937.

23. CLARK, KENNETH. *The Nude*. New York, Doubleday and Co., Inc., 1959.

24. COMMAGER, HENRY STEELE. *The American Mind*. New Haven, Yale University Press, 1950.

25. COUNT, EARL W. *4000 Years of Christmas*. New York, Henry Schuman, 1948.

26. CRAVEN, AVERY and WALTER JOHNSON. *The United States, Experiment in Democracy*. Boston, Ginn, 1947.

27. CRAWLEY, ALFRED ERNEST. *The Mystic Rose. A Study of Primitive Marriage and of Primitive Thought in Its Bearing on Marriage*, ed. Theodore Bestermann. New York, Boni and Liveright, 1927.

28. CUNLIFFE, MARCUS. *The Literature of the United States*. London, Penguin Books, 1954.

29. CURTI, MERLE E. *The Growth of American Thought*. New York, Harper, 1943.

30. DAVIS, ALLISON and ROBERT J. HAVIGHURST. "The Measurement of Mental Systems," *Scientific Monthly*, 66 (April 1948), 301–16.

31. *Dictionary of American Biography*, ed. Allen Johnson. (Auspices of the American Council of Learned Societies.) New York, Charles Scribner's Sons, 1928–44.

32. DOBSON, JAMES O. *Worship*. New York, Macmillan, 1941.

33. DOLLARD, JOHN and NEAL E. MILLER. *Personality and Psychotherapy. An Analysis in Terms of Learning, Thinking, and Culture.* New York, McGraw-Hill, 1950.

34. DOUGLASS, TRUMAN B. "Protestantism," *Handbook of Christian Theology.* New York, Meridian Books, Inc., 1958.

35a. DURKHEIM, ÉMILE. *The Elementary Forms of the Religious Life,* trans. J. W. Swain. New York, Macmillan, 1915.

35b. —— *Suicide,* trans. John Spaulding and George Simpson. Glencoe, Ill., Free Press, 1951.

36. DWIGHT, TIMOTHY. *Travels in New-England and New-York,* Vol. *1* of 4 vols. New Haven, T. Dwight, 1821.

37. ELKIN, FREDERICK. *A Study of the Relationship between Popular Hero Types and Socal Class.* Ph.D. Dissertation, University of Chicago, 1951. Deposited in the University of Chicago Library.

38. ELLARD, GERALD. *Christian Life and Worship.* New York, Bruce Publishing Co., 1933.

39a. FARIS, ELLSWORTH. "The Sect and the Sectarian," *American Journal of Sociology, 60* (May 1955 supplement), 75–89.

39b. —— "Some Phases of Religion that Are Susceptible of Sociological Study," *American Journal of Sociology, 60* (May 1955 supplement), 90.

40. FRAZER, SIR JAMES GEORGE. *The Golden Bough. A Study in Magic and Religion* (abridged ed.). New York, Macmillan, 1927.

41a. FREUD, SIGMUND. *New Introductory Lectures on Psycho-analysis,* trans. W. J. H. Sprott. New York, W. W. Norton, 1933.

41b. —— *The Basic Writings of Sigmund Freud,* trans. and ed. A. A. Brill. New York, Random House, Modern Library, 1938.

41c. —— *The Interpretation of Dreams*, 181–552.

41d. —— *Three Contributions to the Theory of Sex*, 553–632.

41e. —— *Totem and Taboo*, 807–930.

42. FROMM, ERICH. *The Forgotten Language*. New York, Rinehart, 1951.

43. FRYE, ALBERT M. and ALBERT W. LEVI. *Rational Belief. An Introduction to Logic.* New York, Harcourt, Brace, 1941.

44. GENNEP, ARNOLD VAN. *Les Rites de passage.* Paris, Émile Nourry, 1909.

45. *A Guide for the Christian Year (1951–60).* New York, Commission on Evangelism and Devotional Life, 1950.

46. GUNN, JOHN ALEXANDER. *The Problem of Time.* London, Allen & Unwin, 1929.

47. HABENSTEIN, ROBERT W. "The American Funeral Director. A Study in the Sociology of Work." Unpublished Ph.D. dissertation, University of Chicago, 1954.

48a. HENRY, WILLIAM E. *The Thematic Apperception Technique in the Study of Culture-Personality Relations.* (Genetic Psychology Monographs, Vol. 35.) Provincetown, Mass., Journal Press, 1947.

48b. —— "The Business Executive. Psychodynamics of a Social Role," *American Journal of Sociology, 54* (January 1949), 286–91.

49. HILDEBRAND, DIETRICH VON. *In Defence of Purity.* New York, Sheed & Ward, 1935.

50. HODGES, GEORGE. *The Episcopal Church, Its Faith and Order,* rev. of James A. Muller to accord with the new prayer book. New York, Macmillan, 1932.

51. HOOFT, W. A. VISSER'T. "Ecumenism," *Handbook of Christian Theology.* New York, Meridian Books, Inc., 1958.

52. HUIZINGA, JOHAN. *The Waning of the Middle Ages.*

A Study of the Forms of Life, Thought and Art in France and the Netherlands in the XIV and XV Centuries. New York, Longmans, Green, 1948.

53. HUNT, MORTON M. *The Natural History of Love.* New York, Alfred A. Knopf, 1959.

54a. JAMES, EDWIN O. *Christian Myth and Ritual.* London, John Murray, 1933.

54b. —— *Origins of Sacrifice. A Study in Comparative Religion.* London, John Murray, 1933.

55. JOHN OF THE CROSS, ST. "En Una Noche Oscura," trans. John Frederick Nims. *Commonweal, 55,* No. 16 (January 25, 1952), 404.

56. JOHNSON, MARTIN. "The Meanings of Time and Space in Philosophies of Science," *American Scientist, 39* (July 1951), 412–21.

57. JUNG, CARL G. *Psychology and Religion.* New Haven, Yale University Press, 1938.

58. KEATING, JOHN F. *The Agape and the Eucharist in the Early Church; Studies in the History of the Christian Love-Feasts.* London, Methuen, 1901.

59a. KLAPP, ORRIN E. "The Creation of Popular Heroes," *American Journal of Sociology, 54* (September 1948), 135–41.

59b. —— "American Villain-Types," *American Sociological Review, 21* (June 1956), 337–40.

60. KLUCKHOHN, CLYDE. "Myths and Rituals," *Harvard Theological Review, 35* (January 1942), 45–79.

61. KORZYBSKI, ALFRED. *Science and Sanity. An Introduction to Non-Aristotelian Systems and General Semantics.* New York, International Non-Aristotelian Publishing Co., 1941.

62. KROPOTKIN, PETR A. *Mutual Aid. A Factor in Evolution.* New York, Penguin Books, 1939.

63. LECKY, WILLIAM E. *History of European Morals, from Augustus to Charlemagne.* New York, D. Appleton, 1879.

64. LÉVY-BRUHL, LUCIEN. *Primitive Mentality*, trans. Lilian A. Clare. New York, Macmillan, 1923.

65. MACCULLOCH, J. A. and others. "Sacraments," *Encyclopaedia of Religion and Ethics, 10* (1919), ed. James Hastings. New York, Charles Scribner's Sons, 897–915.

66. MALE, EMILE. *Religious Art.* New York, Pantheon Books, Inc., 1949.

67a. MALINOWSKI, BRONISLAW. "Magic, Science and Religion," *Science, Religion and Reality,* ed. J. Needham. New York, Macmillan, 1925, 19–84.

67b. ———— "The Problem of Meaning in Primitive Languages," *The Meaning of Meaning,* C. K. Ogden and I. A. Richards. New York, Harcourt, Brace, 1936, 296–336.

68. MARTINDALE, CYRIL CHARLES. *The Faith of the Roman Church.* New York, Sheed & Ward, 1951.

69. MAUSS, MARCEL. *The Gift. Forms and Functions of Exchange in Archaic Societies,* trans. Ian Cunnison. London, Cohen & West, 1954.

70. MAY, GEOFFREY. *Social Control of Sex Expression.* New York, William Morrow, 1931.

71a. MEAD, GEORGE H. "Social Consciousness and the Consciousness of Meaning," *Psychological Bulletin, 7* (1910), 397–405.

71b. ———— "A Behavioristic Account of the Significant Symbol," *Journal of Philosophy, 19* (1922), 157–63.

71c. ———— *Mind, Self, and Society, from the Standpoint of a Social Behaviorist.* Chicago, University of Chicago Press, 1934.

72. MEAD, MARGARET. *Sex and Temperament in Three Primitive Societies.* New York, William Morrow, 1935.

73. MECKLIN, JOHN M. "The Passing of the Saint," *American Journal of Sociology, 60* (May 1955 supplement), 34–53.

74. MICHEL, DOM VIRGIL. *The Liturgy of the Church.* New York, Macmillan, 1937.

75. MILLER, PERRY G. E. *The New England Mind. The Seventeenth Century.* New York, Macmillan, 1939.

76. MINDSZENTY, CARDINAL JOZSEF. *The Face of the Heavenly Mother.* New York, Philosophical Library, 1951.

77. MOLLEGAN, A. T. "Fall, the (Original Sin)," *Handbook of Christian Theology.* New York, Meridian Books, Inc., 1958.

78. MORISON, SAMUEL ELIOT. *The Maritime History of Massachusetts, 1783–1860.* Boston, Houghton, Mifflin, 1924.

79. MORRIS, CHARLES W. *Signs, Language, and Behavior.* New York, Prentice-Hall, 1946.

80. MURRAY, HENRY A. *Thematic Apperception Test Manual.* Cambridge, Harvard University Press, 1943.

81. NELSON, J. ROBERT. "Church," *Handbook of Christian Theology.* New York, Meridian Books, Inc., 1958.

82. NICHOLS, JAMES HASTINGS. *Primer for Protestants.* New York, Association Press, 1951.

83a. NIEBUHR, H. RICHARD. *The Social Sources of Denominationalism.* New York, Henry Holt, 1929.

83b. ——— "Sects," *Encyclopedia of the Social Sciences, 13,* 624–30. New York, Macmillan, 1937.

84. NYGREN, ANDERS T. S. *Agape and Eros. A Study of the Christian Idea of Love.* London, Society for Promoting Christian Knowledge, 1953.

85. OGDEN, CHARLES K. and I. A. RICHARDS. *The Meaning of Meaning.* New York, Harcourt, Brace, 1936.

86. PARETO, VILFREDO. *The Mind and Society,* trans. Andrew Bongiorno and Arthur Livingston. New York, Harcourt, Brace, 1935.

87. PARRINGTON, VERNON L. *Main Currents in American Thought.* New York, Harcourt, Brace, 1927.

88. PAUCK, WILHELM. "Reformation," *Handbook of Christian Theology.* New York, Meridian Books, Inc., 1958.

89a. PIAGET, JEAN, and others. *The Language and Thought of the Child,* trans. Marjorie Gabain. New York, Harcourt, Brace, 1926.

89b. —— *The Moral Judgment of the Child,* trans. Marjorie Gabain. New York, Harcourt, Brace, 1932.

90. PIDDINGTON, RALPH. *The Psychology of Laughter. A Study in Social Adaptation.* London, Figurehead Press, 1933.

91. *Presbyterian Plan Book.* New York, Department of Stewardship and Promotion of the General Council of the Presbyterian Church in the U.S.A., 1952–53.

92a. RADCLIFFE-BROWN, ALFRED R. "The Sociological Theory of Totemism," *Proceedings, Fourth Pacific Science Congress, 3* (1929), 295–309.

92b. —— *Religion and Society.* London, Royal Anthropological Institute of Great Britain and Ireland, 1945.

92c. —— *The Andaman Islanders.* Glencoe, Ill., Free Press, 1948.

93. RAGLAN, FITZROY R. S. *The Hero. A Study in Tradition, Myth and Drama.* London, C. A. Watts, 1949.

94. RICHARDS, AUDREY I. *Hunger and Work in a Savage Tribe.* Chicago, Free Press, 1948.

95. RIESMAN, DAVID and others. *The Lonely Crowd.* New Haven, Yale University Press, 1950.

96. *The Roman Missal,* ed. Fernand Cabrol, O.S.B. New York, P. J. Kenedy and Sons, 1949.

97. ROSTEN, LEO, ed. *Guide to the Religions of America.* New York, Simon & Schuster, 1955.

98. ROUGEMONT, DENIS DE. *Love in the Western World,* trans. Montgomery Belgion. Revised and augmented edition. New York, Pantheon Books, 1956.

99a. RUSSELL, BERTRAND. *Mysticism and Logic and Other Essays.* New York, Longmans, Green, 1918.

99b. ——— *Marriage and Morals.* Liveright Publishing Corp., 1929.

100. SANDBURG, CARL. *Abraham Lincoln. The Prairie Years and the War Years.* New York, Harcourt, Brace, 1954.

101. SAPIR, EDWARD. "Symbolism," *Encyclopedia of the Social Sciences, 14,* 492–95. New York, Macmillan, 1937.

102a. SHEPHERD, MASSEY H. "Liturgy," *Handbook of Christian Theology.* New York, Meridian Books, Inc., 1958.

102b. ——— "Sacraments," *Handbook of Christian Theology.* New York, Meridian Books, Inc., 1958.

103. SIMMEL, GEORG. "A Contribution to the Sociology of Religion," *American Journal of Sociology, 60* (May 1955 supplement), 1–18.

104. SMALL, ALBION W. "The Church and Class Conflicts," *American Journal of Sociology, 60* (May 1955 supplement), 54–74.

105. SMITH, WILLIAM ROBERTSON. *Lectures on the Religion of the Semites.* New York, D. Appleton, 1889.

106. STAFFORD, THOMAS A. *Christian Symbolism in the Evangelical Churches.* Nashville, Tenn., Abingdon-Cokesbury, 1942.

107. SUMNER, WILLIAM G. "Religion and the Mores," *American Journal of Sociology, 60* (May 1955 supplement), 19–33.

108a. TILLICH, PAUL "The Religious Symbol," *Journal of Liberal Religon, 2,* 13–33.

108b. ——— *The Protestant Era.* Chicago, University of Chicago Press, 1948.

109. TOCQUEVILLE, ALEXIS DE. *Democracy in America*. New York, Alfred A. Knopf, 1945.

110. TROELTSCH, ERNST. *The Social Teaching of the Christian Churches*. New York, Harper Torchbooks, 1960.

111. TURNER, FREDERICK JACKSON. *The Frontier in American History*. New York, Henry Holt, 1921.

112. VAN DOREN, CARL C. *Benjamin Franklin*. New York, Viking Press, 1938.

113. WACH, JOACHIM. *Sociology of Religion*. Chicago, University of Chicago Press, 1944.

114a. WARNER, W. LLOYD. *A Black Civilization. A Social Study of an Australian Tribe*. New York, Harper, 1937.

114b. ——— "The Society, the Individual, and His Mental Disorders," *American Journal of Psychiatry, 94* (1938), 275–84.

114c. ——— and LUNT, PAUL S. *The Social Life of a Modern Community*. ("Yankee City Series," Vol. *1*.) New Haven, Yale University Press, 1941.

114d. ——— and SROLE, LEO. *The Social System of American Ethnic Groups*. ("Yankee City Series," Vol. *3*.) New Haven, Yale University Press, 1945.

114e. ——— and LOW, J. O. *The Social System of the Modern Factory*. ("Yankee City Series," Vol. *4*.) New Haven, Yale University Press, 1947.

114f. ——— *The Living and the Dead*. ("Yankee City Series," Vol. 5.) New Haven, Yale University Press, 1959.

115. WATTS, ALAN W. *Easter, Its Story and Meaning*. New York, Henry Schuman, 1950.

116. WEBER, MAX. *The Protestant Ethic and the Spirit of Capitalism,* trans. Talcott Parsons. New York, Charles Scribner's Sons, 1948.

117. WEBSTER, HUTTON. "Holidays," *Encyclopedia of the*

Social Sciences, 7, 412–15. New York, Macmillan, 1937.

118. WECKLER, JOSEPH E., JR. "Ritual Status in Polynesia." Unpublished Ph.D. dissertation, University of Chicago, 1940.

119. WECTER, DIXON. *The Hero in America. A Chronicle of Hero-Worship.* New York, Charles Scribner's Sons, 1941.

120. WEISS, JOHANNES. *Earliest Christianity, a History of the Period A.D. 30–150.* New York, Harper Torchbooks, 1959.

121. WELLER, FORREST L. *The Changing Religious Sect. A Study of Social Types.* Unpublished Ph.D. Dissertation, University of Chicago, 1945.

122. WHITEHEAD, ALFRED NORTH. *Symbolism, Its Meaning and Effect.* New York, Macmillan, 1927.

123a. WHORF, BENJAMIN L. "Time, Space and Language," *Culture in Crisis. A Study of the Hopi Indians,* ed. Laura Thompson. New York, Harper, 1950.

123b. ——— *Language, Thought and Reality.* Cambridge, Mass., Technology Press, Massachusetts Institute of Technology, 1956.

124. YERKES, ROBERT M. and H. W. NISSEN. "Pre-Linguistic Sign Behavior in Chimpanzees," *Science, 89* (June 1939), 585–87.

INDEX

Adam, 374; as autonomous son, 332; and Christ, 280, 334; as father, 333; as symbol, 334–5

Advent, 351, 367, 400–1

African Bantu: ancestor worship, 40–1; sacred symbolism, 25; social system, 29–36

Age: divisions, 40; and social structure, 101

Altar, 85, 296, 321

American Legion: and Memorial Day, 221, 222, 241, 243; and war, 255, 256

Ancestors: and Christian ethic, 125; Puritan, 138–9; souls of, 104; and totems, 27; worship of, 32–3

Annunciation, 302, 371, 372, 377

Anxiety: of the church, 266; and death, 258; and doctors, 204; and survival, 11; and transition rites, 193, 209

Architecture, church, 60

Arnold, Benedict: and Jewish group, 147–52; in Yankee City history, 127, 147–52

Art, and symbols, 64–5, 158

Arunta. *See* Australian aborigines

Australian aborigines: and death rites, 187; family and clan, 25–9, 31; and gods, 356; myths, 100; sacred symbolism, 25

Autonomy: of Adam, 332; family, 17, 19, 21, 81; and graveyards, 183; individual, 12, 20, 56, 392;

of local communities, 13, 252; moral, 16, 86; of soul, 282

Baptism, 53, 194, 318; as birth and death rite, 165; as rite de passage, 165, 297; as sacrament, 197, 352, 375; as sacred ceremony, 363, 373

Baptismal font, 373, 376–7

Baptist Church, 54; and faith, 55; ritual, 53, 75

Beliefs, 5, 6, 54, 213; Christian, 267, 327; of church, 266; and myths, 100; non-rational, 339; sacred, 18, 167, 257, 361

Bible, 283, 284, 285; as revealed truth, 55; as source of authority, 394

Birth, 194, 197; of Christ, 268, 367, 400–1; and death, 379

Blood, sacred, 323

Bride of Christ, the church as, 280, 282, 285–91, 305

Cabrol, Dom Fernand, 369, 399–400

Calendar, 381–9, 397; church, 75, 351, 356; function of, 382; sacred, 357–8; symbols of, 381

Calvinism, 56, 66, 136; and asceticism, 82; and liturgy, 348

Candle, 373, 374

Catholic: doctrine, 84; doctrine and family life, 272–3, 274, 279; dogma and sexual act, 277;

443

266; and sex, 278–9, 281; and society, 190; and vicars, 198; word of, 394
Gods: ancestral, 4; Australian, 356; Bantu, 35, 40
Grave, 168
Graveyards, 161; of historical significance, 214. *See* Cemetery
Greek Orthodox Church, 58

Heaven and Hell, in Christian belief, 55
Hildebrand, Dietrich Von, 273, 282–3, 291
Holidays, 162, 216
Holy coitus, 372; and sacred procreation, 373–80
Holy days, 162, 216, 220
Holy Saturday, 165
Holy Spirit or Holy Ghost, 65, 69–70, 268, 303, 331, 355, 371, 372
Holy Week, 314, 351, 369
Hostility, as symbolically expressed, 187–8
Huizinga, Johan, 71
Hymns, 62, 63

Immaculate Conception, 303, 309
Incest, 266, 272, 292
Indians: and Puritans, 136–7; in Yankee City hierarchy, 136

Jesus, 267, 313, 374; in Protestant liturgy, 68. *See* Christ
Jewish: graveyards, 181; Passover, 327; symbols, 24, 147; theological system, 70; worship, 40
Joseph, 267, 309
Judas Iscariot, and Benedict Arnold, 148
Jung, Carl G., 93

Knights of Columbus, 146, 241
Kropotkin, Petr A., 336

Lamb of God, 312
Language: of art and religion, 64–5; referential, 63; as symbol system, 158, 411
Lecky, William E., 66, 83
Lent, 351
Light and dark, 403
Lincoln: as collective representation, 247–51; and Memorial Day rites, 221, 234, 236–7, 239–40, 243
Liturgical: cycle of seasons, 346, 406; revival, 347, 348; year, 353–4, 399
Liturgies: of Easter, Holy Week, Lord's Supper, Mass, 314
Liturgy: in Protestantism, 67–8, 77–8; of Trinity, 370
Logic, structural and non-rational, 297
Lord's Supper, 53, 314, 317
Love: in Christian concepts, 269; and family, 187; mystical, 284; romantic, 117
Lower-class, churches, 65–6
Lutheran Church, 53, 54

Males: and freedom, 81; and sexuality, 293–5; as superordinate, 120, 178–9, 296
Malinowski, Bronislaw, meaning of signs, 417
Marriage: act, 273; of consecrated virgin, 288–9; and procreation, 272; rite, 194, 197, 271, 279; as sacrament, 352; as sacred ceremony, 363; sacred and profane, 280; as social relation, 281, symbols of, 298
Martyrs, 103–4
Mary. *See* Mother, Virgin Mary